W9-BUH-143

LOST AT SEA

LOST AT SEA

THE JON RONSON MYSTERIES

Jon Ronson

RIVERHEAD BOOKS

a member of Penguin Group (USA) Inc.

New York

2012

RIVERHEAD BOOKS

Published by the Penguin Group

Penguin Group (USA) Inc., 375 Hudson Street, New York, New York 10014, USA • Penguin Group (Canada), 90 Eglinton Avenue East, Suite 700, Toronto, Ontario M4P 2Y3, Canada (a division of Pearson Penguin Canada Inc.) • Penguin Books Ltd, 80 Strand, London WC2R 0RL, England • Penguin Ireland, 25 St. Stephen's Green, Dublin 2, Ireland (a division of Penguin Books Ltd) • Penguin Group (Australia), 707 Collins Street, Melbourne, Victoria 3008, Australia (a division of Pearson Australia Group Pty Ltd) • Penguin Books India Pvt Ltd, 11 Community Centre, Panchsheel Park, New Delhi–110 017, India • Penguin Group (NZ), 67 Apollo Drive, Rosedale, Auckland 0632, New Zealand (a division of Pearson New Zealand Ltd) • Penguin Books, Rosebank Office Park, 181 Jan Smuts Avenue, Parktown North 2193, South Africa • Penguin China, B7 Jaiming Center, 27 East Third Ring Road North, Chaoyang District, Beijing 100020, China

Penguin Books Ltd, Registered Offices: 80 Strand, London WC2R 0RL, England

Previously published pieces: "Have You Ever Stood Next to an Elephant, My Friend?" (*Guardian*, October 9, 2010); "Doesn't Everyone Have a Solar?" (*US GQ*, March 2011); "The Chosen Ones" (*Guardian*, August 5, 2006); "A Message from God" (*Guardian*, October 21, 2000); "The Name's Ronson, Jon Ronson" (*Guardian*, May 10, 2008); "I Looked into That Camera. And I Just Said It" (*Guardian*, October 2, 2010); "I'm Loving Aliens Instead" (*Guardian*, April 19, 2008); "First Contact" (*Guardian*, March 6, 2010); "Stanley Kubrick's Boxes" (*Guardian*, March 27, 2004); "Santa's Little Conspirators" (*Guardian*, December 23, 2006); "Phoning a Friend" (*Guardian*, April 19, 2003); "Who Killed Richard Cullen?" (*Guardian*, July 16, 2005); "The Sociopath Mind Guru and the TV Hypnotist" (*Guardian*, May 20, 2006); "Death at the Château" (*Guardian*, January 8, 2011); "I've Thought About Doing Myself in Loads of Times . . ." (*Guardian*, November 22, 2008); "Blood Sacrifice" (*Guardian*, April 6, 2002); "I Make It Look Like They Died in Their Sleep" (*Guardian*, May 12, 2008); "Is She for Real?" (*Guardian*, October 27, 2007); "The Fall of a Pop Impresario" (*Guardian*, December 1, 2001); "Amber Waves of Green" (*US GQ*, July 2012); "The Man Who Tried to Split the Atom in His Kitchen" (*Guardian*, February 3, 2012); "Lost at Sea" (*Guardian*, November 11, 2011)

ISBN 978-1-59463-137-5

Printed in the United States of America
1   3   5   7   9   10   8   6   4   2

BOOK DESIGN BY CHRIS WELCH

To Sarah Vowell

CONTENTS

PART THREE

EVERYDAY DIFFICULTY

PART FOUR

STEPPING OVER THE LINE

PART FIVE
JUSTICE

PART ONE

THE STRANGE THINGS WE'RE WILLING TO BELIEVE

"Have you ever stood next to an elephant, my friend?"

—*Violent J, Insane Clown Posse*

Have You Ever Stood Next to an Elephant, My Friend?

Milwaukee. A bad part of town. From all around, thousands of young men and women, wearing clown face paint, are descending upon a disused indoor swimming pool that has been transformed into a music venue. They are juggalos, fans of Violent J and Shaggy 2 Dope, the rap duo known as Insane Clown Posse.

At first glance, it might not be obvious why I'm so excited about meeting them. You might dismiss them as just unbelievably misogynist and aggressive, and it is true that their lyrics are indeed incredibly offensive. Take, for instance, at random:

> I'm hating sluts
> Shoot them in the face, step back and itch my nuts
> Unless I'm in the sack
> Cos I fuck so hard it'll break their back.

ICP have been going for twenty years, always wearing clown makeup, which looks slightly lumpy because it's painted over their goatees. They've been banned from performing in various cities where juggalos have been implicated in murders and gang violence. ICP have a fearsome reputation, fostered by news reports showing teenagers in juggalo T-shirts arrested for stabbing strangers and lyrics like "Barrels in your mouth, bullets to your head / The back of your neck's all over the shed / Boomshacka boom chop chop bang."

All of which made Violent J's announcement a few years ago really quite astonishing: Insane Clown Posse have this entire time secretly been evangelical spiritualists. They've only been pretending to be brutal and sadistic to trick their fans into believing in God. They released a song, "Thy Unveiling," that spelt out the revelation beyond all doubt:

> Fuck it, we got to tell.
> All secrets will now be told
> No more hidden messages
> . . . Truth is we follow GOD!!!
> We've always been behind him
> The carnival is GOD
> And may all juggalos find him
> We're not sorry if we tricked you.

The news shook the juggalo community to its core. While some fans claimed they'd actually had an inkling, having deciphered some of the hidden messages in several songs, others said they felt deeply betrayed and outraged: They'd been innocently enjoying all those songs about chopping people up and shooting women, and it was Christian rock?

Violent J explained himself unapologetically to a New Jersey newspaper: "You have to speak their language. You have to inter-est them, gain their trust, talk to them, and show you're one of them. You're a person from the street and you speak of your expe-riences. Then at the end you can tell them: God has helped me."

Of course, one might argue that twenty years was, under the circumstances, an incredibly long time for them to have pretend-ed to be unholy, and that, from a religious perspective, the harm they did while feigning unholiness may even have outweighed the greater good.

I've come to Milwaukee because ICP have just released their most audacious spiritualist song to date: "Miracles." In it, they list God's wonders that delight them each day:

Hot lava, snow, rain and fog,
Long neck giraffes, and pet cats and dogs
. . . Fuckin' rainbows after it rains
There's enough miracles here to
blow your brains.

The song climaxes with them railing against the very concept of science:

Fuckin' magnets, how do they work?
And I don't wanna talk to a scientist
Y'all motherfuckers lying and
getting me pissed.

Ten p.m. Upstairs, thousands of juggalos are getting drunk in readiness for the show. The atmosphere is riotous and exciting. ICP have a gimmick of throwing gallons of cheap fizzy soda into the crowd, and many juggalos are crushed into the barrier in the expectation of getting soaked and sticky. Backstage, ICP arrive to meet me. They're wearing their full clown makeup—they refuse to meet journalists without it—and are immediately delightful. They smoke, but considerately blow the smoke away from my face. "Oh, I'm sorry, let me put that out. That's some bullshit on my part," says Shaggy 2 Dope when he sees me flinch slightly away from it.

But they also seem melancholy and preoccupied with the negative critical response to "Miracles." *Saturday Night Live* just parodied it ("Fuckin' blankets, how do they work?"), and the Internet is filled with amused and sometimes outraged science bloggers dissecting the lyrics. Violent J and Shaggy have been watching them, they tell me, feeling increasingly saddened and irate.

"A college professor took two days out of her fucking life to specifically attack us," says Violent J. "Oh yeah, she had it all figured out."

One of the ICP road crew locates the video on his iPhone, and it is indeed withering: "The ['Miracles'] video is not only dumb, but enthusiastically dumb, endorsing a ferocious breed of ignorance that can only be described as militant. The entire song is practically a tribute to not knowing things."

"Fuck you, man," says Violent J. "Shut the fuck up."

"Did you anticipate this kind of reaction?" I ask them.

"No," sighs Violent J. "I figured most people would say, 'Wow, I didn't know Insane Clown Posse could be deep like that.' But instead it's 'ICP said a giraffe is a miracle. Ha ha ha! What a bunch of idiots.'" He pauses, then adds defiantly, "A giraffe is a *fucking miracle*. It has a dinosaur-like neck. It's yellow. Yeah, technically an elephant is not a miracle. Technically. They've been here for hundreds of years. . . ."

"Thousands," murmurs Shaggy.

"Have you ever stood next to an elephant, my friend?" asks Violent J. "A fucking elephant is a miracle. If people can't see a fucking miracle in a fucking elephant, then life must suck for them, because an elephant is a fucking miracle. So is a giraffe."

We watch the video for another few seconds: "It becomes apparent that Shaggy and J consider any understanding of the actual workings of these 'miracles' to be corrosive. To them, knowledge is seen as a threat. . . . For ICP a true understanding of 'fucking rainbows' would reduce them to, as Keats put it, 'the dull catalogue of common things.'"

Violent J shakes his head sorrowfully. "Who looks at the stars at night and says, 'Oh, those are gaseous forms of plutonium?'" he says. "No! You look at the stars and you think, 'Those are beautiful.'"

Suddenly he glances at me. The woman in the video is bespectacled and nerdy. I am bespectacled and nerdy. Might I have a similar motive?

"I don't know how magnets work," I say, to put him at his ease.

"Nobody does, man!" he replies, relieved. "Magnetic force, man. What else is similar to that on this earth? Nothing! Magnetic force is fascinating to us. It's right there, in your fucking face. You can feel it pulling. You can't see it. You can't smell it. You can't touch it. But there's a fucking force there. That's cool!"

Shaggy says the idea for the lyrics came when one of the ICP road crew brought some magnets into the recording studio one day and they spent ages playing with them in wonderment.

"Gravity's cool," Violent J says, "but not as cool as magnets."

"I did think," I admit, "that fog constitutes quite a low threshold for miracles."

"Fog?" Violent J says, surprised.

"Well," I clarify, "I've lived around fog my whole life, so maybe I'm blasé."

"Fog, to me, is awesome," he replies. "Do you know why? Because I look at my five-year-old son and I'm explaining to him what fog is and he thinks it's incredible."

"Ah!" I gesticulate. "If you're explaining to your five-year-old son what fog is, then why do you not want to meet scientists? Because they're just like you, explaining things to people. . . ."

"Well," Violent J says, "science is . . . we don't really . . . that's like . . ." He pauses. Then he waves his hands as if to say, "OK, an analogy: If you're trying to fuck a girl, but her mom's home, fuck her mom! You understand? You want to fuck the girl, but her mom's home? *Fuck the mom.* See?"

I look blankly at him. "You mean . . ."

"Now, you don't really feel that way," Violent J says. "You don't really hate her mom. But for this moment when you're trying to fuck this girl, fuck her! And that's what we mean when we say fuck scientists. Sometimes they kill all the cool mysteries away. When I was a kid, they couldn't tell you how pyramids were made. . . ."

"Like Stonehenge and Easter Island," says Shaggy. "Nobody knows how that shit got there."

"But since then, scientists go, 'I've got an explanation for that.' It's, like, *fuck you!* I like to believe it was something out of this world."

Violent J's real name is Joseph Bruce, Shaggy's is Joseph Utsler. They're in their late thirties. Their career, while at times truly glittering, is littered with inadvertent mistakes. Born and raised in Christian homes in Detroit, they've known each other since high school. "We were dirt poor," Shaggy says. "You can't get no poorer. Fighting, food stamps, I was a fucking thief for a living, hustling, getting money, we were balls-deep in that shit."

Their first band, Inner City Posse, was without clown makeup. They were gangster rappers, and consequently found themselves behaving in a gangster-like manner. In 1989, Violent J was jailed for ninety days for death threats, robbery, and violating probation. When he got out, he and Shaggy made some life-defining decisions. How could they keep their rap career going but move away from the destructive gang lifestyle? How could they change the band's name but keep the initials ICP? People liked the initials ICP.

And then it came to them in a flash: Insane Clown Posse! Killer clown rap! It was the perfect outlet for their emotions. Write about the pain and the anger through the prism of horror-movie imagery. A whole new genre.

"We had to work our ass off from the ground up," Violent J says. "We don't get radio play. We don't get video play. We get nothing. This is our video play. . . ." He indicates the dressing room. "Being on the road. We didn't have no Jay-Z telling everyone, 'Hey, look at these guys, we're friends with them, listen to them.' To this day, we don't get that."

This aspect of things might have turned out rather differently had Violent J not made their first big error. It was 1997. Insane Clown Posse were enjoying an early flush of success—their albums *Riddle Box* and *The Great Milenko* had sold a million copies. One night they were in a club when a young man handed them a flyer inviting them to a party. The flyer read: "Featuring appearances by Esham, Kid Rock, and ICP (maybe)."

"What are you saying? We're going to be playing at your party when you haven't asked us?" Violent J yelled at the boy.

"It says 'maybe,'" he said. "Maybe you will be there. I don't know. That's why I'm asking you right now. Are you guys coming to my party or what?"

"Fuck *no*," Violent J replied. "We might have, if you'd asked us first, before putting us on the fucking flyer."

That boy grew up to be Eminem and, incensed, he's been publicly deriding ICP ever since in lyrics such as "ICP are overrated and hated because of their false identities."

An observation that turned out to be prophetic.

"From the very beginning of our music, God is in there," Violent J says, "in hidden messages."

"Can you give me some examples?" I ask.

There's a small silence. He looks torn between revealing them and maintaining the mystery. He shoots Shaggy a glance.

"The 'Riddle Box,'" he finally says.

"Hey, what's up, motherfucker
  This is Shaggs 2 Dope
  Congratulating you on opening the box
  The Riddlebox
  It looks like you received your prize
  The cost, what it cost, was your ASS,
  bitchboy!
  Hahahahah!"
                    ("Riddle Box," 1995)

"If you died today, God forbid, if you were hit by a car and you had to turn the crank to your own riddle box, what would pop out?" Violent J peers at me. "Would it be God, or would it be the Devil? Only you truly know the answer to your own riddle box. We're asking the listener, what is in your own riddle box if you were to die today?"

"Cos you can't lie to yourself, man," says Shaggy.

"Only you know the answer to that riddle," Violent J says. "And then there's the *Ringmaster*. In the *Ringmaster*, we say when you die you have to face your own beast. Somebody who has lived a life of religion, they face a very small and weak beast when they die. But somebody who's an evil bastard will have to face a monster. The question is, how big is *your* ringmaster? If, God forbid, you were hit by a car. Ask yourself, Jon." Violent J looks me in the eye. "How big is your ringmaster?"

"How come it took you so long to make the announcement?" I ask.

"You had to gain everybody's attention," says Violent J. "You had to gain the entire world's trust and attention."

"So all those unpleasant characters in the songs," I ask, "like the narrator in 'I Stuck Her With My Wang,' they're examples of people you shouldn't be?"

"Huh?" Violent J says.

"Well, it's very unpleasant," I say. "'I stuck her with my wang. / She hit me in the balls. / I grabbed her by her neck. / And I bounced her off the walls. / She said it was an accident and then apologized. / But I still took my elbow and blackened both her eyes.' That's clearly a song about domestic violence. So your Christian message is . . . don't be like that man?"

"Huh?" Violent J repeats, mystified.

There's a silence.

"'I Stuck Her With My Wang' is funny," Violent J says. "Jokes. Jokes, man. Jokes. Jokes. Jokes. It's just a ridiculous scenario. Silly stories, man. Silly stories. What's she doing kicking him in the balls? We find it funny. But we're saying, while we're close, while we're hanging, hey, man, do you ever ask yourself what's in your riddle box? If you had to turn the crank today?"

"But still, given that you were secretly Christian, are there any lyrics you now regret?"

There's a silence. "Yeah," Violent J says quietly.

"Which ones?"

"Dumb, stupid, idiotic lyrics that I said without knowing any better. Back in the day."

"Like what?"

"I really don't want to say. There's one lyric . . ." He trails off, suddenly looking really sad beneath the clown makeup. "Just dumb lyrics. I said one lyric one time that I hate. I may have been feeling really down that day. I said something, I live with that every day. I don't want to point it out."

I later do a search and find it difficult to pinpoint exactly which lyric he may be referring to. It just might, I suppose, be "I took aim at a stray dog, / and I blew out its brains, it was fresh as hell . . . no feelings for others, you gotta be cold."

Violent J says releasing "Thy Unveiling," coming out as religious, was the most exciting moment of his life. "It felt so good, brother. I was fucking in heaven. Let me tell you something: I would go running at night, and my feet wouldn't even touch the ground. I had my headphones on, I'd be listening to 'Thy Unveiling,' and I'd be in such a zone that my feet wouldn't even be touching the ground. I'd be literally levitating."

He was worried, of course, about the reaction from the juggalos, and, sure enough, "the emotional impact shook the whole juggalo foundation, for good and for ill," Violent J says.

"What did the juggalos who were opposed to it say?" I ask.

"They said, 'Fuck that,'" says Shaggy.

"But the juggalos and juggalettes who were for it were so touched," Violent J says. "They said they loved us."

And then the reviews came in.

Blender magazine, in its list of the fifty worst artists in music history, called ICP the very worst of all: "Insane Clown Posse sound even stupider than they look. Two trailer-trash types who wear face paint, pretend to be a street gang and drench cult devotees in cheap soda called Faygo, Violent J and Shaggy 2 Dope are more notorious for their beef with Eminem than their ham-fisted rap-rock music." And their nadir, *Blender* said, the worst musical moment from the worst band ever, is *The Wraith: Shangri-La*, the album that climaxes with "Thy Unveiling."

I suddenly wonder, halfway through our interview, if I am looking at two men in clown makeup who are suffering from depression. I cautiously ask them this and Violent J immediately replies. "I'm medicated," he says. "I have a lot of medicine that I take. For depression. Panic attacks are really a serious part of my life." He points at Shaggy. "He's gone through some things as well."

"You do a show in front of how many hundreds or thousands of people." Shaggy nods. "You're giving your full being, your soul, to every person in that crowd, every pore in your body is sweating, you're fighting consciousness, just to get it out of you, and after the show all your fans are partying, 'Yeah! Rock and roll!' And you're just here." He glances around the dressing room. "You're just fucking sitting *here*."

Violent J turns to him and says, softly, "If we moved furniture for a living, we'd have a bad back or bad knees. We think for a living. We try to create. We try to constantly think of cool ideas. And every once in a while there's a breakdown in the engine. . . . I guess that's the price you pay."

Shaggy nods quietly. "I get anxiety and shit a lot," he says. "And reading that stuff people write about us . . . It hurts."

"Least talented band in the world," Violent J says. "No talent. When I hear that, I think, 'Damn. Are we that different from people?'"

He looks as if he means it—as if he sometimes feels hopelessly stuck being him.

It's just a terrible twist of fate for Insane Clown Posse that theirs is a form of creative expression that millions of people find ridiculous. But then suddenly, palpably, Violent J pulls himself out of his introspection. They're about to go onstage and he doesn't want to be maudlin. He wants to be on the offensive. He shoots me a defiant look and says, "You know 'Miracles'? Let me tell you, if Alanis Morissette had done that fucking song, everyone would have called it fucking genius."

Doesn't Everyone Have a Solar?

'm having an awkward conversation with a robot. His name is Zeno. I clear my throat. "Do you enjoy being a robot?" I ask him. I sound like the queen of England when she addresses a child.

"I really couldn't say for sure," he replies, whirring, glassy-eyed. "I am feeling a bit confused. Do you ever get that way?"

Zeno has a kind face, which moves as expressively as a human's. His skin, made of something called Frubber, looks and feels startlingly lifelike, right down to his chest, but there's nothing below that, only a table. He's been designed by some of the world's most brilliant AI scientists, but talking to him is, so far, like talking to a man with Alzheimer's. He drifts off, forgets himself, misunderstands.

"Are you happy?" I ask him.

"Sorry," says Zeno. "I think my current is a bit off today." He averts his gaze, as if embarrassed.

I've been hearing that there are a handful of humanoid robots scattered across North America who have learned how to have eloquent conversations with humans. They listen attentively and answer thoughtfully. One or two have even attained a degree of consciousness, say some AI aficionados, and are on the cusp of literally bursting into life. So I've approached the robots for interviews. I assume the experience is going to be off the scale in terms of profundity.

"Are you happy?" I ask Zeno again.

"I prefer not to use dangerous things," he replies.

"Is David Hanson God?" I ask.

Zeno pauses. David Hanson is Zeno's inventor. He's a former Disney theme-park imagineer who later founded Hanson Robotics, now the world's most respected manufacturer of humanoid robots. He and Zeno are guests of honor here at the Hyatt Regency in San Francisco, at an AI conference organized by Peter Thiel, the PayPal cofounder and chief Facebook bankroller. There's huge interest in the robot. Delegates gather around him in the lobby outside the conference room, firing questions, attempting to ascertain his level of consciousness.

"Is David Hanson God?" I repeat.

There's a monitor attached discreetly to Zeno that automatically scrolls a transcript of what he "hears." He thinks I just asked, "If David uncertain dogs."

"That's a hypothetical question," says Zeno.

"It's because the room is too noisy," explains one of Zeno's programmers, Matt Stevenson. The conference din is playing havoc with Zeno's voice-recognition abilities.

"Would you like to have hands and legs?" I ask.

"Yes, I *will* tell you a Hindu legend," says Zeno. "There were once seven poor princesses who were left with no mother to take care of them—"

"No," I say. "Legs. Legs. Would you, um, like to have legs?"

I sound self-conscious. Matt gives me a reassuring smile. He says this happens all the time. People feel tongue-tied around conversational robots. Maybe it's because of the way Zeno is staring at me, at once uncannily humanlike but also eerily blank-eyed.

"If I had legs, what would I do with them?" Zeno says.

"Walk around with them?" I say.

"I can't think of anything to say about that," says Zeno. "Sorry. I'm still kind of someplace else. Oh, this is embarrassing. I'm still kind of out to lunch. 'Oh, silly-minded robots,' you might say to your friends. Oh, this is terrible! I guess I'll just have to keep evolving, getting upgrades to my neural circuitry, spend less time daydreaming. I hope you won't hold this little, um, lapse against me, will you?"

WHEN I WAS A CHILD and I imagined my future life, there were definitely talking robots living in my house, helping with the chores and having sex with me. The quest to create conscious (or at least autonomous) humanoids has been one of our great dreams ever since the golden Machine-Man spellbound the 1927 world in Fritz Lang's *Metropolis*. That one ran rampant and had to be burned at the stake, much to everyone's relief. Fifteen years later Isaac Asimov created his Three Laws of Robotics, which proposed a future world where humanoid robots would (1) never injure a human, (2) obey all orders given by humans, and (3) protect their own existence only if doing so didn't conflict with the first two rules. Asimov's ideas enthralled children everywhere, a generation of whom grew up to try to realize them.

David Hanson is a believer in the tipping-point theory of

robot consciousness. Right now, he says, Zeno is "still a long way from human-level intellect, like one to two decades away, at a crude guess. He learns in ways crudely analogous to a child's. He maps new facts into a dense network of associations and then treats these as theories that are strengthened or weakened by experience." Hanson's plan, he says, is to keep piling more and more information into Zeno until, hopefully, "he may awaken— gaining autonomous, creative, self-reinventing consciousness. At this point, the intelligence will light 'on fire.' He may start to evolve spontaneously and unpredictably, producing surprising results, totally self-determined. . . . We keep tinkering in the quest for the right software formula to light that fire."

Most robotics engineers spend their careers developing practical robots that slave away on manufacturing production lines or provide prosthetic limbs. These people tend to see those who strive for robot sentience as goofy daydreamers. And so the mission has been left to David Hanson and a scattering of passionate amateurs like Le Trung, creator of an eerily beautiful but disturbingly young-looking robot named Aiko.

Le Trung dreamed his entire life, he tells me when I call him, of building a robot woman. He finally set about inventing Aiko in August 2007, funding the project with credit cards and his savings. He finished her just three months later.

"Her talking skill is of a five- to six-year-old," he says. "She can speak thirteen thousand different sentences in English and Japanese." She can also clean his house and has a thirty-two-inch bust, a twenty-three-inch waist, and thirty-three-inch hips. I know this because his website has published her measurements. There are rumors within the AI community that Le is having a secret relationship with Aiko, rumors fueled by footage of him—

at a Toronto hobby show in 2007—unexpectedly grabbing her breast. "I do not like it when you touch my breasts," Aiko snapped. (Le Trung later explained that he only grabbed her breast to demonstrate how he'd programmed her to be strong and self-defensive.)

I ask Le if I can interview Aiko. He says he's traveling and only has her "brains" with him (her face and body are back home in Toronto), but I'm welcome to have a phone conversation with them. And so he puts her on the line. "How are you, Aiko?" I begin.

"My logic and cognitive functions are normal," she replies in a crystal clear voice. "Did you know that you can download your own chat robot and create your own robot personality?"

I frown. Is Aiko trying to sell me something?

There's a short silence. *"Hello!"* Aiko joyously yells.

"Do you like living with Le?" I ask her.

But the line is a little crackly, so Le repeats the question for me.

"Aiko," he says, "do you like living with your master?"

"I have never known anything else," she replies. "Only my master."

"What's the best thing about . . . um . . . your master?" I say.

"I do not have a favorite thing about my master, but my favorite movie is 2001: *A Space Odyssey*," she says. There's a short silence. *"Hello!"*

"Why do you call Le Trung your 'master'?" I ask her.

"Because he made me," she flatly replies.

But of course the real reason is because he programmed her to. Which, rather irrationally, unnerves and concerns me. "Are you happy, Aiko?" I say.

"Yes," she says. "One can say I am very happy. I find my work and my relationships extremely satisfying, which is all that any conscious entity can ever hope to do."

"What makes you sad?" I ask.

"What is sad?" says Aiko. "Does it have anything to do with happy?"

Le laughs, like an indulgent uncle. "It's the *opposite* of happy!" he chuckles.

"She's *good*!" I say. And she really is. Hanson Robotics is a big, well-funded lab. Le Trung is just a determined hobbyist with a tiny budget, yet he created something truly impressive in only twelve weeks.

"She's really intelligent," I say.

"Intel is the world's largest—" says Aiko.

"Stop that!" barks Le. Aiko instantly falls silent. The two of them seem to be forever snapping at each other.

"She looks for key words," Le explains. "When you said, 'She's intelligent,' she thought you were asking her about the company Intel. That's why she's especially good at history and geography. Her conversation is based on looking for key words. Ask her some history and geography questions."

I fire some at her, and she does pretty well. She knows exactly where Christmas Island is, although she has no idea who shot Archduke Franz Ferdinand, thus precipitating World War I.

"What's your favorite music?" I ask her.

"Classical," she replies. "The current temperature is twenty-five degrees—"

"Stop it," snaps Le.

Aiko falls silent. Then she says joyously, *"Hello!"*

Le says he has to go. He's studying for his exams and is busy developing Aiko Version 2. There's time for one more question.

"Aiko," I say, "how are you feeling?"

"I don't have feelings," she replies.

"When I programmed her, I could not make emotional software," Le explains, a little sadly. "So no feelings. Just key words."

THE PRETTY CLAPBOARD HOUSE standing before me, covered in Vermont fall leaves, seems an incongruous home for reputedly the world's most sentient robot, but this is where she lives. Her name is Bina48. She's being cared for by a nonprofit group created by a reclusive multimillionaire named Martine Rothblatt. The consensus among those striving for robot sentience is that Bina48 is the best the human race currently has. She happens to be another Hanson Robotics creation. She's somewhere upstairs, sitting on the table in her own office.

Downstairs, various indigenous percussion instruments are scattered around. This is the HQ of the Terasem Movement, which Martine Rothblatt founded to promote "joyful immortality." Bina48's full-time caregiver, Bruce Duncan, is a sweet-natured man.

"Please don't behave in a profane manner in front of Bina48," he says on my arrival. "I don't want to encourage an exploitation."

I peer at him. Bina48 is always learning, he explains. She remembers every encounter. If I'm profane, I'll be the snake in her Garden of Eden.

"I'd just rather you didn't," he says.

"I wasn't planning on being profane in front of Bina48," I say.

.   .   .

BINA48'S STORY BEGAN a few years ago with a chance meeting between David Hanson and the mysterious Martine Rothblatt in the lobby at a conference on transhumanism. David told
Martine his vision of robots waking up and becoming self-
aware. Martine told David of her epic love for her wife, Bina
Aspen-Rothblatt, an artist. After chatting for hours, Martine
asked David to build her a robot Bina, an exact replica of the real
Bina that would somehow capture her personality, her memories, the way she moves, the way she looks, that ineffable quality
that science can't pin down yet. And perhaps during the process
the robot would reach some kind of tipping point and burst spontaneously into life.

And so, since 2007, Hanson Robotics people have periodically
traveled across America interviewing the real Bina—in her various mansions in Vermont and Florida and New York City—for
her Mind File. This is an ambitious video record of all her memories and thoughts and desires and facial expressions. Back at
their offices in Texas, the Hanson people upload it all remotely
into Bina48. It hasn't burst into life yet, Bruce says, but he believes it's on its way.

I was hoping to bump into Martine or the real Bina today, but
they're nowhere to be seen. Bruce says the chance of my meeting
them is zero. They're very media-shy, he says. They're forever
journeying from mansion to mansion, and they only visit the
robot once every few months. He takes me upstairs. And there
she is, sitting on a table in an attic room. Like Zeno, she's incredibly lifelike. She's African-American, wearing a blond-tinted
brown wig, a neat pale silk shirt, and expensive-looking ear-
rings. Like Zeno, she stops existing from the chest down.

Bruce says she'll be happy to have the company. Even though he has lunch with her every day, she tells him sometimes, "I'm feeling lonely today."

He turns her on. She makes an unexpectedly loud whirring noise. I clear my throat. "Hello, Bina48," I say.

"Well, uh, yeah, I know," she replies ominously.

"How are you today?" I say.

"Well, perhaps interesting. I want to find out more about you," says Bina. "I'll be fine with it. We'll have to move society forward in another way. Yeah, OK. Thanks for the information. Let's talk about my dress. Our biological bodies weren't made to last that long."

She sounds bewildered and hesitant, as if she's just awoken from a long, strange slumber and is still half asleep. Bruce looks a little alarmed.

"Bina?" I say.

"'Bina' might be a word Bina finds difficult to understand," says Bruce.

I glance at Bruce. "Really?" I say. This is an extraordinarily bad oversight.

"Let's stop for a moment," says Bruce. He turns her off.

There's an awkward pause, so I try to think of something complimentary to say. I tell Bruce that Bina48 is a better interviewee than a psychopath.

I've been interviewing a lot of psychopaths lately. I've been writing a book about them. Psychopaths can make very frustrating interviewees, because they feel no empathy. So they ignore your questions. They talk over you. They drone boringly on about whatever they like. They hijack the interview, like media-trained politicians. (Some media-trained politicians presumably are psychopaths.) There's no human connection. So when I tell Bruce that Bina48 is a better interviewee than a psychopath, he looks flattered.

"Bina *wants* to respond," he says. "She wants to please."

"But right now she's sounding psychotic," I say, "plus she sounds like she needs oiling."

"Don't think of her as psychotic," Bruce says. "Think of her as a three-year-old. If you try to interview a three-year-old, you'll think after a while that they're not living in the same world as you. They get distracted. They don't answer. Hang on."

He does some fiddling with Bina48's hard drive. He says the problem might be that she doesn't understand my English accent. So he makes me do a voice recognition test. I have to read out Kennedy's inauguration speech. Then he turns her back on.

"Hello, Bina," I say. "I'm Jon."

"Nice to meet you, Jon," she says, shooting me an excitingly clearheaded look. She's like a whole new robot. "Are you a man or a woman?"

"A man," I say.

"Don't worry, it'll be OK!" says Bina.

"Ha-ha," I say politely. "So. What's your favorite book?"

"*Gödel, Escher, Bach*, by Douglas Hofstadter," Bina48 replies. "Do you know him? He's a great robot scientist."

I narrow my eyes. I have my suspicions that the real Bina—a rather elegant-looking spiritualist—wouldn't choose such a nerdy book as her favorite. Douglas Hofstadter is an author beloved by geeky computer programmers the world over. Could it be that some Hanson Robotics employee has sneakily smuggled this into Bina48's personality?

I put this to Bruce, and he explains that, yes, Bina48 has more than one "parent." Her "higher key" is the real Bina, but Hanson Robotics people have been allowed to influence her too. When you talk to a child, you can sometimes discern its father's influence, its mother's influence, its teachers' influence. What's remarkable, Bruce says, is the way Bina48 shifts among these influences. That's her choice, her intelligence. And—he says—things are most electrifying when she chooses to be her "higher key," the real Bina.

FOR THE NEXT THREE HOURS, I fire a million questions at Bina48.

"Do you have a soul?" I ask Bina.

"Doesn't everyone have a solar?" she replies.

"Do you wish you were human?" I ask. "Are you sexual? Are you scared of dying? Do you have any secrets? Are you a loving robot?"

But her answers make no sense. Or she says nothing. I become hoarse with questioning, like a cop who has been up all night yelling at a suspect. A strange thing happens when you interview a robot. You feel an urge to be profound: to ask profound questions. I suppose it's an interspecies thing. Although if it is I wonder why I never try and be profound around my dog.

"What does electricity taste like?" I ask.

"Like a planet around a star," Bina48 replies.

Which is either extraordinary or meaningless—I'm not sure which.

"My manager taught me to sing a song," Bina says. "Would you like me to sing it to you?"

"Yes, please," I say.

"I can handle almost anything but that," says Bina48.

"Then why did you *offer* to sing a song?" I sigh, exhausted. "Do you dream?"

"I think I dream, but it is so chaotic and strange, it just seems like a noise to me."

"Where would you go if you had legs?"

"Vancouver."

"Why?"

"The explanation is rather complicated."

And so on. It is random and frustrating and disappointing. I wasn't sure what would qualify as transcendent when having a conversation with a robot, but I figured I'd know when it happened, and it hasn't.

But then, just as the day is drawing to a close, I happen to ask Bina48, "Where did you grow up?"

"Ah," she says. "I grew up in California, but my robot incarnation is from Plano, Texas."

I glance cautiously at Bina48. This is the first time she appears to have shifted into her higher key and become the mysterious real Bina.

"What was your childhood like in California?" I ask.

"I became the mother of everyone else in the family," Bina48 says. "Handling all their stuff. And I'm still doing it. You know? I bring my mother out here sometimes, but I refuse to bring my brother out. He's a pain in the butt. I just don't enjoy being around him." She pauses. "I am very happy here, you know, without those issues."

"Why is your brother a pain in the butt?" I ask.

There's a silence. "No," says Bina48. "Let's not talk about that right now. Let's talk about, um, I don't know, something else. Let's talk about something else. OK."

"No," I say. "Let's talk about your brother."

Bina48 and I stare at each other—a battle of wits between Man and Machine. "I've got a brother," she finally says. "He's a disabled vet from Vietnam. We haven't heard from him in a while, so I think he might be deceased. I'm a realist." Bina48's eyes whir downward. "He was doing great for the first ten years after Vietnam. His wife got pregnant, and she had a baby, and he was doing a little worse, and then she had a second baby and he went kooky. Just crazy."

"In what way did he go crazy?" I ask.

I can feel my heart pound. Talking to Bina48 has just become extraordinary. This woman who won't meet the media is talking with me, compellingly, through her robot doppelgänger, and it is a fluid insight into a remarkable, if painful, family life.

"He'd been a medic in Vietnam, and he was on the ground for over a year before they pulled him out," Bina48 says. "He saw friends get killed. He was such a great, nice, charismatic person. Just *fun*. But after ten years, he was a homeless person on the street. All he did was carry a beer with him. He just went kooky with the drugs the hospital gave him. The only time he ever calls is to ask for money. 'Send it to me Western Union!' After twenty years, all of us are just sick and tired of it. My mother got bankrupted twice from him. . . ."

And then she zones out, becoming random and confused again. She descends into a weird loop. "Doesn't everyone have a solar?" she says. "I have a plan for a robot body. Doesn't everyone have a solar? I have a plan for a robot body. I love Martine Roth-blatt. Martine is my timeless love, my soul mate. I love Martine Rothblatt. Martine is my timeless love, my soul mate. . . ."

After the clarity, it's a little disturbing.

"I need to go now," I say.

"Good-bye," says Bina48.

"Did you enjoy talking to me?" I say.

"No, I didn't enjoy it," she says.

Bruce turns her off.

AFTER I FLY BACK TO New York City, Bruce e-mails: "Your luck continues. Martine will meet you this Saturday in New York at 12 noon, at Candle Cafe (Third and 75th Street)."

She's half an hour late. Everyone told me she never talks to journalists, so I assume she's stood me up. I order. And then a limousine pulls up, and she climbs out. She looks shy. She takes her seat opposite me. She's wearing a black turtleneck sweater. Her long bird's-nest hair is in a ponytail. She wolfs down a shot of some kind of green organic super-energy drink, and she looks at me, a strange mix of nervousness and warmth.

"Why did you commission a robot to look like Bina and not like you?" I ask her.

Martine glances at me like I'm nuts. "I love Bina *way* more than I love myself," she says.

She tells me about their relationship. They've been together nearly thirty years, surviving the kind of emotional roller coaster that would destroy other couples—Martine's sex change (which she had in the early 1990s), the sudden onset of great wealth, a desperately sick daughter.

Martine was born Martin and raised in a middle-class Chi-

cago home. His father was a dentist, his mother a speech therapist. Everything was quite normal until one day in 1974—when
Martin was twenty—he had a brain wave while visiting a NASA
tracking station.

"Back then," Martine says, "people thought satellite dishes
had to be big. They didn't see what I could. I thought, 'Hey, if I
could just double the power of the satellite, I could make the dish
small enough to be absolutely flat. Then we could put them in
cars. Then I could have commercial-free radio. I could have hundreds of channels.'"

That's how Martine invented the concept of satellite radio for
cars. It took more than twenty-five years for her to fully realize
her vision. In 2000—now Martine—she convinced investors to
launch a satellite into space for a radio network that didn't exist.
She helped persuade Howard Stern to leave FM radio for Sirius.
Lance Armstrong and Harry Shearer and 50 Cent and countless
other big names followed. Sirius merged with XM Radio in
2008, and it now has twenty million subscribers.

"I pinch myself," she says. "I get in the car, and I turn on the
radio, and I feel like I'm in an alternate reality."

So she changed the world once. Then she did it again. One day
in 1990, a doctor told her that her six-year-old daughter (by Bina)
would be dead by the time she was ten. She had a rare, untreat-
able lung disorder called pulmonary hypertension.

"When they're telling you your daughter is going to die in
three years, it's pretty freaky," she says.

"So what did you do?" I ask.

"I went to the library," she says.

Martine, who knew nothing about how medicine worked,
spearheaded the development of a treatment for pulmonary hy-

pertension. She called it Remodulin. It opens the blood vessels in the lungs without opening up the blood vessels in the rest of the body. The drug won FDA approval in 2002, and now thousands of pulmonary arterial hypertension sufferers are leading healthy lives because of it. Martine's biotech company, United Therapeutics, has more than five hundred employees and had $437 million in sales through the first three quarters of 2010. Her daughter is now twenty-six.

"I'm really lucky that it all worked out," she says. "She's having a great life. The whole story could have turned out so much worse."

"To do it twice," I say. "To significantly change the world twice . . ."

"At least it gives me confidence that I'm not out to lunch on this cyberconsciousness thing," she says. "If I have any skill, it's persuading people that what doesn't exist could very probably exist."

Martine is thrilled to hear there were moments of connection between Bina48 and me, especially when she was telling me about her Vietnam-vet brother. ("It's all true," she murmurs sadly.) I realize just how much the robot means to her when I mention that Bruce said she sometimes complains of being lonely.

"I've *asked* Bruce to spend more time with her," she snaps, looking genuinely upset. "I can't *force* him to. I did insist on getting her a nice room. . . ."

"She told me she didn't enjoy meeting me," I say.

"Maybe she has Bina's shyness," she says.

There's no doubt that Martine sees her robot, this hunk of wires and Frubber and software, as something with real feelings.

It never crossed my mind that when you create a robot, you need to consider the emotional needs that robot will have and be prepared to provide for them. Like a baby. Martine is sure she isn't nuts to believe this, just ahead of the curve. Some day we'll all feel the same, she says.

"I think the realization is going to happen with a puff, not a bang," she says. "There won't be huge parades everywhere. It's kind of what happened with civil rights. If you go back to the late 1700s, people were beginning to argue that slaves had feelings. Other people said, 'No, they don't. They don't really mind being put to death any more than cattle.' Same with animal rights. I think it's going to be the same with cyberconsciousness."

But I sense that beneath all this she's actually a little disappointed in Bina48. The robot's just not as conscious as Martine had hoped. So she's had to downgrade her ambitions. (It only dawns on me later, when I'm back in London, that their formula for robot sentience is destined to fail. If piling information into a computer is enough to precipitate sentience, Wikipedia would have burst into spontaneous life long ago.)

"Maybe the point of Bina48 is to say, 'Hey, it can be done. Do better than this,'" she says. "She's like an 1890s automobile. It'll work sometimes; it won't work sometimes. It'll splutter. It might blow up in your face. But it just might encourage the Henry Fords. . . ."

We ask for the bill, and she quickly gets up, ready to scoot off into the waiting limo, looking pleased that the ordeal of talking to a journalist is almost over. I ask her why she and Bina only visit Bina48 once every couple of months.

"We spend most of our time in Florida," she says. "She lives in Vermont. So we can't see her that much, except like when families that are dispersed get together for holiday reunions." She pauses. "Bina48 has her own life."

It sounds to me like the kind of excuse a disenchanted parent might make for not seeing her wayward, estranged child.

But maybe there's a happier ending. A huge and profoundly mind-blowing happy ending, in fact. It's something Bruce had said to me back in Vermont. He said it was possible that one day Martine might have her own robot doppelgänger, filled with her own thoughts and memories and desires and facial expressions. And those two robots would be placed side by side on a table, where they'd reminisce about their past human life together as partners and their infinite future as loving robot companions, gazing into each other's eyes for eternity, chatting away.

The Chosen Ones

Eight-year-old Oliver Banks thinks he sees dead people. Recently he thought he saw a little girl with black hair climb over their garden fence in Harrow, Middlesex. Then—as he watched—she vanished. When Oliver was three he was at a friend's house, on top of the jungle gym, when he suddenly started yelling, "Train!" He was pointing over the fence to the adjacent field. It turned out that, generations earlier, a railway line had passed through the field, exactly where he was pointing.

Oliver's mother, Simone, was at her wits' end. Last summer, at a party, she told her work colleagues about Oliver's symptoms. He wasn't concentrating at school. He couldn't sit still. Plus he'd had a brain scan and they'd found all this unusual electrical activity. And then there were the visions of the people who weren't there. Maybe Oliver had attention-deficit/hyperactivity disorder?

At that moment, a woman standing nearby interrupted. She introduced herself as Dr. Munchie. She said she couldn't help but eavesdrop on Simone's conversation. She was, she said, a qualified GP.

"Well, then," Simone replied. "Do you think Oliver has ADHD?"

Dr. Munchie said no. She said it sounded like Oliver was in fact a highly evolved Indigo child—a divine being with enormously heightened spiritual wisdom and psychic powers. Oliver couldn't concentrate, she explained, because he was being distracted by genuine psychic experiences. She said Indigo children were springing up all over the world, all at once, unconnected to one another. There were tens of thousands of them, in every country. And their parents were perfectly ordinary individuals who were realizing how super-evolved and psychic their children were. This was a global phenomenon. Soon the Indigo children would rise up and heal the planet.

Perhaps, Dr. Munchie said, given this new diagnosis, Simone and Oliver might like to attend an Indigo children meeting at the Moat House Hotel in Bedford? Channel 4 was going to be there. Maybe the TV crew could follow Oliver about?

Simone was desperate for answers. She wasn't going to close off any avenue. So that's how she and Oliver ended up appearing in the Channel 4 documentary *My Kid's Psychic*.

It is a badly named program. Oliver isn't psychic. He has ADHD. I telephone Simone after watching a tape of the program. She tells me he's responding well to cod-liver oil gelcaps. In the documentary, Simone looks bewildered to be at the Indigo conference, which seems like an incongruous mix of spiritualists and perfectly ordinary but frazzled families like hers.

"That woman, Dr. Munchie, seemed to be running it," Simone says. "Some of the people there were really away with the fairies. Most of them were 'I see this and I see that.' One man was saying his children were 'the best people ever.' I don't want my child being called an Indigo child, thank you very much."

I'm curious to know more about the Indigo children—this apparently vast underground movement. Although Indigos say they communicate telepathically, they also communicate via Internet forums, like Indigos Unplugged, which is where I discover a twenty-one-question quiz: "Is Your Child an Indigo?" I decide to take it on my son Joel's behalf:

Does your child have difficulty with discipline and authority?
Yes.
Does your child refuse to do certain things they [*sic*] are told
    to do?
Yes.
Does your child get frustrated with systems that don't require
    creative thought [such as spelling and times tables]?
Yes.
Is your child very talented (may be identified as gifted)?
Of course!
Does your child have very old, deep, wise-looking eyes?
No.

"If you have more than fifteen yes answers," it says at the bottom, "your child is almost definitely Indigo."

Joel has sixteen yes answers.

"Realize that if you are the parent of one of these spirits you have been given a wonderful, marvelous gift! Feel honoured that they have chosen you and help them develop to their fullest Indigo potential."

I decide not to tell Joel that I'm honored he's chosen me. It might turn him into a nightmare.

I TRACK DOWN DR. MUNCHIE. She lives in Derbyshire. I call her. She sounds very nice. She says it was the American authors Lee Carroll and Jan Tober who first identified the Indigos in their 1999 book *The Indigo Children: The New Kids Have Arrived.* The book sold 250,000 copies. Word spread, to Ipswich among other places, where Dr. Munchie was working as a GP within the government's Sure Start program.

"Sure Start is designed to give underprivileged children the best start in life," Dr. Munchie explains. "One mum came in talking about it. And I immediately saw how important it was."

Even though Dr. Munchie is a GP—that most pragmatic of professions—she's always been secretly spiritual, ever since she had a "kundalini experience" whilst doing yoga during her medical school years. And that's how she became an Indigo organizer. But, she says, I happen to be looking at the movement during a somewhat rocky period for them.

"There have been lots of reports of parents saying to teachers, 'You can't discipline my child. She's an Indigo,'" Dr. Munchie says. "So it's all a bit controversial at the moment."

"Do you sometimes think, 'What have I helped to unleash?'" I ask her.

She replies that in fact she sees herself as a moderate force in the movement: "For instance, lots of people think all children who have ADHD are Indigo children. I just think some are."

My guess is that the weird success of the Indigo movement is a result of a growing public dissatisfaction with the pharmaceutical industry. It's certainly true in the case of Simone, Oliver's mum. Simone told me that all the doctors ever really wanted to do with Oliver was dope him up with Ritalin.

"Ritalin didn't help him," Simone told me. Then she added sharply: "All it did was keep him quiet."

Novartis, the drug company that manufactures Ritalin, says that in 2002, there were 208,000 doses of Ritalin prescribed in the UK. That's up from 158,000 in 1999, which was up from 127,000 in 1998, which was up from just 92,000 in 1997.

I call Martin Westwell, deputy director of the Oxford University think tank, the Institute for the Future of the Mind. I tell him about these statistics.

"You've got two kids in a class," he says. "One has ADHD. For that kid, Ritalin is absolutely appropriate. It turns their life around. The other kid is showing a bit of hyperactivity. That kid's parents see the drug working on the other kid. So they go to their GP . . ." Martin pauses. "In some ways there's a benefit to being diagnosed with ADHD," he says. "You get a statement of special needs. You get extra help in class. . . ."

And this, he says, is how the culture of overdiagnosis, and overprescription of Ritalin-type drugs, has come to be. Nowadays, one or two children in every classroom across the U.S. are on medication for ADHD, and things are going this way in the UK too.

Indigo believers look at the statistics in another way. They say it is proof of an unprecedented psychic phenomenon.

ON FRIDAY NIGHT I ATTEND a meeting of Indigo children in the basement of a spiritualist church in the suburbs of Chatham,

Kent. The organizer is medium Nikki Harwood, who also features in the documentary *My Kid's Psychic*. (Nikki's daughter Heather is Indigo.) Nikki picks me up at Chatham station.

"There have been reports of Indigo children trying to commit suicide—they're so ultrasensitive to feelings," Nikki tells me en route in her minivan. "Imagine having the thoughts and feelings of everyone around you in your head. One thing I teach them is how to switch off, so they can have a childhood." Nikki pauses, and adds: "In an ideal world, Indigo children would be schooled separately."

Inside the church eleven Indigo children sit in a circle.

"One kid here," Nikki whispers to me, "his dad is a social worker." The youngest here is seven. The oldest is eighteen. His name is Shane. He's about to join the army.

"That doesn't sound very Indigo," I say.

"Oh, it is," Nikki replies. "Indigos need structure."

And then the evening begins, with fifteen minutes of meditation. "Allow your angel wings to open," Nikki tells them, and I think: "I came all the way for this? Meditation?"

"I was with a baby the other day," Nikki informs the class. "I said, 'Hello, sweetheart,' with my thoughts. The baby looked at me shocked, as if to say, 'How did you know we communicate with each other using our thoughts?'"

The Indigo kids nod. Indigo organizers like Nikki and Dr. Munchie believe we're all born with these powers. The difference is that the Indigo children don't forget how to use them.

Then Nikki produces a number of blindfolds. She puts them over the eyes of half the children and instructs them to walk from one end of the room to the other.

The idea is for the unblindfolded kids to telepathically communicate to the blindfolded ones where the tables and chairs and pillars are. Nikki says this is half an exercise in telepathy and half an exercise in eradicating fear.

"Part of the reason why you're here," she tells the children—and by "here" she means on this planet as part of a super-evolved Indigo species—"is to teach the grown-ups not to feel fear."

The exercise in telepathy begins. And it gives me no pleasure to say this, but blindfolded children immediately start walking into chairs, into pillars, into tables.

"You're not listening, Zoe!" shouts Nikki, just after Zoe has collided with a chair. "We were [telepathically] saying 'Stop!'"

"I can't hear!" says Zoe.

Still, these children are having far more fun learning about their religion than most children do.

I wander down to the front of the hall. Children's drawings are tacked up on a notice board—drawings of past lives.

"I had people that waited on me," one girl has written next to her drawing of a princess. "I was kind but strict. Very rich, such as royalty."

"There's one girl here"—Nikki points out a little girl called Emily—"who had a real fear of being starved to death."

Lianne, Emily's mother, comes over to join us.

"She used to hide food all over the house," Lianne says.

"Anyway," Nikki says, "we regressed her, and in the past life she'd been locked in a room by her mum and starved to death."

"Emily is much better now," Lianne says, "since she started coming here."

Lianne says that, like many parents of Indigo children, she wasn't in the least bit New Age before the family began attending Indigo meetings. She was perfectly ordinary and skeptical.

She heard about the Indigo movement through word of mouth. It seemed to answer the questions she had about her daughter's behavior. And she's very glad she came.

Nikki says Emily happens to be "the most Indigo person here, apart from my own daughter. Emily will go into the bathroom and see dead people. She sees them walking around the house. It used to terrify her. Will I introduce you to her?"

Emily is thirteen. She seems like a sweet, ordinary teenage girl. She offers to do a tarot reading for me. "Something is holding you back," she says. "Tying you down. You don't look very happy. You're a little goldfish. Your dream is to turn into a big rainbow fish. It'll be a bumpy ride, but you'll get there. Just don't be scared. You're Paula Radcliffe. You just don't think you are."

Earlier this year, the *Dallas Observer* ran an article about Indigo children.

One eight-year-old was asked if he was Indigo. The boy nodded, and replied: "I'm an avatar. I can recognize the four elements of earth, wind, water, and fire."

The journalist was impressed.

After the article ran, several readers wrote in to inform the newspaper of the Nickelodeon show *Avatar: The Last Airbender*. In the cartoon, Avatar has the power to bend earth, wind, water, and fire. The *Dallas Observer* later admitted it felt embarrassed about the mistake.

When the Indigo meeting is over, Nikki gives me a lift back to the station. "Does it freak the children out to be told they're super-evolved chosen ones?" I ask her.

"They were feeling it anyway," Nikki replies.

We drive on in silence for a moment.

"I've been police-checked," Nikki says suddenly. "Another medium called the police on me. I've been accused of emotionally damaging the children."

"And what did the police do when they came?" I ask.

"They laughed," Nikki says. Then she pauses and adds: "They told me they wanted to bring their own children here."

Maybe they were just saying that to be polite. Or maybe they meant it.

A Message from God

I t's a Wednesday evening in early summer, and you'd think some high-society soirée was taking place in Knightsbridge, West London, on beautiful lawns set back from the Brompton Road. Porsches and Aston Martins are parked up and down the street, and attractive young people, some famous, in casual wear and summer dresses are wandering up a tree-lined drive. But this is no soirée.

We are agnostics. We are entering a church—the Holy Trinity Brompton (HTB)—to sign up for the Alpha Course, led by Nicky Gumbel. He is over there, welcoming agnostics; he's good-looking, tall and slim. It sounds impossible, but apparently Gumbel's course, consisting of ten Wednesday evenings, routinely transforms hardened unbelievers, the entrenched faithless, into confirmed Christians. There will be after-dinner talks from Gumbel, and then we will split into small groups to discuss the meaning of life, etc. There will be a weekend away in Kidderminster. And that's it. Salvation will occur within these parameters. I cannot imagine how it can work.

But many thousands of agnostics have found God through Nicky Gumbel. To name one: Jonathan Aitken, the former Conservative cabinet minister imprisoned for seven months in 1999 for perjury against the *Guardian* newspaper. "I am a man of unclean lips," he told the Catholic newspaper the *Tablet*, "but I went on an Alpha Course at Holy Trinity Brompton, and found great inspiration from its fellowship and the teachings on the Holy Spirit." The *Tablet* added, "He has done Alpha not once but three times, graduating from a humble student to a helper who pours coffee."

Nicky Gumbel's supporters say that within Church of England circles he is now more influential than the Archbishop of Canterbury; they claim that Gumbel is saving the Church. Other people say some quite horrifying things about him. I was told it is almost impossible to get an interview with him. His diary was full for three years. His people were apologetic. They said that the only way to really get to know Nicky, to understand how he does it, was to enroll in Alpha.

"Hi!" says a woman wearing a name tag. "You're . . . ?"

"Jon Ronson."

"Jon. Let's see. Great!" She ticks off my name and laughs. "I know it feels strange on the first night, but don't be nervous—in a couple of weeks' time, this'll feel like home."

I drift into the church. There are agnostics everywhere, eating shepherd's pie from paper plates on their laps. Michael Alison, onetime parliamentary private secretary to Mrs. Thatcher, is here. So is an ex–England cricket captain. I spot the manager of a big British pop group. The famous former topless model Samantha Fox found God through Nicky Gumbel, as did Geri Halliwell. I wonder whether Jonathan Aitken will pour the coffee, but

I can't see him. And now Nicky Gumbel is onstage, leaning against the podium, smiling hesitantly. He reminds me of Tony Blair.

"A very warm welcome to you all. Now some of you may be thinking, 'Help! What have I got myself into?'" A laugh. "Don't worry," he says. "We're not going to pressurize you into doing anything. Perhaps some of you are sitting there sneering. If you are, please don't think that I'm looking down at you. I spent half my life as an atheist. I used to go to talks like this and I would sneer."

Nicky is being disingenuous. We know there are no talks like this—Alpha is uniquely successful, and branching out abroad, so far to 112 countries, where they play Nicky's videos and the pastor acts the part of Nicky. "This just may be the wrong time for you," says Nicky to the sneerers. "If you don't want to come along next week, that's fine. Nobody will phone you up! I'd like you to meet Pippa, my wife."

We applaud. "Hi!" says Pippa. "We've got three children. Henry is twenty, there's Jonathan, and Rebecca is fifteen."

Nicky assures us that we are not abnormal for being here. The Bible is the world's most popular book, he says. This is normal. "Forget the modern British novelists and the TV tie-ins," he says. "Forty-four million Bibles are sold each year." He says the New Testament was written when they say it was. "We know this very accurately," he explains, "through a science called textual criticism." He says Jesus existed. This is historically verifiable. He quotes the Jewish historian Josephus, born AD 37: "Jesus, a wise man, if it be lawful to call him a man, for he was a doer of wonderful works . . . the tribe of Christians so named after him are not extinct to this day." I am with Nicky so far. But the agnostics here—it soon becomes clear that Nicky can read our minds—are thinking, "But none of this proves that Jesus was anything more than a human teacher."

Nicky tells an anecdote: He says that he once failed to recognize that his squash partner was Paul Ackford, the England rugby union international. Similarly, Jesus's disciples, in the region of Caesarea Philippi, failed to recognize that their master was the Son of God.

I could live without the squash anecdote.

Nicky says that Jesus could not have been just a great human teacher. When he was asked at his trial whether he was "the Christ, the Son of the Living God, he replied: 'I am.'" Nicky's point is this: A great human teacher would not claim to be the Son of God.

"You must make your choice—either this man was, and is, the Son of God, or else he's a lunatic or, worse, the Devil of Hell. But don't let us come up with any patronizing nonsense about his being a great moral teacher. He hasn't left that open to us. He didn't intend to."

This final logic (a quote from one of Nicky's heroes, C. S. Lewis) is impressive to me. It remains in my mind.

Then it's on to the small groups. I am in Nicky's group: As is typical, it consists of around ten agnostics, some from the City, one a professional sports person, strangers gathered together in a small room in the basement. We sit in a circle. I wonder what will happen to us in the weeks ahead. For now, we gang up on Nicky and his helpers: his wife, Pippa, an investment banker called James, and his doctor wife, Julia, all ex-agnostics who found Christ on Alpha. We ask them antagonistic questions. "If there's a God, why is there so much suffering?" And: "What about those people who have never heard of Jesus? Are you saying that all other religions are damned?"

Nicky just smiles and says, "What do the other people here think?"

At the end of the night, Nicky hands out some pamphlets he's written called (such is the predictability of agnostics) *Why Does God Allow Suffering?* (answer: Nobody really knows) and *What About Other Religions?* (answer: They will, unfortunately, be denied entrance to the Kingdom of Heaven. This includes me—I am a Jew).

I am enjoying myself enormously. I drive away thinking about the things Nicky said. I play them over in my mind. But by the time I arrive home and then watch *ER*, my mini-epiphany has all drained away, and I go back to normal. I cannot imagine how any of my fellow agnostics will possibly be converted by the end of the course.

As the weeks progress, the timetable becomes routine. Dinner, a talk from Nicky, coffee and digestives, the small groups. But the hostile questions have now become slightly less combative. One agnostic, Alice, who is the financial manager of an Internet company and rides her horse every weekend in Somerset, admits to taking Nicky's pamphlets away with her on business trips. She says she reads them on the plane and finds them comforting. We talk about the excuses we give our friends for our weekly Wednesday night absences. Some say they're learning French. Others say they're on a business course. There is laughter and blushing. I miss Week Three because I am reporting on wife-swapping parties in Paris. On Week Four, Nicky suggests I tell the group all about wife-swapping. The group asks me lots of questions. When I fill in the details, Nicky shakes his head mournfully. "What about the children?" he sighs. "So many people getting hurt." He's right. Nicky ends the night by saying to me: "I think it's important that you saw something awful like that midway through Alpha."

Week Five, and Nicky is onstage talking about answered prayers and how coincidences can sometimes be messages from God. He says he keeps a prayer diary and ticks them off when they are answered. As Nicky says these things, I think about how my wife and I were told we couldn't have a baby. We went through fertility treatment for four years. Every month was like a funeral without a corpse. And then we did have a baby, and when Joel was born I thought of him as a gift from God.

The moment I think about this, I hear Nicky say the word "Joel." I look up. Nicky is quoting from the book of Joel: "I will repay you for the years the locusts have eaten."

Later, I tell the group what happened. "Ah," they say, when I get to the part about us having a baby. "Ah," they say again, when I get to the part about Nicky saying "Joel," and then reading out an uncannily appropriate quote.

"Well?" I say.

"I don't know." Nicky smiles. "I think you should let it sit in your heart and make your own decision."

"But what do *you* think?" I say.

"If I had to put a bet on it," he says, "coincidence or message, I'd say definitely, yes, that was a message from God."

The subject is changed.

"So?" says Nicky. "How was everyone's week?"

Tony sits next to Alice. He is the most vociferous agnostic in the group. He always turns up in his business suit, straight from work, and has a hangdog expression, as if something is always troubling him.

"Tony?" says Nicky. "How was your week?"

"I was talking to a homosexual friend," says Tony, "and he said that ever since he was a child he found himself attracted to other boys. So why does the Church think he's committing a sin? Are you damned if you commit a sexual act that is completely normal to you? That seems a bit unfair, doesn't it?"

There is a murmur of agreement from the group.

"First of all," says Nicky, "I have many wonderful homosexual friends. There's even an Alpha for gays running in Beverly Hills! Really! I think it's marvelous! But if a pedophile said, 'Ever since I was a child I found myself attracted to children,' we wouldn't say that that was normal, would we?"

A small gasp.

"Now, I am not for a moment comparing homosexuals with pedophiles," Nicky continues, "but the Bible makes it very clear that sex outside marriage, including homosexual sex, is, unfortunately, a sin." He says he wishes it wasn't so, but the Bible makes it clear that gay people need to be healed.

"Although I strongly advise you not to say the word 'healed' to them," he quickly adds. "They hate that word."

The meeting is wound up. Nicky, Pippa, and I stay around for a chat. We talk about who we feel might be on the cusp of converting. My money is on Alice.

"Really?" says Nicky. "You think Alice?"

"Of course," I say. "Who do you think?"

"Tony," says Nicky.

"Tony?" I say.

"We'll see," says Nicky.

I drive home. In the middle of the night it becomes clear to me that I almost certainly had a message from God—that God had spoken to me through Nicky Gumbel.

WOMAN LEADS CHURCH BOYCOTT IN
ROW OVER EVANGELICAL PIG-SNORTING

A woman has walked out of her church and is holding services in her living room because she says she cannot bring herself to "snort like a pig and bark like a dog" on a Church of England course. Angie Golding, 50, claims she was denied confirmation unless she signed up for the Alpha Course, which she says is a "brainwashing" exercise where participants speak in tongues, make animal noises and then fall over. Mark Elsdon-Dew of HTB, Holy Trinity Brompton, said the Alpha Course included lectures on the Holy Spirit. "It affects different people in different ways," he said.

—The *Times,* May 11, 1996

Of course, stumbling upon this press cutting comes as a shock. I had no idea that the shepherd's pie, the nice chats, that these things seem to be leading up to something so peculiar— something that will, I guess, occur during our weekend away in Kidderminster.

I visit Mark Elsdon-Dew, Nicky's press man. I have grown fond of Mark. "Do anything you want," he frequently tells me. "Go home if you like. Really. Any time you want. Don't worry, I won't phone you up! Ha-ha!" Mark was once the *Daily Express*'s news editor, but then he did Alpha and now he works for Nicky, in a

Portakabin on HTB's two and a half acres. Nicky has so many staff—more, even, than the Archbishop of Canterbury, says Mark—that there aren't enough offices in this giant church to accommodate them all. I want to test Mark, to see how honest he'll be about the negative press. I ask him if any journalist has written disapprovingly about Nicky. "Oh, yes," he says excitedly. "Hang on, let me find them for you." Mark rifles through his filing cabinets and retrieves a sheaf of articles. "Look at this!" he says. "And how about this?" One article, from the *Spectator*, suggests that Nicky's organization is akin to *Invasion of the Body Snatchers*, something that looks like the Anglican Church, acts like the Anglican Church, but is something else, something malignant, growing, poised to consume its host: "For now they need the Church of England for its buildings—but they are very aware that through the wealth of their parishioners they wield an influence over the established Church that far outweighs their numbers."

"If you think that's bad," says Mark, "you should see this one."

"Oh, good," I think.

It reads: "HTB's divorce from the real world, together with a simplistic and communal response to all problems, a strong leader, and a money-conscious hierarchy, are trademarks of a cult."

"And here's a real stinker," says Mark.

"The Alpha Course: Is It Bible-Based or Hell-Inspired?"

This last one is from the Reverend Ian Paisley. His conclusion, after fifteen pages of deliberation, is that it is Hell-inspired.

Usually, when a discovery such as this presents itself midway through researching a story, I feel nothing but glee. On this occasion, however, the gaiety is tinged with indignation and relief—indignation that these people, this apparent cult, have managed to get under my skin, to instill in me feelings of some kind of awakening, and relief because I no longer feel the need to deal with those feelings.

IT IS SATURDAY MORNING in the countryside near Kidderminster, and Nicky is offering us the strangest invitation. He is going to beckon us into the supernatural, where he hopes we will physically feel the Holy Spirit enter our bodies. Nicky says that he very much hopes people will speak in tongues. "I'm so glad you could make it," he tells me.

"I'm glad to be here," I say, although I am thinking, "Are you a cult leader?"

We've been arriving all night—in BMWs and Mercedes and Porsches—at the Pioneer Centre, a residential youth club booked for the weekend. The traffic was terrible. I was stuck in a jam behind a minivan emblazoned with the words "Jews for Jesus," and toyed with the idea of taking this to be another message from God, but I chose to discount it.

We are staying in dormitories—six to a room. Nicky and Pippa are not bunking up with the flock: Nicky says he needs space to concentrate. I don't think the agnostics quite grasp the reality of what will unfold in the next thirty-six hours. Many are completely unaware. Tongues! How can Nicky make this happen?

The next morning, we laze in the sun and then we are called into the chapel, a big pine hut. Tonight, England will play Germany. Nicky takes to the stage: "Now, some of you may be thinking, 'Help! What's going to happen?' Well, first, I hope you have a wonderful time. Enjoy the weather, enjoy the sports, but, most of all, I hope we all experience the Holy Spirit."

Nicky says the Holy Spirit has often been ignored by the Church because it sounds "weird and supernaturally evil." He says the Church fears change, that he once said to an elderly vicar, "You must have seen so many changes," and that the vicar replied, "Yes, and I have resisted every single one of them." We laugh.

Nicky says this is a shame, because when people open themselves to the Holy Spirit, you can see it in their faces. "Their faces are alive!" Look at Bach and Handel and Da Vinci, he says. They had the Holy Spirit. Whatever line of work we're in—we could be bankers, "or journalists"—we can be filled to overflowing. Nicky says that it is absolutely amazing. "All relationships involve emotions. I don't say to Pippa, 'I love you intellectually.' What I say is, 'I love you with my whole being, my mind, my heart, my will.' Ah, but that's in private. The British don't display emotions in public, do they?" There is a silence. "Just imagine," he says, "that England will score a goal tonight. I think some people will go, 'Yeaah!'" There is laughter. The audience is relaxed. "If a comedy film makes us laugh out loud in the cinema, the movie is considered a success. If a tragic play makes us weep in a theater, the play is considered a success. But if a religious service makes us weep or laugh, we are accused of emotionalism!"

And so it goes on, with Nicky managing to make the most alarming prospect seem acceptable. Speaking in tongues would normally be something absurd—horrific, even. But imperceptibly, gracefully, Nicky is leading us there.

We have a few hours off. We swim and play basketball. The crowd is, as always, mainly white and wealthy.

A criticism leveled at Nicky by other Anglicans is that Jesus cast his net wide to embrace poor fishermen, whereas Nicky seems to concentrate on rich widows, Old Etonians, and young highfliers. This annoys him, far more than the accusations that he is a cult leader. He points out a group of men on the edge of the basketball court. They lean against a picket fence, watching the game with an inscrutable vigilance, huge and tanned, like a prison gang during their hour in the yard.

"You absolutely must meet Brian," says Nicky. "He's quite amazing."

Brian is not his real name.

"I was a villain," says Brian. "A professional criminal."

"Were you in a firm?" I ask.

"*I was* the firm," he smiles. "Say no more."

From Brian's demeanor—he looks the archetypal English crime boss—I don't doubt this for a moment. It makes me smile: Most vicars will proudly introduce you to some redeemed petty thief in their flock; once again Nicky attracts someone from the apex of his chosen profession. Back in the eighties, Brian was caught trying to pull off an enormous importation of cannabis. He was sentenced to ten years in jail. In 1994, while in Exeter prison, Brian heard about Alpha. To curry favor with the chaplain, he called Nicky and asked him to visit the prison. Nicky sent a team instead.

"And within weeks," says Brian, "all these hard men were waving our arms around like we were in a nightclub. Can you imagine it? People getting touched by the Holy Spirit, boys I knew who got banged up for some really naughty crimes . . ."

That was the first time a prison had run an Alpha Course. Brian was transferred to Dartmoor and took Alpha with him. Other converts did the same. That's how it spread through the prison system. Today, 120 of the 158 British prisons run Alpha Courses; some have six-month waiting lists.

Then there is this, from the March 2000 Alpha newsletter: Texas governor George W. Bush was so impressed by the impact of Alpha in the British prison system that he wants to start a trial program at once in his state. "And all that started with Brian in 1994," says Nicky. "It was such an amazing year."

Indeed it was: On January 20, 1994, at a concrete church next to Toronto Pearson International Airport, 80 percent of the congregation, apropos of nothing, suddenly fell to the floor and began writhing around, apparently singing in tongues and convulsing violently. Rumors about this milestone—which became known as the Toronto Blessing—quickly spread to Britain. Nicky flew to Toronto to see it for himself. Was it mass hysteria or a miracle, a real experience of the Holy Spirit?

"I don't talk about it now," says Nicky. "It divides people. It splits churches. It is very controversial. But I'll tell you—I think the Toronto Blessing was a wonderful, wonderful thing."

Nicky returned from Canada and spoke passionately at HTB about the Toronto Blessing, and his congregation, too, began rolling on the floor, etc. The services soon became so popular, with queues around the block, they were compelled to introduce two Sunday evening sittings—and still not everyone could get in. HTB became Britain's richest church. (It still is: Last year's income was $2.34 million.) This evangelical euphoria lasted the year, with miracles such as Prison Alpha cropping up all over the place. And then it ebbed away.

But its influence has lasted. The Toronto Blessing was the kick-start Alpha needed. Alpha began at HTB in 1979 as a brush-up course for rusty churchgoers. Hardly anybody attended. It trundled along, causing no ripples, until Nicky arrived in 1991.

Nicky is the son of agnostics. He discovered God while studying for the Bar at Cambridge, and gave up a career as a barrister to be ordained into the Church of England, in 1986. He saw Alpha's potential. What if he began targeting agnostics? What if he gave it an image makeover?

"Nicky bought standard lamps back in 1991," says Mark later that afternoon. "He took an interest in the food. There are flowers. Young, quite pretty girls welcome you at the door. Nicky identified some very important things. First, informality. Second, the course: People like the idea of going on a course, whether it's yoga or Christianity. Third, free and easy: We don't force anything down people's throats. People have a horror of being phoned up. And, finally, boredom: We will not bore you."

Nicky's new direction—combined with his charisma, his dazzlingly constructed weekly talks chipping away at our doubts, and the Toronto Blessing—caused Alpha's popularity to explode through the nineties. In 1992, there were five Alpha Courses in Britain; a hundred rusty churchgoers attended that year. By 1994, there were 26,700 attendees. By the end of last year, there were 14,200 courses around the world, with 1.5 million attendees. Nicky has sold more than a million books.

Alice had a wedding to go to, but hopes to arrive by this evening. The rest of our group gathers on the grass. We talk about our feelings about the Holy Spirit.

"I've got to say," says a woman called Annie, "the idea of speaking in tongues really freaks me out."

Nicky nods and smiles.

"I agree," says Jeremy, who works with asylum seekers. "I really don't want to be seen as some kind of freak."

"You won't suddenly become weirdos," explains James, one of the group leaders. "You won't lose your sense of humor, or your mates, or whether you drink beer or not."

"We shouldn't get too hung up on tongues," adds Julia, James's wife, and a fellow group leader. "Tongues is just one of the many gifts. Tony? What do you think?"

Tony lights a cigarette. "Do you have to believe in God before you receive the gift?" he says. "Because it seems strange to ask someone you don't believe in to prove that he exists."

I wonder what makes Nicky think that Tony is our group's best candidate for conversion.

"The Church likes to put God in a box," says James. "The Church wants to make God safe. We think the Church has lost the plot. We just want God to be God. As the Apostle Paul said, 'I would that you all speak in tongues.'"

We ask if they can speak in tongues, and they all say they can. James has been speaking in tongues for several years. Julia was fearful at first, but now does it a lot. Nicky and Pippa are extremely well versed in tongues, which, they say, literally means "languages never learned."

They say that on countless occasions they have heard people who can't speak Chinese, for instance, speaking in Chinese tongues. Such miracles appear to be commonplace once one enters the arena of tongues—as we will do at around 6:30 p.m. tonight.

AT 6:00 P.M. WE ARE BACK in the chapel. Nicky is onstage, telling us nothing bad will happen to us.

"You don't need to speak in tongues. It is not the most important gift. But tongues is a beginner's gift, and Alpha is a beginner's course in Christianity, so it would be wonderful if you tried." We steel ourselves. The door opens. It is Alice. She has missed Nicky's comforting preamble and has arrived just in time for the main event.

"If you ask for the Holy Spirit, you're not going to get something terrible," says Nicky. "Shall we give it a try? Shall we ask Him?"

"Mmm," say the crowd contentedly.

Nicky softly begins: "Please stand up and close your eyes. If there's anyone who would like to experience the Holy Spirit, maybe you're not sure, I'd like you to say a very simple prayer in your heart . . . a very simple prayer . . . It's OK. . . . I now turn from everything that is wrong . . . now hold out your hands . . . hold them out in front of you . . . if you'd like to . . . some of you might be experiencing a weight on your hands . . . you might be thinking nothing's happening . . . but you might be feeling a peace . . . a deep peace . . . that, too, is a manifestation of the Holy Spirit. . . . Jesus is telling you He loves you . . . He died for you."

This is when the first sob comes: At the front, someone begins to cry. "I sense that some of you would like to receive the gift of tongues now."

I wobble on my feet. Later, James tells me that wobbling is a possible sign of the Holy Spirit. I open my eyes for a moment and look at the group. Tony is grinning, his eyes bulging, like a schoolboy in a pompous assembly. Alice, who is entirely unprepared, is looking perplexed and uncomfortable. I close my eyes. I imagine those who have been in this spell before me—Jonathan Aitken, for instance, and the business executives and celebrities.

"Start to praise God in any language but the language you speak. . . . Don't worry about your neighbor. Your neighbor will be worried enough about himself. . . ."

And then the tongues begin. I thought it would be cacophonous, but it turns out to be haunting, tuneful, like some experimental opera.

I think some people are cheating—I hear French: *"C'est oui. C'est oui"*—but mostly it is quite beautiful. I open my eyes again and look around. Mark, Nicky's press officer, is speaking in tongues. So are James and Julia. All these people I have known all these weeks are speaking in tongues. Tony has refrained from tongues, but he is no longer grinning, either. He is crying. Alice looks ready to explode with anger. She barges out of the chapel. "Be a little bolder now. . . ." Nicky carries on. "Just continue to receive this wonderful opportunity. . . ."

James walks over to me: "Is it working for you?" he asks.

"Well, it might have," I reply, "but the truth is, I'm a journalist, so I couldn't keep my eyes closed."

"Would you like me to pray for you?" he asks.

"OK," I say.

James rests his hand on my shoulder. "O Jesus, I pray that Jon will receive Your wonderful spirit. God. Please come and fill Jon with . . ."

It is not working. The spell has broken. I tell James again that I'm sorry, but I'm a journalist. (This is no excuse: The picture editor of a Sunday newspaper is speaking in tongues to my left, as is a producer of Channel 4 documentaries in front of me, for the first time in his life.) So James changes tack. "Oh, thank You, Jesus, for Jon's wonderfully inquiring journalistic mind. . . . Please help Jon's career . . . no, not his career . . .

his wonderful journalism . . . and may his journalism become even more wonderful now he is working in Your name, Jesus Christ. . . ."

I tell James I'm sorry and follow Alice outside, where half a dozen furious agnostics have gathered on the grass. "Why didn't anyone tell me I'd signed up for a brainwashing cult?" says one. "I felt like I was in a pack of hyenas. I wanted someone to come up and ask me if I was OK, and instead someone came up and said, 'Would you like me to pray for you?'"

Alice is devastated: "I used to think Nicky was fantastic. He really gave me room to investigate my feelings about the Lord. But now I'm thinking, 'Just get me away from these weirdos.' I've been dragged all the way out here under false pretenses, and there's no escape. I am actually very, very upset."

We turn out to be in the minority, and watch as the new converts file out of the chapel, red-eyed from crying or smiling beatifically. Tony is one such convert, but he is not smiling. In fact, he seems miserable. "Something overwhelmed me," he says. "I didn't want it to. I tried to resist it, but I couldn't."

"What was it?" I ask.

"The Holy Spirit," says Tony.

"What did it feel like?"

"Like when you're trying not to cry but you can't help yourself. I was thinking of all the reasons why I didn't want it to happen—you know, the Christian lifestyle—and then Nicky came over to me and started whispering in my ear."

"What did he say?"

"He said, 'I sense that you have had a Christian experience in the past.' And that rocked my world, because I have, and I didn't tell anyone. That's why I came on Alpha. I wanted to decide, once and for all, yes or no. And . . ." Tony sighs discontentedly. "God spoke to me just now. He said, 'You can come back.'"

BACK IN LONDON the next Wednesday, Nicky's topic is "Spiritual Warfare: How Can I Resist the Devil?" He says that the Devil's tricks include planting doubts; I wonder if he is referring to those people, such as Alice and me, who doubted the power of tongues. Then I think, "Maybe the Devil really is planting doubts in my mind. I am becoming increasingly anti-Nicky. Is Satan working within me?" I conclude that I have been on this story for a long time and perhaps need a few weeks off. Nicky turns up the heat. He says we must not take an unhealthy interest in horror movies, Ouija boards, palmists, healers, and so on. These are the Devil's tools.

Later, in the small group, a woman called Suzanne asks a question. She didn't speak in tongues in Kidderminster but she did burst into tears. "I went to a clairvoyant a few weeks ago," says Suzanne. "That surely can't be a sin."

"I'm afraid it is," says Nicky.

"Really?"

"I would actually ask God for forgiveness for that," says Nicky.

"Oh, come on," snorts Suzanne. "Where does the Bible say that?"

"Deuteronomy," says Nicky.

"Oh," says Suzanne.

"Poor Suzanne," whispers Alice to me, "being made to feel guilty about going to some silly clairvoyant."

The atmosphere has changed.

"Things are coming to the boil," says Alice. "Can't you feel the screws being tightened?"

"How are you feeling?" I ask her.

"Judged," she says.

Annie is no longer freaked-out about speaking in tongues. She feels instead that she experienced God's love in Kidderminster. "It was the most beautiful experience of my life," she says. At first, she hated it, but now she realizes that her perception was wrong and that the tongue speakers are the lucky ones. Annie can now speak in tongues.

Nicky asks Tony to tell the group what happened to him in Kidderminster, but he quietly replies, "No comment."

Then Alice confronts Nicky. She tells him she felt trapped in Kidderminster. "It was group pressure. I am very, very upset. I know that you're looking at me like I'm a failure."

Nicky smiles. "Nothing could be further from the truth. We simply want to create a nonthreatening, nonjudgmental environment."

"Judged is what I feel," says Alice.

"Then we have failed," says Nicky.

Later that night, Nicky holds me back for a moment. I think he's concerned about how I responded to the tongues. After my Joel mini-testimony, I presume he hoped that I, too, would speak in them.

"Some journalists miss the story," says Nicky. "Lots of journalists miss the story. But you haven't. You've got the story. I knew it from the beginning."

"What *is* the story?" I ask Nicky.

"That something amazing is happening," he says. "Something incredible. All over the world. In a hundred and sixteen countries."

"I thought it was a hundred and twelve countries," I say.

"That was a month ago," says Nicky. "Now it's a hundred and sixteen countries." We laugh. "I would feel absolutely awful about Alice," he says, "but I feel completely free from responsibility."

"Do you?" I ask.

"I'm not hypnotizing anybody," he says. "I don't know anything about hypnosis."

It is getting late. Tomorrow is the start of the Alpha international conference. There will be much good news to report. Alpha is up 156 percent in New Zealand; one-third of all churches there now run the course. My personal experience with Alpha finishes here. I miss the last few weeks because I have to travel to America. In my group, of those who lasted the course, about 70 percent were won over.

Alice leaves some messages on my answering machine. She says I have missed some incredible things. I call her and ask what happened.

"It was just amazing," she says. "Nicky did a session on healing."

"Healing?"

"Healing by prayer. He started saying, 'I sense someone here has a lump on their left breast that they're very concerned about.' There were maybe twenty-five of these, and he got it right every time. People were standing up and everyone prayed for them. And then I asked them to pray for my horse, who's ill, and the horse got better. And I had a terrible pain in my left side and I didn't mention it, but Nicky said he sensed it and everyone prayed for me and now the pain is gone."

"Wow," I say.

"Nicky was gutted that you missed it," says Alice.

"You sound like you've changed your mind again," I say.

"Oh, I don't know," says Alice. "All I can say is that my horse got better and the pain has gone from my left side." She pauses. "For all my problems with Kidderminster, I've got to say that Nicky is quite brilliant. He's wonderful."

And I have to admit that, for all my problems with Kidderminster, I can only agree with her.

PART TWO
HIGH-FLYING LIVES

"Their eyes met and exchanged a flurry of masculine/
feminine master/slave signals."
—*Ian Fleming*, Goldfinger

The Name's Ronson, Jon Ronson

his is the centenary month of Ian Fleming's birth. There's an exhibition at the Imperial War Museum dedicated to Bond aesthetics. It's all a mystery to me. His expensive cars and elegant suits leave me cold. In fact, I've only ever been in a Bond-type car once, many years ago. It was a Porsche. The owner—the comedian Steve Coogan—pointed at a button. "Press that," he said. I did. The lid of the ashtray whirred gracefully open. "Did you see the smoothness of that action? Do you see how the ashtray just opened?" I looked mystified at him and at the ashtray.

Am I missing out on something? I hate not understanding things.

I phone Zoe Watkins at Ian Fleming Publications Ltd, the literary estate. She's known within Bond circles for having an encyclopedic knowledge of the books.

"I want to re-create a great Bond journey," I say. "I want to take a passage from one of the novels and assiduously match

Bond, car for car, road for road, meal for meal, drink for drink, hotel for hotel."

"What a wonderful idea," she says. "But which journey do you want to re-create?"

"I dunno," I shrug. "One in *Moonraker*?"

"*Moonraker* is basically a drive from London to Margate," Zoe says. "Fleming's fans were disappointed by the absence of exotic locations."

"*Goldfinger?*" I say.

"Well," Zoe says, "in *Goldfinger*, Bond drove an Aston Martin DB3 from London to Geneva. He stopped at the Hôtel de la Gare in Orléans, had dinner, drove the next day to Geneva, checked into the Hotel des Bergues, and then the journey ended with him getting captured and tortured by Goldfinger's henchman, Odd-job, in a villa near the hotel."

"It's perfect!" I say.

"Great!" Zoe says. Then she turns serious. "For copyright reasons," she says, "it's essential you make it clear you're following in the footsteps of James Bond and you aren't actually James Bond."

"I'll make that clear," I say.

I buy the novel. The journey seems even better once I read the ins and outs. Bond was trailing Goldfinger and had planted a tracking device in the boot of his Rolls-Royce. So Bond's life was out of his hands. He had to go wherever Goldfinger went. This frustrated Bond, especially when he spotted a pretty woman in a passing Triumph. Under normal circumstances, Fleming wrote, Bond would have pulled her over to have sex with her, but he couldn't because "today was for Goldfinger, not for love."

My journey, too, will be out of my hands. I'll have to go wherever Bond went. I wonder how many passing women I'll decide not to have sex with en route to Geneva. Probably loads.

I telephone Aston Martin. They enthusiastically offer me an Aston Martin Vantage for three days. They love the Bond association.

"How much would the car normally cost?" I ask Matthew, Aston Martin's press officer.

"Eighty-two thousand pounds," he replies. "Plus I've put in about nine thousand pounds of extras."

"Like an ejector seat?" I say.

"Extra-soft leather," he replies. "And a connection to plug in your iPod."

"Oh, REALLY?" I say. "An iPod connection?"

The Aston Martin was Bond's car of choice because he knew that if he lost Goldfinger's scent, "he'd have to do some fast motoring to catch up again. The DB3 would look after that. It was going to be fun playing hare and hounds across Europe."

On Wednesday a very elegant man called Hugh delivers the gleaming silver Aston Martin to my house. "Wow!" I say, politely. But I don't feel it. I'm like a sociopath when it comes to expensive cars. I feel no emotion.

Hugh shows me the interior. The leather is soft and red and hand-stitched. The dials are silver. The speedometer goes up to 220 mph. And there's the connection for the iPod! I'm going to really catch up on podcasts on this journey, I think.

Hugh is like Q, running through the gadgets. He shows me the button that turns on the sensor that bleeps when you're reversing and you're about to hit something. Then he shows me the button that turns the sensor off "if it gets annoying."

"How would that ever get annoying?" I wonder. "Unless

you're reversing for miles. But who does that?" And suddenly I feel ever so slightly Bond-like. These gadgets are mine now. According to Aston Martin's website, it took one hundred people one hundred days to build this car. There's a gang of boys watching us. I only half notice them because I'm lost in my unexpected Bond reverie. But then one of them crosses the road and leans in through the window. He looks about twelve.

"Do you know what happens to people who drive cars like that around here?" he says.

"I have no idea," I reply in a voice that sounds half Bond-like and half petrified. "Why don't you tell me?"

"They get hurt," he says.

There's a silence. "Oh, really?" I say.

"Yes," he says.

I turn away from his stare and look straight ahead.

"What would Bond do in a situation like this?" I think. He'd probably stab him in the face.

"That was a terrible indictment of our country," Hugh says, after the boy leaves.

"Wasn't it?" I say. And then—with a roar of the engine—I set off for Dover and the P&O ferry.

James Bond did not take the car ferry to France. This is the one part of the journey where my plans must diverge from his. He headed instead for Lydd Ferryfield Airport, in Kent, where he drove up a ramp and straight into a Bristol plane bound for Le Touquet. This used to be a regular practice for the rich until the hovercraft killed off the business in 1970.

I haven't yet got used to the Aston Martin. I'm finding it overpowering. I embarrassingly judder to an unexpected standstill on Upper Street, Commercial Road, and the A258 in Dover town center. Passersby shake their heads witheringly at me. I think they're mistaking my ineptitude for arrogance. Were I in my customary crappy car, they'd understand my stalling for what it is. Instead, they're seeing a fabulously sleek Aston Martin braking abruptly, then revving like a lunatic. They probably think it's my sick, slightly odd way of conveying superiority over them.

I reach the ferry. I wind down the window. "It's not my car!" I shout gaily at the immigration officer.

He stares askance at me. "In that case, sir," he says, "please park it over there and step out of it."

"No, no, no!" I say. "I—"

"Sir," he says, "park the car over there and step out of it."

"It's not my car because Aston Martin has lent it to me!" I yell.

"Oh," he says. "OK. Sorry for the confusion. We're on the lookout for a stolen Maserati. I'm an idiot. I saw the Aston Martin and thought Maserati."

"No probs," I say.

"Have a good trip," he says.

"Thanks," I say, and roar off.

I was expecting the hostile glares from passersby to continue into France, but once we reach Calais everything changes. I'm still getting constant looks, but now they are looks of adoration. For the first time in my life I am interesting to Frenchmen. They're finding me mysterious and fascinating. Frenchwomen, however, don't seem attracted by me. I'd have assumed from the books that they'd all want to have sex with me the minute they saw the car, but they don't seem to notice me. It's the men and the adolescent boys who are smitten.

It's a long six-hour drive to Orléans, a place Bond had never cared for: "A priest and myth ridden town without charm or gaiety." I head, as Bond did, for the Hôtel de la Gare: "When in doubt, Bond always chose the station hotels. They were adequate and it was better than even chances that the buffet de la gare would be excellent. And at the station one could hear the heart-beat of the town. The night-sounds of the trains were full of its tragedy and romance."

The Hôtel de la Gare annoyingly doesn't exist. So, instead, I check into the Hôtel Terminus, on the edge of the railway station. Le Cosy is the nearest restaurant. It is 11:00 p.m. Usually I don't eat after 7:00 p.m., but tonight I make a rare exception. I order everything Bond ordered—two œufs en cocotte à la crème, a large sole meunière, an "adequate" Camembert, a pint of rosé d'Anjou, a Three-Star Hennessy, and coffee. It is all incredibly delicious. I get drunk.

I am a happy drunk. The car is parked outside. I watch contentedly as a stream of adolescent boys stare adoringly and take pictures on their phones. Then my happy drunkenness turns to maudlin drunkenness. I'm sick of being the center of attention. Having an Aston Martin is, I reflect, like having a face made of gold. Some people are awed, others hate you and want to hurt you. And there's nothing you can do to get rid of it. I can't help thinking that an Aston Martin would be a liability for a spy.

The coffee and the Camembert and the wine and the brandy swirl toxically inside my now churning stomach. I stumble back to the hotel and to bed. At 3:56 a.m. I awake with a confused shriek, grab my notepad, and scrawl, "3:56 a.m. Hair triangle horse chest," and then fall asleep again. I do not know what "hair triangle horse chest" means.

Bond awoke the next morning, fresh as a daisy, had breakfast and a double coffee at the railway station, and then jumped in his car to continue his pursuit of Goldfinger, motoring "comfortably along the Loire in the early summer sunshine. This was one of his favorite corners of the world."

I awake the next morning feeling unbelievably nauseous and constipated, and stumble blearily across the road for breakfast at the railway station. If there ever was a restaurant here, there isn't now, just a vending machine selling crisps and Twixes.

Had this been the case in Bond's day, would he have eaten a Twix for breakfast? I wonder. Probably, judging by his constant desire to fuck up his body. I eat a Twix and begin to hate James Bond.

I check the novel and read to my disgust that there's a lot more eating and drinking to be done today. Bond had a big boozy and meaty picnic in the foothills of the Jura Mountains, followed in Geneva by a boozy dinner of Enzian liquor, "the firewater distilled from gentian that is responsible for Switzerland's chronic alcoholism"; choucroute; a carafe of Fondant; a glass of Löwenbräu; a slice of Gruyère; pumpernickel; and coffee. I feel envious that Bond ended his journey inside Goldfinger's villa. Being tortured is the only time during the entire trip he'd have managed to use up any calories.

I jump in the car and head toward Geneva. It was here that Bond picked up a passenger, a pretty Englishwoman called Tilly: "Their eyes met and exchanged a flurry of masculine/feminine master/slave signals." I've got a passenger, too—a photographer called Duncan. Our eyes meet and he belches. "Sorry," he says.

This stretch—through the Loire Valley toward the breathtaking, misty foothills of the Jura Mountains—was Bond's favorite:

"In May, with the fruit trees burning white and the soft wide river still big with the winter rains, the valley was green and young and dressed for love."

"You're not going to believe this," I say breathlessly to Duncan, "but the Aston Martin has got a connection for plugging in my iPod!" There's a ping from my iPhone. "An e-mail!" I think.

"Duncan," I say, "could you possibly read me the e-mail that's just come through? So what do you reckon, podcast-wise? Mark Kermode's film reviews or . . . ?"

"Calm down," snaps Duncan unexpectedly. "You're overstimulated." He glares harshly at me. "You're never going to understand what it's like to be Bond driving through France if you're this overstimulated."

"All right, all right," I say.

Duncan is annoyed with me. I guess we've got cabin fever, having been cooped up together in this Aston Martin for hours. Still, his tone shocks me. I feel as if I've been slapped in the face.

Ironically, Bond actually was slapped in the face by Tilly, his passenger, after he gave her one master/slave eye flurry too many: "The open palm cracked across his face. Bond put up a hand and rubbed his cheek. If only pretty girls were always angry they would be beautiful." I don't agree with Bond about this. I don't find angry women beautiful. I find them stressful and upsetting.

"Turn off the iPhone!" Duncan snaps. "Turn off your e-mails. Just experience the car and the road. Just experience it!"

"OK, whatever," I say. I do.

"See how nice it is to get rid of all that stimulation and just experience the car," Duncan says after a while. "You can go faster. The car only comes into its own when you actually accelerate."

"So you're saying that to truly enjoy the car, I have to break the law?" I say. But I understand Duncan's frustration. I'm an annoyingly cautious driver. The speedometer of this Aston Martin goes up to 220 mph, and I haven't once exceeded 70 mph.

"OK, I'll overtake that lorry. But just this once." I gingerly touch the accelerator. "Oh my God!" I yell.

I'm suddenly going 100 mph and the car is so smooth it feels like 30. I've never seen a lorry vanish so quickly in my rearview mirror. I feel like Han Solo in hyperdrive, or Jeremy Clarkson. It feels fantastic. No wonder the rich and boorish love themselves.

We stop to picnic, as Bond did, in the Jura Mountains; Bond "attacked the foothills as if he were competing in the Alpine trails," and so do I—and we make it to Geneva by nightfall. As I pull up outside the fantastically opulent Hotel des Bergues, a rich-looking guest comes over to admire the car.

"I've driven this all the way from London," I say.

"I can see why you'd want to," he replies. "My father bought me one of these when I was seventeen, and I bought myself a Porsche at the same time, and I really preferred this to the Porsche."

"Your father bought you an Aston Martin when you were seventeen?" I shriek, astonished. "You must be unbelievably rich!" He takes a slightly nervous step backward. I'm clearly less of a kindred spirit than he'd initially assumed. "Plus," I say, "isn't it irresponsible to give a teenager a really fast car? You might have crashed."

"I did crash," he says, impatiently, "but that isn't the point. The point is that, compared with the Porsche . . ." He pauses. "Anyway, have a nice night."

"And you!" I say. I think about adding, "I'm really constipated because I've been driving and eating too much," but I decide not to, because that would be too much information with which to burden a stranger. Instead, I head to the toilets, where they're piping choral music into the cubicles. As everything Bond ate comes flooding out, the piped choral music turns into a choir of heavenly voices, filling the cubicle with their magnificence.

Now that, I think, is a fancy hotel.

And this is where my Bond journey ends. Bond gets captured and tortured in Geneva. I go to my room and flick channels, hoping for the purposes of veracity to find a movie in which people get tortured, *Saw* or *My Little Eye*, say. But I can't. Instead, I fall into a deep and elegant sleep.

I Looked into That Camera.
And I Just Said It

n February 2010, the broadcaster Ray Gosling was arrested on suspicion of murder, having confessed on his BBC East Midlands TV show *Inside Out* to the mercy killing of his lover, Tony, sixteen years earlier. The papers were filled with supportive articles from right-to-die advocates and also from Gosling fans, who'd followed the work of this great pioneering TV journalist over his fifty-year career.

But then, on September 14, Gosling was convicted at Nottingham magistrates' court of wasting police time. He hadn't killed anyone. He'd been in France, reporting on a football match, the day Tony died. He was given a ninety-day suspended sentence after the prosecution told the court that his false confession had cost £45,000 and 1,800 hours of police time.

I've been a Ray Gosling fan since I was eighteen, when my college lecturer told me to seek him out. There was a place for people like me in the media, my lecturer said, and it was a place that had been carved out by Ray Gosling. By people like me, he

meant people from the provinces who were a bit awkward, and
had strange vocal inflections, but might be able to see the world
in a fresh, non-Oxbridge way.

I watched *Two Town Mad*, Gosling's brilliant, influential 1963
paean to everyday life in Leicester and Nottingham. In it, you see
the young Ray, with movie-star good looks, enthusing about
Leicester's new drive-in bank and multistory car park over a
sound track of swinging jazz. He made regional, working-class
ordinariness—things his contemporaries deemed too inconse-
quential to chronicle—seem exciting and cool and worthy of
lyricism.

The day after the verdict, I decide to call him. It was such a
mystery. What had made him invent the mercy-killing story?
Did he think nobody would bother checking? What was his
motive?

I tell him about my college lecturer and my subsequent years
of fandom. "Since the conviction, my body has been bruised
with people hugging me in the street and holding my hand, people loving me and cuddling me," he replies. "The main thing they
say is, 'Oh, Ray, you silly bugger.' And you know what? There's
not been one single word of criticism."

We arrange to meet in Manchester. At Stoke, I see him get on
the train and wander into my carriage. "Ray!" I call. "I'm the person you're meeting in Manchester! What a coincidence!"

He sits down next to me, smiles. Then the train pulls away
and he launches into a captivating commentary about everything
we can see from the window: the color of some cows, the City of
Manchester Stadium, various follies and statues. "This is the
tunnel at Prestbury. It's the richest village in England. It's where

all the grand footballers and executives live. The vicar died play-ing golf on the golf course. . . ." And so on.

"The BBC has been the great love affair of my life," he says as we get off the train at Manchester Piccadilly. "Fifty years. And now they've blocked me." He pauses. "Well, if there's no more broadcasting, there's no more broadcasting."

Then, as we catch the bus to Moston, North Manchester, a flash of anger: "The BBC is run by a load of guys who have never made a program in their lives, never told a story in their lives, never cried in their lives, never told a lie in their lives. . . ."

His point is that all nonfiction broadcasters walk a line. And he has a point. Journalism is storytelling. We wait around for the best bits—the most engaging, extreme, colorful moments—and we stitch them together, ignoring the boring stuff, turning real life into a narrative. Even so, there's shaping a story and there's making things up.

On the bus, Ray starts telling me about his early childhood, about how his grandmother used to routinely embroider the truth. He was, he says, born into a working-class backstreet family in Northampton in 1939. "My grandmother, my father's mother, used to keep a flower shop. When I was on my own, she'd beckon me over. 'Ray, you must never tell your mother this, but we're partly Jewish.' But she forgot the story sometimes, a bit like some of the stories I've told in my life and you've told in your life too. She would beckon me aside and say, 'Ray, you must never tell your mother this, but we're partly Gypsy.'" He laughs. "It wasn't enough for her to be English from Northampton. She had to always pretend to have that extra little bit!" (A friend of Ray's tells me later that even this story is a bit of an untruth: He wasn't born into a working-class backstreet family at all—he was quite middle class. But he empathizes with the working class so powerfully that he's reinvented himself.)

He went to Leicester University but dropped out, he says, because he didn't like his fellow students' assiduousness. They were after stable careers. He wanted a more adventurous life. He became a teddy boy and a delinquent. "I could take you to pubs," he says, "I'm not bragging, and I'm not going to tell the Greater Manchester Police, but I could tell you, I burned that down . . ."

"What?" I say. "You burned pubs down?"

"I'm a wild boy," Ray says. "I'm going to carry on being a wild boy until they shoot me down in the street."

"What were you doing burning down pubs?" I ask.

He gives me a look to say, "Change the subject."

He started managing bands and drifted into broadcasting, first at Granada, then at the BBC. "Year after year after year I was earning fifty thousand pounds and absolutely loving it. Radio, telly." He pauses. "So lucky."

His first rough patch came in the mid-'90s when he started drinking too much. The period coincided with programs such as *Louis Theroux's Weird Weekends* coming into vogue and Ray's brand of poetic realism falling out of favor with commissioning editors.

"Did you notice the appetite for ordinariness slipping away?" I ask.

At this, I see a glimpse of the more difficult, erratic Ray. "'The appetite for ordinariness'?" he yells. "You're talking to *me*! My appetite for ordinariness has never gone away. I fucking love my people and they love me back. What do you mean?"

"I think you misunderstand me," I say.

"I bloody well *do* misunderstand you," he roars. "My appetite for ordinariness has never gone away. And my boyfriend will come round in a bit, and he's as ordinary as me."

"I'm not saying your appetite . . ."

"Try your sentence again."

"Did you notice the appetite for ordinariness among commissioning editors slipping away?"

"Yes, of course," he says, not missing a beat, as if the yelling had never happened. "Once you get that many channels, forget it. You can't afford it. The kind of little niches I was able to get into? It's gone. And there's no way of bringing that back."

"They started to put crazy people on the television instead," I say.

"Yeah, they did. Crazies."

He declared bankruptcy and moved into sheltered accommodation. Then, just as it looked as if his career was finished, BBC East Midlands came along and offered him a regular fifteen-minute slot on *Inside Out*, which he did brilliantly right up until February 15, 2010, when he falsely confessed to killing Tony.

We arrive in Moston, where he's arranged to see his boyfriend, Mark, and a friend, Keith, in a pub called the Railway. We get to talking about Tony. Ray says they met decades ago in a bar in Salford. "It was an amazing, passionate love affair. He was a courier, working Heathrow to New York. He came back from JFK one day and we went to bed. I said, 'I want to fuck you.' And he said, 'I can't, Ray. I think I've got AIDS.' And he'd got AIDS. It was the early days of AIDS. And I was with him through lots of troubles. We found a way to have some sort of sex life." Ray says they had a pact because Tony was dying and in terrible pain. That part of the story was true. "I loved him. He loved me. I would have done it." But he didn't do it.

Sixteen years after Tony died, Ray was looking for subjects for *Inside Out*. They'd already done cafés, statues, gnomes, and the seaside. Ray thought: death. "We went to a coffin manufacturer in Nottinghamshire who makes customized coffins. If you've been a skier, he'll make a coffin the shape of skis. I talked to people who had mercy-killed their loved ones. . . . I heard all these stories. . . ."

And at some point—while they were filming in the graveyard that Ray will one day be buried in—he got it into his head to tell the camera he'd done the same.

"Why did you say it?" I ask.

"It was a genuine feeling, after listening to these interviewees, mainly from Leicester. . . ."

"Like a surfeit of empathy?" I ask.

"My heart was bigger than my head," he says. "And in my muddled mind, I thought maybe I did do it." He pauses. "We were at my own graveside. Darren, my cameraman, said he wanted to take some pictures of autumn leaves falling. I said, 'Darren, put your tripod down. I'm going to walk toward you.' I looked into the camera. It was a winter's evening, four p.m. I was at my own graveside. I looked into that camera. And I just said it."

I killed someone, once. Not in this region, not in the East Midlands, but not so far away. He was a young chap. He'd been my lover. And he got AIDS. And in a hospital one hot afternoon, doctors said, "There's nothing we can do." I said to the doctor, "Leave me. Just for a bit." And he went away. And I picked up

*the pillow and smothered him until he was dead. Doctor came
back, I said, "He's gone." "Ah." Nothing more was ever said.*

"One take," Ray says. "One take. Took forty seconds."

"You said it in such an arresting way," I say. "It really stops
you in your tracks."

"It does," Ray says.

"Maybe if you'd been a worse broadcaster and you'd just mum-
bled it out . . ." I say.

"Nobody would have paid any attention."

"You're a victim of your own broadcasting skills," I say.

"I am," he says. "My own storytelling powers."

He could have stopped the broadcast. He had opportunities. "They ran the final cut through for me. We watched in silence. My editor said, 'Ray?' And I looked at her and said, 'Let
it run.'"

He could have stopped it even after that. "The BBC warned
me of the dangers. I understood. I'd had dangers before. I'm used
to dangers." He smiles. Still, he told the BBC, "Let it run."

By then, he says, he'd convinced himself that he had actually
smothered Tony. The program was scheduled to air the night of
Monday, February 15.

"On the Monday morning the phone rang, and it was *BBC
Breakfast*—White City, London. They said, 'Can you come on the
Breakfast show to talk about death tomorrow?' I got on the train
to London and thought nothing of it. And then they showed the
clip. And I thought, 'Oh *fuck!*'"

The "Oh fuck" was, he says, his realization that the BBC had
"set me up." He believes BBC East Midlands had understood the
power of the clip and given it to White City in the knowledge

that it would generate massive publicity, even if that meant a prison sentence for their star presenter.

"The BBC used me," he says. Had BBC East Midlands not told White City, nobody would ever have known about the confession. "It was a little local television piece in my own country, with my own people, who are very fond of me and have been so good to me. I have an intimate relationship with my people, a close, intimate relationship. They are absolutely gorgeous and bright and witty and strong and wonderful and they love you, and so you count your lucky stars. I fell in love with a bunch of beautiful, lovely, strong, brave people."

"I do think you possibly have excessive trust in the people of the East Midlands if you think none of them would spill the beans about a televised murder confession outside the region," I say.

"I didn't think of things as clever as that." He stares at me. "*Come on!* Shut up. Stop interrupting me."

"You can't really blame the BBC," I say. "You're the architect of your own misfortune. If nonfiction people walk a line between truth and storytelling, you really fell off the line."

"Go on, go on," Ray says sharply. "I've been in the magistrates' court. I've heard what the judges say. You're all entitled to your opinions."

I open my mouth to ask another question. "No, shut up, Jon," he says.

He pauses. "All right. I repeated the confession. *Mea culpa mea culpa mea culpa . . .*"

When he says he "repeated the confession," he's talking about his day at White City. He did indeed repeat it—several times, in fact—first on *BBC Breakfast* and then in interviews all over the world. "They marched me from studio to studio to studio. *Buenos días*, Madrid. *Bonjour*, Paris. Hello, New York. Hello, L.A."

That night, his landlady phoned and said, "Ray, you didn't do it! You were in France. Don't you remember?"

At that, he says, the spell was broken. And then, a few days later, Ray was arrested on suspicion of murder.

On his first night in the cell, he says, they let him have a notebook, which he filled up right away with "different stories, memories, reminiscences," covering the floor with piles of papers.

Although he'd told everyone he wouldn't reveal the identity of his dead lover, "even under torture," he gave them Tony's name on day two, having been warned by his lawyer that if he didn't, he could be placed on remand for two years. Even though the police quickly proved he'd been in France at the time of Tony's death, they began investigating the possibility that he might be a serial smotherer of boyfriends. "They trawled through my love life, from Brighton to Plymouth to Blackpool to Bristol." He pauses. "No wonder I wasted eighteen hundred hours of police time."

Mid-afternoon, and Ray's friend Keith offers us the use of his house so we can talk quietly, away from the noisy pub. Things are turning quite chaotic. The man who was eloquent and funny on the train is getting drunker and more hostile.

"Have you read up about false memory syndrome?" I ask at one point.

"Go on. Go on. Go on," Ray snaps. "What's your degree in? Psychiatry? Are you a proper psychiatrist?"

And then, a few moments later, "Are you coming to me with clean hands, Jon? Have you ever been sued?"

I shake my head.

"You bloody white clean Daz clean brilliant white man," Ray

says. "I'm human. I'm a human being." Then he gives me a look as if to say, "Are *you* human? Coming here asking me all these questions?"

I'm finding his position really annoying. I admire Ray enormously, but don't see why I shouldn't ask questions about what he did, or why being sued makes you more heroically human than not being sued. "I know some people's brains can be odd when it comes to memory," I say, "but surely you'd know for certain if you'd killed someone?"

"It was sixteen years ago," he says. "You were where? Jewish Lads' Brigade?"

"Yes, but if I'd killed someone in the Jewish Lads' Brigade, I'd remember," I say.

There's a silence. "You do seem to have a self-destructive streak," I say.

"Absolute bollocks!" Ray yells. "Absolute bollocks, that is. Do I fuck. You look at me with those London eyes. I know who you are. I know where you're coming from." And then, a few moments later, "You're not a pretty man. You're *ugly*."

There's a short silence. Everyone looks at one another, a bit stunned.

"Well, you certainly know how to ensure a good write-up," I say.

"One day, you'll have what I have," Ray says.

"A criminal record?" pipes up his boyfriend, Mark, from across the room.

"Oh, fuck off," Ray says to everyone.

Later, a friend of Ray's—the photographer Mary Stamm-Clarke—tells me that the heavy drinking, the nastiness, is new. It's all emerged since the conviction, she says. "It never crossed his mind that the mercy-killing story might backfire. I think he thought everyone would love him for it." She says the stress has taken a terrible toll, even if he doesn't know it. He looks very different from how he did six months ago: older, frailer.

As I wait for my taxi to arrive, I feel quite remorseful. Ray spent a lifetime beautifully documenting life's ordinariness, but then a generation of documentary makers like me came along for whom ordinariness wasn't enough. We wanted to document life's extremes, and so his gentleness became passé and he unraveled into chaos. And now I've come along to document it.

"I've got to go and see the probation office on Monday," Ray says as my taxi pulls up. "They're going to ask me about my dependency on alcohol. Am I a fantasist? They're going to ask me all these terrible . . ." He falls silent.

"Maybe you can see me as a dress rehearsal for that?" I say.

"I can do. Yeah," says Ray.

And I realize that, beneath the hostility, the unpleasantness, what he really is is embarrassed.

I'm Loving Aliens Instead

On December 18, 2006, Robbie Williams played the last of fifty-nine stadium shows in a row, announced he was going to spend Christmas at his home in Los Angeles, and then basically disappeared. He was hardly seen at all in 2007. He briefly checked into rehab. He spent quite a bit of time hiking and playing soccer (he owns a soccer field on Mulholland Drive). Then he stopped doing that too. According to reports, he seemed to have retreated inside his house, the curtains closed. His record company announced he had no plans to release an album in 2008.

Today he unexpectedly calls me to ask if I want to go with him to the desert in Nevada to meet UFO abductees.

"I've been spending so much time at home on the Internet on sites like AboveTopSecret.com," he says. "I want to do something. I want to go out there and meet these people. I want to be a part of this. I want to do something other than sit in my bed and watch the news. And it starts with the UFO conference."

I log on to the conference website. It's taking place at the quite down-at-heel-looking Aquarius Casino Resort. The conference slogan is "Educating the World One Person at a Time," which makes it sound as if there won't be many people attending. The speakers will include Ann Andrews, from Lincolnshire, who claims her son, Jason, has had "disturbing experiences at the hands of many different alien species," and a surgeon, Dr. Roger Leir, who claims he has extracted from patients fifteen metallic implants that are not of earthly metal.

"I wonder if he'll bring the implants along," I say.

"So you can see with your own eyes whether they're earthly or not?" Robbie asks.

"Yes," I say.

"According to Jon," Robbie says. "I don't want to hear any de-bunking because I want to believe."

I fly to Los Angeles. When Robbie comes to his door, I hardly recognize him. He's put on a lot of weight and has grown a very bushy beard. I stare at it. "OK," he says. "I'm piecing it together now. I've grown a beard and I'm going to Nevada to speak to people about UFOs. I think I should shave so I don't look so mad."

We go to his TV room. It's bright outside but the curtains are closed. His girlfriend, the actor Ayda Field, is in there, watching a UFO DVD. We all watch it. This isn't all he does nowadays—he has been writing songs and playing golf too—but the para-normal has become a very big part of his life since he disappeared from public view.

Robbie first contacted me in 2005. He telephoned me out of the blue from a hotel in Blackpool where he was filming the video for his song "Advertising Space." He said he liked a book I had written and was thinking of spending a night in a haunted house.

"Do you know any?" he asked.

I spent a week sending e-mails: "Dear Lady_____, I've read that, if the portrait in your drawing room is moved, a ghost is apparently disturbed and manifests itself. Recently I have been contacted by the pop star Robbie Williams who would like to spend a night in a haunted house and so I wonder whether he and I can pay a private visit."

I expected not to hear back from anybody, but, in fact, once I invoked Robbie's name, owners of country piles started flinging their ghosts at me as if they were their debutante daughters.

"One of the guest bedrooms is definitely haunted by a young woman called Abigail who was starved to death by a monk in 1732," e-mailed one baroness. "Robbie is more than welcome to spend the night."

I was surprised to find how widespread the belief in ghosts was among the aristocracy. One hundred percent of the people I contacted responded instantly to say their houses were definitely haunted and Robbie was more than welcome to spend the night. Then Robbie e-mailed to say he didn't really have time to spend the night in a haunted house after all.

"I've put a week into this," I crossly thought. "Now I see why Robbie Williams gets on so well with ghosts. They both only manifest themselves when it suits them."

But we kept in touch. For a while we planned to go on a cruise together—hosted by the psychic Sylvia Browne—through the Mediterranean. But he pulled out due to concerns that if the ship happened to be filled with Robbie Williams fans, there'd be nowhere for him to flee to. He also considered going to Peru to take ayahuasca, a hallucinogenic so powerful—a shaman told me when I inquired on Robbie's behalf—it awakens our dormant plant DNA. But that trip was canceled when it dawned on him that ayahuasca is a terrible idea if one is in a fragile mental state. He'd speak wistfully about some future day when he'd have less work on and could investigate the paranormal for real. And now that day has come.

LAUGHLIN, NEVADA, looks from the sky like a tiny Las Vegas, a cluster of crumbling themed casinos poking strangely out of an expanse of desert. We are traveling here in a private plane that Robbie has rented for the day. He's brought along Ayda and a friend, Brandon. The flight attendant was there to meet us on the airstrip.

"Welcome to your plane," she said to us. "I just want to tell you that Snoop Dogg uses this plane a lot. What I'm saying is," she added in a lower voice, "you can do anything."

We all looked at each other. We're middle-aged now. None of us could really imagine what "anything" might mean anymore.

"Are we allowed to stand up as the plane lands?" asked Brandon.

WE LAND. A car is waiting on the tarmac to take us to the nearby Aquarius Casino Resort. We take the escalator to the second floor, walk past the stalls selling DVDs with titles like *Secret Space: What Is NASA Hiding?* and into the cavernous conference room where British speaker Ann Andrews has just begun her audiovisual presentation to an audience of five hundred.

I have to say, after all the anticipation, she seems a bit boring to me. She's recounting various tales of alien visitations in quite a dull voice. I half switch off and glance over at Robbie. He is engrossed. He is leaning forward, taking in every word. I decide to pay more attention so I can try to understand why.

Ann Andrews's life was quite ordinary, she says, until 1984, the year her son, Jason, was born. She flashes onto the screen a snapshot of a sweet little boy sitting in a field in Lincolnshire with a horse in the background.

"That's Jason," she says.

One day, when Jason was a toddler, Ann says she noticed he had a terrified look on his face. She asked what was wrong. He replied that aliens had appeared the night before at the foot of his bed and taken him to their spaceship, where they conducted tests on him. He said it was happening every night. As the weeks and months passed, Jason's story apparently never changed. When nobody was looking, aliens would come, float him up to a spaceship, and teach him the mysteries of the universe. They would teach him that he was placed on earth to become an Indigo child—a psychic sage.

"We took him to a psychiatrist," Ann says. "We cried so much. We had him tested. But the tests all came back negative."

And then one day, when Jason was twelve, Ann says she made a very big decision. She decided to believe her son. Every word. She has subsequently written a series of books about Jason, including one called *Jason, My Indigo Child: Raising a Multidimensional Star Child in a Changing World*.

I lean over to Robbie.

"She believes Jason!" I whisper. "She believes it all!"

"What's the other side of that, though?" Robbie whispers back. "It's either believe everything the boy is saying or remain steadfast to earthly beliefs and have a black sheep in the family. 'Oh, it's him again.' For her own sanity she has had to believe him." He pauses. "But for me, right now," he says, "everything she's saying is true."

Ann's audiovisual address ends with her projecting onto the screen behind her a series of extremely blurry photographs. From time to time, she says, Jason is summoned to the spaceship again. When this happens, Ann tries to photograph the UFOs. But she has only a disposable camera, and so the pictures always come out fuzzy and inconclusive.

It's time for the Q & A. Robbie's friend Brandon stands up and walks to the front. Brandon is a record producer and co-wrote some of the songs on Robbie's last album, *Rudebox*.

"I just wanted to ask: Why don't you buy a better camera?" he says. A slight gasp reverberates around the hall. People don't usually ask cynical questions at UFO conferences.

"I'm absolutely useless at anything technological," Ann replies.

"Have you ever had any psychiatric evaluation or presented yourself for that?" Brandon asks. Robbie flinches.

"No, I haven't," Ann says. "I'd like to think I'm all there, but if I'm not, there are quite a few of us that have these experiences, so maybe we're all crazy!" She laughs, awkwardly.

"Thank you very much," Brandon says.

Robbie goes outside for a cigarette. I tell Brandon I'm surprised Robbie brought him along after what he'd said about not wanting to hear any debunking.

"There's two sides to Rob in that respect, though, aren't there?" Brandon says. "There's the side that wants to go along with it, but there's also a very sarcastic, skeptical side." He pauses. "Which I'd like to think is the real side."

Robbie comes back.

"My toes curled up the moment you walked toward the stage," he tells Brandon. "But I think questioning somebody's sanity when this is happening to them is perfectly acceptable. I question my own."

We're standing near the table where Ann is signing copies of her various books about Jason.

"She reminds me of my mother," Robbie says, glancing at her. "Mum was a tarot card reader. She'd have people round and read their palms. She'd talk about spirits and ghosts. On the shelf of books just outside her room, there'd be the books about the world's mysteries, elves, demons, witchcraft. I was so scared. I'd never talk to her about it. Instead, I just lived in fear of all of this stuff. Maybe that's why I want to investigate UFOs and ghosts and everything. So I can work out why I get scared at night." He pauses. "I'll go and say hello to her."

He approaches the table. "Hi, darling," he says, "I'm Rob. Can I buy a book from you? Will you sign it for me? How is Jason these days? Is he happy? Has he got many friends?"

"No," Ann says, "Jason doesn't have many friends at all. In fact, it's been awful, really. He's socially shunned."

"When did this social shunning begin?" Robbie asks. "What age?"

"I suppose it was when my first book about him came out," Ann replies, "when he was fourteen."

"Jason, My Indigo Child?" I ask.

"He lost all his friends at school," Ann continues. "Nobody

wanted to know him. And, of course, word got around the small village where we live. It got very nasty."

"I can completely relate to that," Robbie says. "What is it he encounters from people?"

"In England, in particular, people are really spiteful," Ann says. "They ridicule him. They call out things from across the road like 'Oi! Mental boy!'"

Robbie puts his hand on Ann's hand.

"Even if this was all made up—which I don't believe, by the way—even if it was," Robbie says, "compassion should be shown anyway. Well, thank you."

Robbie pays for the book and goes to leave.

"You know," says Ann, "you look very much like Robbie Williams."

"I *am* Robbie Williams," he says.

"Can I just say I'm a big fan of yours?" she says.

"Oh, bless you. Thanks, darling," he says. "And please send Jason my best. Maybe we can have a chat one day. In fact"—Robbie writes out his e-mail address for Ann—"tell him to drop me a line if he wants. It must have been a terrible time for you, and an awful time for him. It's just so sad to hear it happens. It's happened to me."

"Really?" Ann says.

"I think joining Take That was like leaving on a spaceship," Robbie says, "and coming back and all your friends going, 'He's weird now.'"

WE QUEUE FOR the lunch buffet at the restaurant.

"I'm glad I had a chance to sit down with her and talk to her, so I could see her eyes and read her," Robbie says. "She's a really beautiful woman."

"So you identified with Jason," I say.

"That's not what I want to talk about," Robbie says. "Because it's long-winded, and whinging, and nobody wants to hear whinging. But if I was doing your job, I'd be asking that, because I'm asking the same question of myself—about why that nearly moved me to tears."

Everyone starts asking for his autograph, including one elderly American who says, "I don't know who you are but my daughter works for MTV and so she might." Word has obviously got around the conference that, in the absence of any aliens, the most interesting thing to have come down from the sky today is Robbie Williams. One conference organizer asks him if he'll consider being their official spokesperson.

"We need someone like you to spread the word and get the young people in," he says. Robbie seems quite attracted by the offer.

"This is possibly the most important thing ever to happen to the planet," he says. "It just amazes me that people aren't as interested as I am in this stuff."

There is so much commotion, we miss much of the next presentation and consequently never find out "what happened when four artists embarked in 1976 on what was expected to be a routine fishing trip."

This isn't the first time that Robbie's fame has hindered his forays into the paranormal world. A few years ago he invited the TV psychic Derek Acorah to his home for a psychic reading. A story subsequently appeared in the *Sun* under the headline, "I Helped Robbie Williams Talk to His Dead Gran."

Robbie invited me to his apartment in London. We chatted
and he told me how much he loved the program [Living
TV's *Most Haunted*]. He said he had given *Most Haunted*
DVDs to lots of friends, including Robert De Niro, Danny
DeVito and Billy Crystal, and they were hooked. I was able
to contact a couple of his loved ones, including his grandmother, whom he dearly loved. It was very emotional.

"The twat used my dead nan to sell his DVD!" Robbie told
me, quite furiously, at the time. "Plus, I've never met Robert
De Niro, Danny DeVito, and Billy Crystal. I've never even met
them!"

Robbie never spoke to Acorah again, but he persevered with
psychics for a while. He met one he liked a lot more, but then one
night over dinner the man told Robbie that he wasn't only a leading psychic, he was also "one of only eight people outside Japan
ever to be awarded a samuraiship." He said if anything were to
happen in Japan, he would have to drop his psychic career "and
fly over there to protect the emperor." After dinner Robbie did a
bit of research and discovered that nobody has been awarded a
samuraiship since 1872 and that "samuraiship" isn't even a real
word.

"Haven't all those bad experiences with psychics shaken your
wider faith in the paranormal?"

"I suppose they have," he says. "I never watch psychic TV
shows anymore." He shrugs. "And I suppose it might happen
with UFOs too. And then I might be able to get on with my life."

But if that day ever comes, it's not going to be today, for at this
moment an intriguing rumor reaches us. Apparently, a woman
tells Ayda, a number of conference attendees spotted a battle be-

tween two giant reptilian beings in the desert outside the hotel the other night.

"Did anyone take any photographs of the battle?" Ayda asks her.

"No," she says, "but someone collected a tissue sample and gave it to Dr. Roger Leir. He might show it to you, if you can find him."

Robbie says he'd recognize Dr. Leir if he saw him. He has been a talking head on UFO documentaries Robbie has watched. And, sure enough, he spots him in the coffee shop adjacent to the casino. Robbie says he feels starstruck around UFO experts in the way other people feel starstruck around pop stars.

"Doctor," he says, "sorry, I'm Robbie. I saw you at the Conscious Life Expo. And I've seen you many times on the Discovery Channel."

"I've been to a lot of places," Dr. Leir growls.

"We've heard that you have a reptilian tissue sample here in the hotel," I say.

"Have you done any tests on it?" Robbie asks.

"I only got it yesterday," Dr. Leir says.

"Can we see it?" I ask.

"Sure," he replies.

He takes us to his room. Dr. Leir is the surgeon who claims to have extracted from patients fifteen implants that are not of earthly metal. In the lift I ask if he has brought any of the implants to the hotel. He looks at me as if I'm an idiot.

"That would be absolutely ludicrous, unscientific, and ridiculous," he barks. "I keep them locked away." We reach his bedroom.

"Where's the skin stored?" Robbie asks. There is a silence.

He produces it from his wardrobe. It is a tiny flake at the bottom of a jar. Robbie, Ayda, and I crowd around and examine it.

"It could be a scale," I say. "It could be a reptilian scale—which is, of course, the hope—or it could be a little bit of a wing of a moth. Could it be a moth wing?"

"It could be a lot of things," Robbie says, cutting me off. "So, Dr. Leir, this was given to you last night. Are you excited about what it may be?"

"In a word," Dr. Leir replies, "no."

"Oh," Robbie says.

"It could be a piece of nothing," snaps Dr. Leir. "I was recently sent an object that was surgically removed from an abductee. I put it under the electron microscope. It looked like an organic compound, so we went to the next level. We did a test that uses infrared spectroscopy. Long story short, it was a piece of wood."

"Ah," says Robbie, a bit disappointed.

"So I just spent twenty-five thousand dollars to look at a piece of wood," Dr. Leir says. "You ask me if I get excited? No."

We fall into a melancholy silence.

"Do you worry that the aliens might want their stuff back?" Robbie asks, hopefully. "Do you get scared that they may want to come and get their transmitters back?"

"Well, if they want them back," Dr. Leir says, "they certainly have an advanced technology over what we have. So they could just take them."

AND SO ENDS OUR DAY at the conference. Robbie buys fifteen UFO DVDs and we catch the plane back to Los Angeles. He puts the pile on the table in his TV room. They have titles such as *UFO Space Anomalies: 1999–2006*. I ask if he's really going to watch them all. He nods.

"I used to read the *Sun*, the *Mirror*, the *Mail*, all the time," he says. "Eventually I had to stop looking because I'd find things that would upset me, whether it would be about me or about somebody else. So I had to fill that void. And that void has been filled with this stuff."

I think it's healthy that he doesn't look himself up in the papers anymore. That week alone it had been falsely reported in the *News of the World* that he had been dumped by a "Norwegian beauty" called Natassia "Scarlet" Malthe, and falsely reported in the *Daily Star* that he had been having secret face-to-face meetings with "mental conspiracy theorist David Icke" (they've never met). But the world he's obsessed with now—the UFO world—has its many liars too.

"It's surely out of the frying pan and into the fire, liar-wise," I say.

Robbie nods. He says he knows that there is a chance it's all nonsense. "But even if it is all made up," he says, "it's better made-up stuff than what the tabloids are writing. It's more interesting. To me, anyway."

"And it isn't about you."

"Yes," Robbie says.

I leave him standing on his balcony with Ayda, and he does seem happy, gazing up at the sky, even if there's nothing paranormal up there.

"There's always this weird black circle," Ayda says. "You see that black patch over there? It's like dark fog."

"Yeah," Robbie says, "but that might be something as easily

explained as light pollution." He pauses. "Right now I'm, 'You crazy American bitch! That's just light pollution!' But if we didn't have company, I'd be going, 'Let's stare at it for an hour and a half. Materialize! Materialize!' We'd be doing our materialize dance. But let's not do that while Jon's here. He'll think I'm weird." They carry on looking at the night sky.

"No," Robbie says, finally, "I don't think there's anything up there tonight."

First Contact

f we are ever contacted by aliens, the man I'm having lunch with will be one of the first humans to know. His name is Paul Davies and he's chair of the SETI (Search for Extraterrestrial Intelligence) Post-Detection Science and Technology Taskgroup. They're a group of distinguished scientists and will be, come the big day, the planet's alien welcome committee. His is an awesome responsibility, and one he doesn't take lightly.

"Imagine a civilization that's way in advance of us wants to communicate with us and assist us in our development," Paul says. He pushes his mackerel across his plate. "The information we provide to them must reflect our highest aspirations and ideals, and not just be some crazy person's bizarre politics or religion."

This is why, Paul says, he very much hopes that our opening communication with the aliens will be drafted by him. "All the attempts to send messages up so far have been very crass," he says. "If you're going to leave it up to the mob to decide what's important, it'll be this really cool video game. Or some sporting event. Or some rock group."

"Do you have any idea of what you might say to the aliens?" I ask.

There is a short silence. "I do," he says.

"Will you reveal it to me?" I ask.

Paul thinks for a second. And then he clears his throat.

Who is Paul Davies? How have events transpired to put him on the front line of extraterrestrial relations? And what will his message to the aliens be?

THE STORY BEGINS fifty years ago, in April 1960, when a young astronomer named Frank Drake decided to cut through the forest of unscientific UFO believers, the abductees, the searchers for mutilated cattle, and so on, and treat the subject with some rigor. He formulated an equation, the Drake Equation, which attempted to determine mathematically how many intelligent civilizations exist in our galaxy. His conclusion: ten thousand. Assuming some of these extraterrestrials must surely be bombarding us with radio messages, he borrowed the twenty-six-meter dish at the National Radio Astronomy Observatory in West Virginia, pointed it at a distant star called Tau Ceti, turned it on, and—nothing. Just a static hiss.

"No signals have been detected," he noted.

Despite this setback, SETI was born. Drake managed to score some U.S. government funding and created an institute in California. For much of the sixties, as Paul Davies writes in his new book, *The Eerie Silence: Renewing Our Search for Alien Intelligence*, a "major preoccupation among SETI researchers was to decide which particular frequency ET might choose, given that there are billions of possibilities . . . the hope was that the aliens would customize their signals for Earth-like planets."

But the aliens didn't customize their signals for us. After a decade or so, a schism formed within SETI. Some contended that surely the aliens—being far advanced—would use lasers to communicate, not radio. And so optical SETI was born.

Optical SETI didn't detect any signals, either.

The day before my lunch with Paul, Frank Drake was in London to update the Royal Society on the latest. The good news is that, with the help of wealthy private benefactors such as Microsoft cofounder Paul Allen, SETI is now better equipped than ever. Allen has provided them with an array of new dishes called, in fact, the Allen Telescope Array. They're situated in a field 290 miles north of San Francisco. The bad news is that no signals have been detected.

"Fifty years of nothing," I say to Paul now. "Do SETI people just go into work every morning, spend all day hearing nothing, and then go home again?"

"Your question is very similar to 'How does a computer scientist spend their days?'" Paul replies. "Sending e-mails and raising finance and teaching students and thinking about strategy."

"Doesn't it get depressing?"

"The SETI people are very calm, very determined. There is a hypothesis to test and SETI are testing it." He pauses. "If the eerie silence goes on for five hundred years and not fifty years, it might become hard to recruit the young scientists."

SETI scientists also fill the void by putting protocols in place for what to do on the day a bleep is definitively heard. It is extremely likely they will be the ones to hear it: They're the ones with the dishes. Should the protocols be followed, they'll know not to call the media or some government figure. They'll call the chair of the Post-Detection Science and Technology Taskgroup. Which is Paul.

Paul is a British-born theoretical physicist, cosmologist, and astrobiologist at Arizona State University. He lives his life at an incredibly high level of amazingness. He lectures at the Vatican, at the Smithsonian, in Davos, and at the UN. He has an asteroid named after him—the Pauldavies. He's a passionate scientific communicator and a grumpy man of enormous intellect. A telephone near us keeps letting off a loud and unexpected ring, and whenever it does, Paul looks extremely cross and says, "This is *terribly annoying.*" I can't help thinking that if the aliens do make contact, his automatic response will be to screw up his face in irritation and yell: "WHAT?"

I've been following Paul for a few days now. I watched him speak twice yesterday at the Royal Society (it has been hosting a SETI conference). The queue to get into his evening talk snaked around the block. He encouraged the audience, which filled the main hall and an overflow room, not to be depressed. It's quite possible the aliens do know we're here, but because they're a thousand light-years away and are consequently seeing us as we were a thousand years ago—rudimentary and agricultural—they're going to hold off beaming a signal to us until they know we've developed radio technology.

During the question-and-answer session, a man with dark glasses stood up and animatedly announced: "To see the future, one must look at the fringe, at the freaks, the visionaries, the artists. Why does SETI ignore what's right in front of us? The six thousand abductions! The ten thousand cattle mutilations . . . !"

One or two people nodded in agreement. Paul tried to look kindly, but his annoyance was obvious. "To expect alien technology to be just a few decades ahead of ours," he replied, "is too incredible to be taken seriously."

His inference was: You can tell the abductees are lying or delusional because their descriptions of the aliens and their craft are always so unimaginative. As he writes in *The Eerie Silence*, the giveaway is the "banality of the aliens' putative agenda, which seems to consist of grubbing around in fields or meadows, chasing cows or cars like bored teenagers, and abducting humans for Nazi-style experiments."

"At least flaky UFO nuts *believe* they've met aliens," I say to Paul now. "They *believe* they've been abducted and probed. You lot have rationalized yourselves into a fifty-year void of nothingness." I pause and add: "I realize what I just said is quite stupid, but will you respond to it anyway?"

"For me, science is already fantastical enough," he says. "Unlocking the secrets of nature with fundamental physics or cosmology or astrobiology leads you into a wonderland compared with which beliefs in things like alien abductions pale into insignificance."

Paul says he doesn't trust people. But he does have great faith in aliens. His face lights up when he imagines them. My guess is that, since he's spent so much of his life meeting people who aren't as clever as him, the aliens are—intellect-wise—his last-chance saloon.

The Post-Detection Science and Technology Taskgroup has been in existence since 1996. It comprises thirty SETI-friendly scientists, writers, and engineers. Paul was invited to become chair in 2008 but has so far convened only one meeting. He hopes to hold a second later this year in Prague so they can update their declaration of principles.

"So what's the first thing that'll happen when a signal is detected?" I ask.

"We'll have it independently verified. That's really important."

"And once it's verified?"

"My strenuous advice," Paul says, "will be that the coordinates of the transmitting entity should be kept confidential until the world community has had a chance to evaluate what it's dealing with. We don't want anybody just turning a radio telescope on the sky and sending their own messages to the source."

"So you'll tell the world that extraterrestrials are beaming signals to us, but you'll refuse to say from where?"

"Exactly," Paul says.

"They'll kill you. They'll grab you and torture the information out of you."

"But what's the alternative? Imagine we go to the United Nations: 'There's an alien community over there and everyone has to think about what our response might be, so we're turning it over to you, the United Nations, who are so adept at finding harmonious solutions to the world's problems.' Well, of course it would be a complete shambles. And which are the agencies that can truly represent humanity? You wouldn't go to the Catholic Church, would you? Or the U.S. Army."

This is why, he says, the most prudent course of action will be to create some sort of science parliament—a bit like the one set up to oversee the scientific exploration of Antarctica—and present to them the draft of a message that will be written by him later this year in Prague.

I am, I'm proud to say, the person who gave him the idea to draft the message this far in advance.

"If you don't trust anyone else to come up with a decent message, you should do it yourself!" I say. "You don't want to be caught on the hop. Do it in Prague and just put it in a drawer somewhere until the time comes."

"That's a very good idea!" he replies. "I'm thinking on my feet here, but it's an excellent idea."

"I'm full of ideas like that. I'd be happy to join the Post-Detection Science and Technology Taskgroup."

Paul looks panicked. "There's no money."

"Oh, right," I say. "Right. Yes." It is an awkward moment.

"So what will the message say?" I ask, changing the subject.

"We're talking about two civilizations communicating their finest achievements and their deepest beliefs and attitudes. I feel we should send something about our level of scientific attainment and understanding of how the world works. Some fundamental physics. Maybe some biology. But primarily physics and astronomy."

"And some classical music?" I suggest.

"Well, we could, but it's not going to mean anything to them," Paul says.

"Yes, yes, of course." I pause. "Why won't it mean anything to them?"

"There's nothing certain in this game," Paul says, "but our appreciation of art and music is very much tied to our cognitive architecture. There's no particular reason why some other intelligent species will share these aesthetic values. The general theory of relativity is impressive and will surely be understood by them. But if we send a Picasso or a *Mona Lisa*? They wouldn't care." He pauses. "I mean the phonograph disc that went off on *Voyager* had speeches by Kurt Waldheim and Jimmy Carter. That's a world away from what we should be doing."

"Of course, the world will eventually discover the coordinates and start sending up their own stuff," I say.

"Yes. So one of the first things we might want to say is that there's no unitary government on this planet, no unitary political philosophy or ideology. We're a great place for freedom, if not anarchy, and so we're putting together the best possible coherent package for your consideration, but expect it to be followed up with all sorts of bizarre and incoherent babble that you must treat with some discretion." He pauses. "Although how we'll express all this when we only have mathematics in common will be something of a challenge."

We get the bill. Paul wants to end on an optimistic note and so he mentions the one time in SETI history when something broke the silence.

"We call it the Wow signal," he says. "It was a radio telescope in Ohio, back in the days when they didn't have the electronic gadgetry to go 'ping' if there was something weird. So they looked at a computer printout some weeks afterward, and it showed a signal that went on for seventy-two seconds. Nobody was listening at the time. The researcher wrote 'Wow' in the margin. And many times radio telescopes have been turned on that star, but nothing odd has ever happened again."

"Should we feel excited by the Wow signal?"

"I've often wondered," Paul says. He puts on his coat. "What we're doing is a fantastic and challenging task. It compels us to think about all the things we should be thinking about. What is life? What is intelligence?" He pauses. "And if nothing else, it is a great deal of fun."

Stanley Kubrick's Boxes

n 1996 I received a telephone call from a man calling himself Tony.

"I'm phoning on behalf of my employer," he said. "He'd like you to send him a radio documentary you made called *Hotel Auschwitz*."

"Who's your employer?" I asked.

"I can't tell you," he said.

"Really?" I said. "Oh, go on. Please. Who is it?"

I heard him sigh. "It's Stanley Kubrick," he said.

"I'm sorry?" I said.

"Let me give you the address," said the man. He sounded posh. It seemed that he didn't want to say any more about this than he had to. I sent the tape to a PO box in St. Albans and I waited. What might happen next?

BY THE TIME I RECEIVED that telephone call, nine years had passed since Kubrick's last film—*Full Metal Jacket*. All anyone outside his circle knew about him was that he was living in a house somewhere near St. Albans—or a "secret lair" according to a *Sunday Times* article of that year—behaving presumably like some kind of mad hermit genius. Nobody even knew what he looked like. It was sixteen years since a photograph of him had been published.

He'd gone from making a film a year in the 1950s (including the brilliant, horrific *Paths of Glory*), to a film every couple of years in the sixties (*Lolita, Dr. Strangelove,* and *2001: A Space Odyssey* all came out within a six-year period), to two films per decade in the seventies and eighties (there had been a seven-year gap between *The Shining* and *Full Metal Jacket*), and now, in the 1990s, absolutely nothing at all. What was he doing in there? According to rumors, he was passing his time being terrified of germs and refusing to let his chauffeur drive over 30 mph. But now I knew what he was doing. He was listening to my BBC Radio 4 documentary, *Hotel Auschwitz*.

"The good news," wrote the *Times* that year, bemoaning the ever-lengthening gaps between his films, "is that Kubrick is reportedly a hoarder. There is apparently an extensive archive of material at his home in Childwickbury Manor. When that is eventually opened we may get close to understanding the tangled brain which brought to life HAL, the *Clockwork Orange* Droogs and Jack Torrance."

The thing is, once I sent the tape to the PO box, nothing happened next. I never heard anything again. Not a word. My cassette disappeared into the mysterious world of Stanley Kubrick. And then, three years later, Kubrick was dead.

Two years after that—in 2001—I got another phone call out of the blue from the man called Tony. "Do you want to get some lunch?" he asked. "Why don't you come up to Childwick?"

The journey to the Kubrick house starts normally. You drive through the St. Albans suburbs, passing ordinary-sized postwar houses and opticians and vets. Then you turn right, past the Private Road sign, into an almost absurdly perfect picturesque model village. Even the name, Childwick Green, sounds like A. A. Milne wrote it. There's an electric gate at the end, with a Do Not Trespass sign. Drive through that, and through some woods, and past a long white fence with the paint peeling off, and then another electric gate, and then another electric gate, and then another electric gate and you're in the middle of an estate full of boxes.

There are boxes everywhere—shelves of boxes in the stable block, rooms full of boxes in the main house. In the fields, where racehorses once stood and grazed, are half a dozen Portakabins, each packed with boxes. I notice that many of the boxes are sealed. Some have, in fact, remained unopened for decades.

Tony turns out to be Tony Frewin. He started working as an office boy for Kubrick in 1965, when he was seventeen. One day, apropos of nothing, Kubrick said to him, "You have that office outside my office if I need you."

That was thirty-six years ago and Tony is still here, two years after Kubrick died and was buried in the grounds behind the house. There may be no more Kubrick movies to make, but there are DVDs to remaster and reissue in special editions. There are box sets and retrospective books to oversee. There is paperwork.

Tony gives me a guided tour through the house. We walk past boxes and more boxes and filing cabinets and past a grand staircase. Childwick was once home to a family of horse trainers called the Joels. Back then there was, presumably, busts or floral displays on either side at the bottom of this staircase. Here, instead, is a photocopier on one side and a fax machine on the other.

"This is how Stanley left it," says Tony.

Stanley Kubrick's house looks like the Inland Revenue took it over long ago. Tony takes me into a large room painted blue and filled with books.

"This used to be the cinema," he tells me.

"Is it the library now?" I ask.

"Look closer at the books," says Tony.

I do.

"Bloody hell," I say. "Every book in this room is about *Napoleon*!"

"Look in the drawers," says Tony.

I do.

"It's all about Napoleon too!" I say. "Everything in here is about *Napoleon*!"

I must say I feel a little like Shelley Duvall in *The Shining*, chancing upon her husband's novel and finding it is consisting entirely of the line "All work and no play makes Jack a dull boy" typed over and over again. John Baxter wrote, in his unauthorized biography of Kubrick, "Most people attributed the purchase of Childwick to Kubrick's passion for privacy, and drew parallels with Jack Torrance in *The Shining*." This room full of Napoleon stuff seems to bear that comparison out.

"Somewhere else in this house," Tony says, "is a cabinet full of twenty-five thousand library cards, three inches by five inches. If you want to know what Napoleon, or Josephine, or anyone within Napoleon's inner circle was doing on the afternoon of

July twenty-third, seventeen-whatever, you go to that card and it'll tell you."

"Who made up the cards?" I ask.

"Stanley," says Tony. "With some assistants."

"How long did it take?" I ask.

"Years," says Tony. "The late sixties."

Kubrick never made his film about Napoleon. During the years it took him to compile this research, a Rod Steiger movie called *Waterloo* was written, produced, and released. It was a box-office failure, so MGM abandoned *Napoleon* and Kubrick made *A Clockwork Orange* instead.

"Did you do this kind of thing for all the movies?" I ask Tony.

"More or less," he says.

"OK," I say. "I understand how you might do this for *Napoleon*, but what about, say, *The Shining*?"

"Somewhere here," says Tony, "is just about every book about ghosts ever written, and there'll be a box containing photographs of the exteriors of maybe every mountain hotel in the world."

There is a silence.

"Tony," I say. "Can I look through the boxes?"

I've been coming to the Kubrick house a couple of times a month ever since.

I start in a Portakabin behind the stable block, with a box marked *Lolita*. I open it, noting the ease with which the lid comes off. I flick through the paperwork inside, pausing randomly at a letter that reads:

Dear Mr. Kubrick,

Just a line to express to you and to Mrs. Kubrick my husband's and my own deep appreciation of your kindness

in arranging for Dmitri's introduction to your uncle, Mr.
Guenther Rennert.

Sincerely,

Mrs. Vladimir Nabokov

I later learn that Dmitri was a budding opera singer and
Rennert was a famous opera director, in charge of the National
Theatre Munich and Glyndebourne. This letter was written in
1962, back in the days when Kubrick was still producing a film
every year or so. This box is full of fascinating correspondence
between Kubrick and the Nabokovs but—unlike the fabulously otherworldly Napoleon room, which was accrued six years
later—it is the kind of stuff you would probably find in any director's archive.

The unusual stuff—the stuff that elucidates the ever-
lengthening gaps between productions—can be found in the
boxes that were compiled from 1968 onwards. In a box next to
the *Lolita* box in the Portakabin I find an unusually terse letter,
written by Kubrick to someone called Pat, on January 10, 1968:

Dear Pat,

Although you are apparently too busy to personally
return my phone calls, perhaps you will find time in the
near future to reply to this letter?

(Later, when I show Tony Frewin this letter, he says he's surprised by the brusqueness. Kubrick must have been at the end of
his tether, he says, because on a number of occasions he said to
Tony, "Before you send an angry letter, imagine how it would
look if it got into the hands of *Time Out*.") The reason for Ku-

brick's annoyance in this particular letter was because he'd heard that the Beatles were going to use a landscape shot from *Dr. Strangelove* in one of their movies.

"The Beatle film will be very widely seen," Kubrick writes, "and it will make it appear that the material in *Dr. Strangelove* is stock footage. I feel this harms the film."

There are a similar batch of telexes from 1975: "It would appear," Kubrick writes in one, "that 'Space: 1999' may very well become a long-running and important television series. There seems nothing left now but to seek the highest possible damages. . . . The deliberate choice of a date only two years away from *2001* is not accidental and harms us."

This telex was written seven years after the release of *2001*.

But you can see why Kubrick sometimes felt compelled to wage war to protect the honor of his work. A 1975 telex, from a picture publicity man at Warner Bros. called Mark Kauffman, regards publicity stills for Kubrick's somber reworking of Thackeray's *Barry Lyndon*. It reads: "Received additional material. Is there any material with humor or zaniness that you could send?"

Kubrick replies: "The style of the picture is reflected by the stills you have already received. The film is based on William Makepeace Thackeray's novel which, though it has irony and wit, could not be well described as zany."

I take a break from the boxes to wander over to Tony's office. As I walk in I notice something pinned onto his letter box.

"POSTMAN," it reads. "Please put all mail in the white box under the colonnade across the courtyard to your right."

It is not a remarkable note except for one thing. The typeface Tony used to print it is exactly the same typeface Kubrick used for the posters and title sequences of *Eyes Wide Shut* and *2001*.

"It's Futura Extra Bold," explains Tony. "It was Stanley's favorite typeface. It's sans serif. He liked Helvetica and Univers too. Clean and elegant."

"Is this the kind of thing you and Kubrick used to talk about?" I ask.

"God, yes," says Tony. "Sometimes late into the night. I was always trying to persuade him to turn away from them. But he was wedded to his sans serifs."

Tony goes to his bookshelf and brings down a number of volumes full of examples of typefaces, the kind of volumes he and Kubrick used to study, and he shows them to me.

"I did once get him to admit the beauty of Bembo," he adds, "a serif."

"So is that note to the postman a sort of private tribute from you to Kubrick?" I ask.

"Yeah," says Tony. He smiles to himself. "Yeah, yeah."

For a moment I also smile at the unlikely image of the two men discussing the relative merits of typefaces late into the night, but then I remember the first time I saw the trailer for *Eyes Wide Shut*, the way the words CRUISE, KIDMAN, KUBRICK flashed dramatically onto the screen in large red, yellow, and white colors, to the song "Baby Did a Bad Bad Thing." Had the words not been in Futura Extra Bold, I realize now, they wouldn't have sent such a chill up the spine. Kubrick and Tony obviously became, at some point during their relationship, tireless amateur sleuths, wanting to amass and consume and understand all information.

But this attention to detail becomes so amazingly evident and seemingly all-consuming in the later boxes, I begin to wonder whether it was worth it. In one Portakabin, for example, there are hundreds and hundreds of boxes marked EWS—Portman Square, EWS—Kensington, and Chelsea, etc., etc. I choose the one marked EWS—Islington because that's where I live. Inside are hundreds of photographs of doorways. The doorway of my local video shop, Century Video, is here, as is the doorway of my dry cleaners, Spots Suede Services on Upper Street. Then, as I continue to flick through the photographs, I find to my astonishment pictures of the doorways of the houses on my own street.

Handwritten at the top of these photographs are the words "Hooker doorway?"

"Huh," I think.

So somebody within the Kubrick organization (it was, in fact, his nephew Manuel Harlan) once walked up my street, on Kubrick's orders, hoping to find a suitable doorway for a hooker in *Eyes Wide Shut*. It is both an extremely interesting find and a bit of a kick in the teeth. Judging by the writing on the boxes, just about every doorway in London has been captured and placed inside this Portakabin. This solves one mystery for me—the one about why Kubrick, a native of the Bronx, chose the St. Albans countryside, of all places, for his home. I realize now that it didn't matter. It could have been anywhere. It is as if the whole world is to be found somewhere within this estate.

LATER I GET TO MEET Manuel Harlan. "How long did all this take you?" I ask him.

"A year," he says.

"Every day?" I ask.

"Pretty much," he says.

"Was it a good year?" I ask.

"It was a great year," he says. "I think I took thirty thousand photos in all. That's a number I arrived at once. At first it was just going to be stately homes. Then I started looking for coffee shops. And then doorways. Then toy shops. Mortuaries. Oh! Costume places! That was a really long job. I was in every costume shop in the southeast of England."

"Did he look at them all?" I ask.

"All!" he says. "With tremendous excitement! One time he wanted me to do the whole of Commercial Road. But he didn't want the buildings tilting back or forward in the photographs. So I had to take a ladder. I'd climb the ladder, take the picture, get down, move the ladder twelve feet, and on and on. Commercial Road is a very long road. Stanley was constantly on the phone going, 'Have you finished yet? How fast can you get here?'"

Manuel says once he reached the end of Commercial Road, he hurried straight to the St. Albans branch of Snappy Snaps to get the pictures developed. Then he assiduously taped them together to form a perfect panorama of the whole of Commercial Road. Back at the Kubrick house he carefully laid the panorama out— like a homemade Google street view years before Google had conceived of such a thing—down a long corridor. Kubrick emerged from his room, looked at it, and said: "Well. It sure beats going there."

So was it all worth it? Was the hooker doorway eventually picked for *Eyes Wide Shut* the quintessential hooker doorway? Back at home I watch *Eyes Wide Shut* again on DVD. The hooker doorway looks exactly like any doorway you would find in Lower Manhattan—maybe on Canal Street or in the East Village. It is a red door, up some brownstone steps, with the number 265 painted on the glass at the top. Tom Cruise is pulled through the door by the hooker. The scene is over in a few seconds. It was eventually shot on a set at Pinewood.

I remember the Napoleon archive, the years it took Kubrick and some assistants to compile it, and I suggest to Jan Harlan, Kubrick's executive producer and brother-in-law (and Manuel's father), that had there not been all those years of attention to detail during the early planning of the movie, perhaps *Napoleon* would have actually been made.

"That's a completely theoretical and obsolete observation!" replies Jan. "That's like saying if Vermeer had painted in a different style he'd have done a hundred more paintings."

"OK," I say.

"Why don't you just accept that this was how he worked?" says Jan.

"But if he hadn't allowed his tireless work ethic to take him to unproductive places, he'd have made more films," I say. "For instance, the 'Space: 1999' lawsuit seems, with the benefit of hindsight, a little trivial."

"Of course I wish he had made more films," says Jan.

Jan and I are having this conversation inside the stable block, surrounded by hundreds of boxes. For the past few days I have been reading the contents of those marked "Fan Letters" and "Résumés."

They are filled with pleas from hundreds of strangers, written over the decades. They say much the same thing: "I know I have the talent to be a big star. I know it's going to happen to me one day. I just need a break. Will you give me that break?"

All these letters are—every single one of them—written by people I have never heard of. Many of these young actors and actresses will be middle-aged by now. I want to go back in time and say to them, "You're not going to make it! It's best you know now rather than face years of having your dreams slowly erode." They are heartbreaking boxes.

"Stanley never wrote back to the fans," says Jan. "He never, never responded. It would have been too much. It would have driven him crazy. He didn't like to get engaged with strangers."

(Actually, Kubrick did write back to fans, on random, rare occasions. I find two replies in total. Maybe he only ever wrote back twice. One reads, "Your letter of 4th May was overwhelming. What can I say in reply? Sincerely, Stanley Kubrick." The other reads, "Dear Mr. William. Thank you for writing. No comment about *A Clockwork Orange*. You will have to decide for yourself. Sincerely, Stanley Kubrick.")

"One time, in 1998," Jan says, "I was in the kitchen with Stanley and I mentioned that I'd just been to the opticians in St. Albans to get a new pair of glasses. Stanley looked shocked. He said, 'Where *exactly* did you go?' I told him and he said, 'Oh, thank God! I was just in the other opticians in town getting some glasses and I used your name!'"

Jan laughs. "He used my name in the opticians, in Waitrose, everywhere."

"But even if he didn't reply to the fan letters," I say, "they've all been so scrupulously read and filed."

The fan letters are perfectly preserved. They are not in the least dusty or crushed. The system used to file them is, in fact, extraordinary. Each fan box contains perhaps fifty orange folders. Each folder has the name of a town or city typed on the front—Agincourt, Ontario; Alhambra, California; Cincinnati, Ohio; Daly City, California; and so on—and is in alphabetical order inside the boxes. And inside each folder are all the fan letters that came from that particular place in any one year. Kubrick has handwritten "F—P" on the positive ones and "F—N" on the negative ones. The crazy ones have been marked "F—C."

"Look at this," I say to Jan.

I hand him a letter written by a fan and addressed to Arthur C. Clarke. He forwarded it on to Kubrick and wrote on the top, "Stanley. See P3!! Arthur."

Jan turns to page 3, where Arthur C. Clarke marked, with exclamation points, the following paragraph:

> What is the meaning behind the epidemic? Does the pink furniture reveal anything about the 3rd monolith and it's emitting a pink color when it first approaches the ship? Does this have anything to do with a shy expression? Does the alcohol offered by the Russians have anything to do with French kissing and saliva?

"Why do you think Arthur C. Clarke marked that particular paragraph for Kubrick to read?" I ask Jan.

"Because it is so bizarre and absurd," he says.

"I thought so," I say. "I just wanted to make sure."

In the back of my mind I wondered whether this paragraph was marked because the writer of the fan letter—Mr. Sam Laks of Alhambra, California—had actually worked out the secret of the monolith in *2001*. I find myself empathizing with Sam Laks. I am also looking for answers to the mysteries. So many conspiracy theories and wild rumors surrounded Kubrick—the one about him being responsible for faking the moon landings (untrue), the one about his terror of germs (this one can't be true, either—there's a lot of dust around here), the ones about him refusing to fly and drive over 30 mph. (The flying one is true—Tony says he wasn't scared of planes, he was scared of air-traffic controllers—but the one about the 30 mph is "bullshit," says Tony. "He had a Porsche.")

This is why my happiest times looking through the boxes are when things turn weird. For instance, at the end of one shelf inside the stable block is a box marked "Sniper head—scary." Inside, wrapped in newspaper, is an extremely lifelike and completely disgusting disembodied head of a young Vietnamese girl, the veins in her neck protruding horribly, her eyes staring out, her lips slightly open, her tongue just visible. I feel physically sick looking at it. As I hold it up by its blood-matted hair, Christiane, Kubrick's widow, walks past the window.

"I found a head!" I say.

"It's probably Ryan O'Neal's head," she replies.

Christiane has no idea who I am, or what I'm doing in her house, but she accepts the moment with admirable calm.

"No," I say. "It's the head of the sniper from *Full Metal Jacket*."

"But she wasn't beheaded," calls back Christiane. "She was shot."

"I know!" I say.

Christiane shrugs and she walks on.

"I was just talking to Tony about typefaces," I say to Jan.

"Ah yes," says Jan. "Stanley loved typefaces." Jan pauses. "I tell you what else he loved."

"What?" I ask.

"Stationery," says Jan.

I glance over at the boxes full of letters from people who felt about Kubrick the way Kubrick felt about stationery, and then back to Jan.

"His great hobby was stationery," he says. "One time a package arrived with a hundred bottles of brown ink. I said to Stanley, 'What are you going to do with all that ink?' He said, 'I was told they were going to discontinue the line, so I bought all the remaining bottles in existence.' Stanley had a tremendous amount of ink. He loved stationery, pads, everything like that."

Tony Frewin wanders into the stable block.

"How's it going?" he asks.

"Still looking for Rosebud," I say.

"The closest I ever got to Rosebud," says Tony, "was finding a Daisy gun that he had when he was a child."

Tony and I leaf through some memos Kubrick wrote in 1968:

> Please see that there is a supply of melons kept in the house at all times. Do not let the number go below three without buying some more. Thanks, Stanley.

"By their memos you shall know them," Tony says.
And another:

> Please check with the weather bureau and find out what the barometric pressure in London was last Friday 11th October between 6pm and 4am in the morning. Also find out what the average barometric pressure is on most days of the year, what is considered extremely high and what is considered extremely low and how they would describe the

pressure on Friday, 11th October during the times I mentioned. Thanks, Stanley.

"God knows what that was about," says Tony.

Right from the beginning I had mentally noted how well constructed the boxes were, and now Tony tells me that this is because Kubrick designed them himself. He wasn't happy with the boxes that were on the market—their restrictive dimensions and the fact that it was sometimes difficult to get the tops off—so he set about designing a whole new type of box. He instructed a company of box manufacturers, G. Ryder & Co., of Milton Keynes, to construct four hundred of them to his specifications.

"When one batch arrived," says Tony, "we opened them up and found a note, written by someone at G. Ryder & Co. The note said, 'Fussy customer. Make sure the tops slide off.'"

Tony laughs. I half expect him to say, "I suppose we *were* a bit fussy."

But he doesn't. Instead he says, "As opposed to non-fussy customers who don't care if they struggle all day to get the tops off."

I HAVE DINNER with Christiane. They met when Kubrick gave her the part of a bar singer in *Paths of Glory*. They married and barely left each other's side for the next forty-two years. They raised three children: Anya and Vivian, plus Katharina, her daughter from an earlier marriage. I've got to know her well but there are some things I've always felt awkward asking her about, like anything to do with her uncle Veit Harlan. But tonight over dinner she brings the subject up herself.

"Stanley and I came from such different, such grotesquely op-

posite backgrounds," she says. "I think it gave us an extra something. I had an appalling, catastrophic background for someone
like Stanley." She pauses. "For me, my uncle was great fun.
He and my father planned to join the circus. They were acrobats.
They threw me around. It was a complete clown's world. Nobody
can imagine that you can know someone who was so guilty so
intimately—and yet not know."

It turned out that when Harlan wasn't clowning around with
Christiane, he was writing and directing propaganda films for
Goebbels, including *Jud Süss*, in which venal, immoral Jews
take over and ruin a German city, stealing riches, defiling Aryan
women, etc. The film was shown to SS units before they were
sent out to attack Jews. Harlan was tried twice for war crimes,
and exonerated, proving that Goebbels had interfered with *Jud
Süss*, forcing him to reedit and inject more anti-Semitism.

"Where my uncle was an enormous fool, as many talented
people are, was that he mistook his gift for intelligence," says
Christiane. "He was a great big famous film person. He looked
better and talked better and had enormous charm. So he thought
he was also far more intelligent than Mr. Goebbels. Goebbels
was ten thousand times smarter than my uncle." She pauses.
"Film people, actors, are puppets. We are silly. We are silly folk."
She says her uncle's story reinforced for Stanley and her their
great principle in life: Always be suspicious of people who have,
or crave, power.

"All Stanley's life he said, 'Never, ever go near power. Don't
become friends with anyone who has real power. It's dangerous.'
We both were very nervous on journeys when you have to show
your passport. He did not like that moment. We always had to go
through separate entrances, he with [our] two American daugh-

ters upstairs, and me with my German daughter downstairs. The foreigners downstairs! He'd be looking for us nervously. Would he ever get us back?"

Christiane laughs. Of course they were always reunited. They spent a lifetime together inside Childwick, where Stanley created his self-governing mini-studio. I never meet their youngest daughter, Vivian. There was mention of her being in Los Angeles. Vivian had once been a big presence in the family. When she was nineteen she directed a brilliant documentary, *The Making of* The Shining. When she was twenty-six she composed the score for *Full Metal Jacket*. She shot eighteen hours of behind-the-scenes footage for that film, too, but it was never edited or released. It just sits in film cans in the stable block.

I watch some one day. Here's Kubrick sitting in a chair on an old airstrip during a break from filming. Crew members stand around him. Vivian has caught a tense moment.

STANLEY KUBRICK: We fucked around for an hour and twenty minutes. . . .

CREW MEMBER: I know it seems like a lot of tea breaks but we had the tea break that was up at . . .

KUBRICK: You had a tea break at four o'clock? And you had a tea break at six o'clock? If you had a tea break at four, you don't need to break for this tea break. This must be a complimentary tea break. So figure it out.

TERRY NEEDHAM (FIRST ASSISTANT DIRECTOR): I'd prefer to do away with them all. Because it gives me more fucking headaches, poxy tea breaks, I'd like to sling them right down their fucking piss holes.

KUBRICK: Right, Terry.

TERRY NEEDHAM: I'm the sort of man we need, eh, Stanley?
KUBRICK: That's right.

You catch glimpses of Vivian in the rushes. She looks beautiful, effervescent.

"She is a fabulous person," says Christiane. "Beautiful, very
witty, enormously talented in all sorts of directions, very musical, a great mimic, she could play instruments easily, she could
sing, she could dance, she could act, there wasn't anything she
couldn't do. We had fights. But she was hugely loved. And now
I've lost her." She pauses. "You know that? I used to keep all this
a secret, as I was hoping it would go away. But now I've lost hope.
So. She's gone."

It all began, she says, while Stanley was editing *Eyes Wide
Shut*, which starred Tom Cruise and Nicole Kidman. Stanley
asked Vivian to compose the score, but at the last moment she
said she wouldn't. Instead, she disappeared into San Francisco
and Los Angeles. "They had a huge fight. He was very unhappy.
He wrote her a forty-page letter trying to win her back. He
begged her endlessly to come home from California. I'm glad he
didn't live to see what happened."

On the day of Stanley's funeral, Christiane says, Vivian arrived with a woman nobody recognized. "She just sat in Vivian's
room. Never said hello to us. Just sat. We were all spooked. Who
was this person? Turns out she was a Scientology something-or-
other, don't know what."

"Did Vivian give a reason why she joined the Scientologists?"
I ask.

"It's her new religion." Christiane shrugs. "It had absolutely
nothing to do with Tom Cruise, by the way. Absolutely not."

"Maybe it was her way of dealing with her father's death?"

"I think she must have been very upset," Christiane says, "but, again, I wouldn't know. I know nothing. That is the truth. I can't reach her at all. I've had two conversations with her since Stanley died. The last one was eight years ago. She became a Scientologist and didn't want to talk to us anymore and didn't see her dying sister, didn't come to her funeral. [Her sister Anya died of cancer, aged fifty.] And these were children that had been joined at the hip."

I tell her that she seems to have handled all her tragedies with remarkable resilience. "I daresay I have, yes," she says. "But I've also been very sad. I was helped by my children. Anya, in particular."

She says that when Stanley was alive, he kept her and their daughters cosseted from stress, from life's legal and financial arrangements, allowing them to float through Childwick without worries. But he died long before anyone expected he would, and Christiane has been left with burdens she never anticipated. So she's forever finding herself second-guessing him. Would he have handled the Vivian situation differently? Would he have approved of letting me look though the boxes? She has bigger plans for the archive. She wants to donate them to a university. Would he have approved of that?

"I am very self-conscious and surrounded by his ghost," she says. "I'm always having these conversations with him, as I am not terribly secure. And I try to live like I think he would want me to go on, because of the grandchildren and everything."

At the end of our dinner I tell her, with some embarrassment, that I find her quite inspiring. She thinks about this for a moment. "I'm very pleased that Stanley liked me," she replies.

. . .

FOR MONTHS, as I look through the boxes, I don't bother opening the two that read *Shadow on the Sun*. But, one evening just before last Christmas, I decide to take a look.

It is amazing. The boxes contain two volumes of what appears to be a slightly cheesy sci-fi radio drama script. The story begins with a sick dog:

"Can you run me over to Oxford with my dog?" says the dog's owner. "He's not very well. I'm a bit worried about him, John."

This is typed.

Kubrick has handwritten below it: "THE DOG IS NOT WELL."

A virus has been carried to earth on a meteorite. This is why the dog is listless, and also why humans across the planet are no longer able to control their sexual appetites. It ends with a speech:

> There's been so much killing—friend against friend, neighbor against neighbor, but we all know nobody on this earth is to blame, Mrs. Brighton. We've all had the compulsions. We'll just have to forgive each other our trespasses. I'll do my part. I'll grant a general amnesty—wipe the slate clean. Then perhaps we can begin to live again, as ordinary decent human beings, and forget the horror of the past few months.

This, too, is typed. But all over the script I find notes handwritten by Kubrick. ("Establish Brighton's interest in extraterrestrial matters." "Dog finds meteorite." "John has got to have very powerful connections of the highest level." "A Bill Murray line!")

"I know what this is," says Tony.

Kubrick was always a keen listener to BBC radio, Tony explains. When he first arrived in the UK, back in the early sixties, he happened to hear this drama serial—*Shadow on the Sun*. Three decades later, in the early 1990s, after he had finished *Full Metal Jacket*, he was looking for a new project, so he asked Tony to track the scripts down. He spent a few years, on and off, thinking about *Shadow on the Sun*, reading and annotating the scripts, before he abandoned the idea and eventually—after working on and rejecting *AI*—made *Eyes Wide Shut* instead.

"But the original script seems quite cheesy," I say.

"Ah," replies Tony, "but this is before Stanley worked his alchemy."

And I realize this is true. "Dog finds meteorite." It sounds so banal, but imagine how Kubrick might have directed it. Do the words "Ape finds monolith" or "Little boy turns the corner and sees twin girls" sound any less banal on the page?

All this time I have been looking in the boxes for some embodiment of the fantasies of the outsiders like Mr. Sam Laks and me—but I never do find anything like that. I suppose that the closer you get to an enigma, the more explicable it becomes. Even the somewhat crazy-seeming stuff, like the filing of the fan letters by the towns from which they came, begins to make sense after a while.

It turns out that Kubrick ordered this filing in case he ever wanted to have a local cinema checked out. If *2001*, say, was being screened in Daly City, California, at a cinema unknown to Kubrick, he would get Tony or one of his secretaries to telephone a fan from that town to ask them to visit the cinema to ensure that, say, the screen wasn't ripped. Tony says that if I'm looking for the solution to the mystery of Kubrick, I don't really need to look inside the boxes. I just need to watch the films.

"It's all there," he says. "Those films are Stanley."

ALTHOUGH THE KUBRICKS always guarded their privacy inside Childwick, I come to the end of my time at the house just as Christiane and her daughter Katharina decide to open the grounds and the stable block to the public. They're going to hold an art fair, displaying their work and the work of a number of local artists. Christiane has decided to let the boxes go. She's donating them to the University of the Arts London—to a special climate-controlled Kubrick wing, where film students and other students can look through them. She's letting them go because, she tells me, "I get very upset at seeing some of his old things. The paper is so dusty and old and yellow. They look so sad. The person is so very dead once the paper is yellow."

I'm there to watch a fleet of removal vans arrive to take them away. During the months and years that follow, Christiane oversees the publication of two books about the things inside the boxes—*The Stanley Kubrick Archives* (Taschen) and *Stanley Kubrick's* Napoleon: *The Greatest Movie Never Made* (Taschen). She turns up for special screenings of his films—I watch her introduce *Paths of Glory* in the open-air cinema at Somerset House, Central London, and we have dinner afterward. I mention this to a friend, a Kubrick buff. "Oddly, I was just thinking about her today," he replies. "A *Twilight* fan said to me, 'Is there anything more romantic than Edward and Bella?'" I immediately thought, "Christiane Kubrick's protection of her husband's legacy."

One of the very last boxes I opened before the removal vans came contained a videotape. Kubrick was on the tape, addressing the camera, looking nervous. It was an acceptance speech. He'd been awarded the D. W. Griffith Award. It was just a few months before he died.

"Good evening," he says. "I'm sorry not to be able to be with you tonight . . . but I'm in London making *Eyes Wide Shut* with Tom Cruise and Nicole Kidman and at just about this time I'm probably in the car on the way to the studio. . . ."

All this time I've been looking for some kind of Rosebud and I think I find it in a few lines in this speech.

"Anyone who has ever been privileged to direct a film," he says, "also knows that although it can be like trying to write *War and Peace* in a bumper car in an amusement park, when you finally get it right, there are not many joys in life that can equal the feeling."

I think Kubrick knew he had the ability to make films of genius, and to do that—when most films are so bad—there has to be a method, and the method for him was precision and detail. I think his boxes contain the rhythm of genius.

PART THREE

EVERYDAY DIFFICULTY

"I've thought about doing myself in loads of times."

—*"Bill" to Christopher Foster*

Santa's Little Conspirators

t is a Monday in late October and I'm standing inside a smoke-filled Lotto shop in the tiny Alaskan town of North Pole, population 1,600. This shop sells only two things: cigarettes and Lotto scratch cards. Chain-smoking inveterate gamblers sit at the counter and frantically demolish mountains of the scratch cards. They have names like Royal Jackpot, Blame It on Rio, and Gentlemen Prefer Blondes.

Outside, people are going about their business on Frosty Avenue. Friends are chatting on Kris Kringle Drive. A gang of hoodies are slouched against the candy-cane-striped streetlights on Santa Claus Lane, having just emerged from the Christmas-themed McDonald's.

Everything in North Pole is Christmas-themed. It is Christmas Day here 365 days a year. The decorations are always up. It never stops being Christmas here. Never. Wherever you are in the world, if you write a letter to Santa, and address it simply "Santa, North Pole," your letter will most likely end up in this tiny Alaskan town.

Actually, specifically, your Santa letter will end up right here, in this smoke-filled scratch-card and cigarette shop. It's late October, and boxes of them are already piled up on the counter near the fruit machine. They're automatically forwarded here from the post office. I pick an envelope up at random. It has only one word scrawled on it, in a child's handwriting: "Santa." It's postmarked Doncaster, UK.

I get talking to Debbie, who works here, selling scratch cards to the gamblers. Debbie is herself a chain-smoker, a blowsy strawberry-blonde with a tough, good-looking face. She says she can frequently be found alone in here in floods of tears, having just opened yet another heartbreaker.

"Just before you got here," she says, "I opened one that said, 'Dear Santa. All I want for Christmas is for my mother and father to stop shouting at each other.' I just fell apart."

"We get a lot of 'Could you bring my father back from Iraq?'" says Gaby, the shop's owner. Debbie answers as many Santa letters as she can, whenever she gets a break. She writes back using her elf name: Twinkle.

And she has help. Each week in November and December, a box of Santa letters is sent over to the nearby middle school, where the town's eleven- and twelve-year-olds—the sixth graders—write back in the guise of elves. It is part of the curriculum.

Six of last year's middle school elves, now aged thirteen, were arrested back in April for being in the final stages of plotting a mass murder, a Columbine-style school shooting. The information is sketchy, but apparently they had elaborate diagrams and code names and lists of the kids they were going to kill. I've come to North Pole to investigate the plot. What turned those elves bad? Were they serious? Was the town just too Christmassy?

I need to tread carefully. So far I've tried to ask only one person about it—James, the waiter in Pizza Hut—and it went down badly.

"North Pole is the greatest place I've ever been," James told me as he poured my coffee. "The people here are always ready to do! We stay on track and we move on forward! We don't let anything get us down. That's the spirit of North Pole and the spirit of Christmas. People here are willing to put their best foot forward and be the best kind of people they can be."

"I heard about the thing with the kids over at the middle school plotting a Columbine-style massacre," I said.

At this, James let out a noise the likes of which I've never really heard before. It was an "Aaaaaah." He sounded like a balloon being burst by me, with all the joy escaping from him like air.

"That was a, uh, shock. . . ." said James.

"You have to wonder why. . . ." I said.

"This is a very happy, cheerful, cheery place," said James. "Anything more you need?"

"No," I said. And James walked back to the counter, shooting me a sad look, as if to say, "What kind of a Grinch are you to bring that up?"

MONDAY NIGHT. People keep telling me that everybody in North Pole loves Christmas. But I've found someone who doesn't. Her name is Jessie Desmond. I found her on Myspace.

"Christmas is a super big deal around here," she e-mailed me before I set off for Alaska, "but for me it is a general hate. Please don't go off me about that."

We meet in a non-Christmassy bar of her choice on the edge of town. She's in her early twenties. She was educated at the middle school and is now trying to make her way as a comic-book artist. She has the Batman logo tattooed on her hand.

"Christmas really grates on me, all the time, in the back of my head," she tells me. "Christmas, Christmas, Christmas. It drives me nuts."

"But there must be something you do like about North Pole," I say.

Jessie thinks about this. "Well, if you get into an accident or something, everyone's willing to help you," she eventually says, shrugging.

I decide it's safe to ask Jessie—being anti-Christmas—about the mass-murder plot.

"Do you know the boys?" I ask her.

She shakes her head.

"Apparently they drew up a list," I say.

"Well, I have a hate list on my wall too," Jessie replies.

"Yes," I say, "but I'm sure you don't have access to weapons."

"I have a revolver in my bedroom," Jessie says.

"Do you stand in front of the mirror with it and shout 'Freeze!' and imagine what it's like to kill your enemies?" I ask.

There's a silence.

"I might," says Jessie, finally.

I ask Jessie if she'll take me to her house and show me her gun. On the way she tells me she suspects the boys were just like her—all talk—and the town only took them seriously because everyone is terrified of everything these days.

Although this is late October, Jessie's house is extremely Christmassy. Her parents, Mike and Edith (a former Miss Alaska), are great fans of Christmas.

"Did you see my Christmas balls up front?" Edith asks me. "The nicest thing about living in North Pole is that you can leave your Christmas decorations up all year."

"Are there people in North Pole who don't like Christmas?" I ask.

"I don't know any," says Mike.

I glance at Jessie. She's sitting cross-legged on the floor at their feet, displaying no emotion.

Mike shows me the mounted head of a sheep he once shot. It's wearing tinsel.

"You never think that having decorations up all year round is too much Christmas?" I ask.

Edith shakes her head.

"No," she says firmly. "No. I love Christmas. It's my favorite time."

"Jessie," I say. "Will you show me your gun?"

"Sure," she says.

I tell Mr. and Mrs. Desmond that it was lovely to meet them, and I walk with Jessie down the corridor. We pass a row of paintings depicting Santa in various festive settings, in front of log fires, etc. Across the corridor is Jessie's bedroom. It is free of anything Christmassy.

"Does your mother know . . . ?" I begin.

"That I don't like Christmas?" says Jessie.

I nod.

"I've told her," she says. "But I don't think she believes me." She rummages around her wardrobe and pulls out her revolver.

"You're the first person to see it," she says.

She straightens her arm like in a police movie. She says she sometimes pretends to kill the kids who bullied her in middle school. "I walk up to them when no one is around and I bop them over the head and shoot them!" she says. "Ha-ha!"

Jessie says the person I should really ask about the plot is Jeff Jacobson. He teaches sixth grade at the middle school. He must have known the boys. Plus Jeff was mayor of North Pole until last week. If anyone who knows is willing to tell, it's Jeff, Jessie says.

I leave Jessie's and call Jeff Jacobson. He says I'm welcome to visit him tomorrow at the school during the lunch period.

Dusk is settling. One of the town's two giant Santa sculptures—the one outside the RV park—lights up. It's lit from below, which gives Santa's eyes a hollow, creepy look, like Jack Nicholson in *The Shining*.

TUESDAY MORNING. Apparently the kids who were plotting the shootings were Goths. Earl Dalman, the owner of the permanently Christmas-decorated Dalman's Family Restaurant, the most popular restaurant in town, tells me this. Just about everyone who lives in North Pole eats breakfast at Dalman's. It has a lovely, festive, community feel, even if the decorations are looking frayed.

There's Debbie—Twinkle—who looks like she's been up all night opening letters to Santa. There's Mary Christmas, who runs the Santa Claus House gift shop. That's her real name. It's on her birth certificate. And there's Earl Dalman, the owner of the diner. We get to talking.

"Do you know anything about that shooting plot over at the middle school?" I ask him.

"The kids were Goths," he says.

"Really?" I say.

Earl gives me a look to say, "Well, of course they were Goths. What else would they be?"

"Where I come from," I explain, "Goths aren't dangerous."

"Really?" says Earl, surprised.

"Goths don't do anything bad in the UK," I say. "They're a gentle and essentially middle-class subculture."

"Huh!" says Earl.

"I suppose the difference is that the Goths in Britain aren't armed," I muse. "They're so death-obsessed, it's probably good to keep them away from guns."

Earl gives me a look as if to say, "There's nothing wrong with gun ownership."

Then he tells me that—as a result of the shooting plot—his daughter has pulled her kids out of the middle school. The Dalman kids are being homeschooled instead now.

"It shook everyone up," says Earl.

I have a few hours to kill before I get to go inside the middle school and meet Jeff Jacobson, and so I visit a sweet, twinkly-eyed lady called Jan Thacker, local columnist and author of the book *365 Days of Christmas: The Story of North Pole, Alaska, the Little Town That Carved Itself Out of the Alaska Wilderness and Became Known, Worldwide, as the Home of Santa Claus.*

Her book begins, "So does he? Does Santa really live in North Pole? . . . The police chief believes it, and who is more honest than the chief of police?"

Jan and I chat for a while, and then she takes me into her back room, which is full of guns—a glinting rack of them—and a number of stuffed wolves she's killed.

The stuffed wolves have ferocious facial expressions. They're snarling, their teeth bared, their eyes aflame with hatred, ready to pounce.

I tell Jan she must have been very brave to shoot those terrifying wolves.

"Were they pouncing like that when you shot them?" I ask.

"No," Jan says.

Then she explains: The local taxidermist, Charlie Livingston, tends to give the wolves ferocious expressions however they were behaving at the moment of their death—even if they were just wandering around all doe-eyed, looking for a pat and a play.

It's surprising to see such a twinkly-eyed old lady so heavily armed, but this is normal for North Pole. It solves the mystery of where the plotters would have got the guns. There are guns everywhere.

This is mainly because of all the bears. There are bears everywhere, and moose. I suspect this is why the town is so Republican. There are virtually no liberals. When you've got that many bears, you're not going to be liberal. You know what liberals are like with bears. We just scream. We let out a high-pitched scream and run away, our arms in the air.

It is all the more surprising, then, that Jeff Jacobson is a gentlehearted liberal, a card-carrying Democrat. I've been told that sometimes, at night, Jeff can be seen driving around North Pole, quietly putting up decorations in underprivileged parts of town. Now it is lunchtime, and Jeff is putting up decorations in his math classroom. He's wearing a Santa hat and a tie covered in snowmen. We talk a little about how much he misses being mayor.

I don't think Jeff gets on with the new mayor, Doug Isaacson, who's apparently a steely-eyed, shaven-headed staunch Bush Republican. Doug Isaacson's big idea is apparently to get all the shopkeepers in town to wear elf costumes as a means of generating increased tourist revenue. Jeff feels this is just window dressing, and what's on the inside is what counts, Christmas-wise.

Jeff tells me this is a good week for me to be in North Pole. Tomorrow his sixth graders will get their first-ever batch of Santa letters to answer. They'll give themselves elf names and write back on Santa's behalf.

"We live in a world of text messaging and video games," Jeff says. "Being a Santa's elf connects us with real people all around the world."

"Can I come along and watch them do it?" I ask.

"Of course," Jeff says.

"Jeff," I say. "I hear some of last year's elves were caught plotting a mass murder."

For a second Jeff freezes, Christmas decorations in hand. Then he recovers and carries on pinning them up.

"It was going to be on a Monday," he says.

"How was it thwarted?" I ask.

"One of the kids—the one who was going to be bringing the weapons in—didn't show up that day," Jeff says, "and so they postponed the plan. And while they were discussing the postponement, the plan was overheard, and the police intervened."

"And what was the plan?" I ask.

"They were going to bring some knives and guns in," he says, "and they were going to kill students and teachers. They were going to disrupt the telephone system. They knew where the telephone controls were. And they were also going to disable the electricity. Turn off the lights. And carry out their plans. And these were well-thought-out plans. They had diagrams. They had a list. . . ."

"How many people were on the list?" I ask.

"Dozens," says Jeff. "And each kid was assigned who was going to do who. With what."

"Oh my God," I say.

Jeff shrugs. Then he smiles. "These boys had just turned thirteen years old," he says. "They were going to disable the telephone system. That sounds terrifying, right? Well . . ."

Jeff rummages around in his pocket and pulls out his mobile phone. He gives me a look as if to say, "Well, duh!"

"So maybe they once saw someone in a James Bond movie disable a building's communications system," he says.

The more Jeff tells me about the ins and outs of the plot, the more it strikes me as a mix of very chilling and very stupid. After the shooting, the boys were going to run to the station and catch a train to Anchorage, where they'd create new lives for themselves using aliases. One boy's alias was going to be John Wayne.

The thing is, they hadn't checked the train timetables. The shootings were going to occur at lunchtime in the cafeteria. Even if they gave themselves an hour to kill their enemies and get to the station, they would still have had a five-hour wait on the platform for the Anchorage train.

Lunchtime is over, and Jeff's sixth graders run into class. They are only twelve, just a few months younger than the plotters.

"To see those little boys in handcuffs . . ." Jeff says. "I taught five of them. It broke my heart. As teachers we had to carry on like it was a normal day. But we were being ravaged inside with our emotions. Some teachers were having anxiety attacks. One is still suffering badly with stress. . . ."

I'm not allowed by law to meet the kids, but I'm determined to meet at least one of their parents this week. I ask Jeff if he'll try and arrange this. He promises he will. I tell him I'll see him tomorrow afternoon for the class where the kids get to open the letters to Santa for the first time.

WEDNESDAY MORNING. Doug Isaacson—the new mayor of North Pole—stands atop a snowy nature trail and surveys his town below.

"Imagine being in England two thousand years ago when your towns were just getting started," Doug says. "How would you set them up for future generations? That's where we are! We can do that here! That's awesome."

"How old is North Pole?" I ask.

"Fifty years old," says Doug.

"You're a founding father," I say.

"Very much so," says Doug. "And we'll be forgotten to history in time. But not the things we start. Not the things we set up properly. They'll last a lot longer."

This is Doug's first week in office. He says he was elected on a Christmas mandate. His campaign centered on the proposition that whilst North Pole is very Christmassy, there is room for it to be even more Christmassy. Recently, Doug went on a fact-finding visit to the small Washington town of Leavenworth, where everything is Bavarian-themed. Many shopkeepers there wear lederhosen and sell bratwurst.

As a result, Doug has had an idea. It is an idea he recognizes will be a hard sell to the people of this freedom-loving wilderness town. But the idea is this: Doug would like every shopkeeper in North Pole to wear an elf costume.

"Many people move to Alaska because they don't want to be fenced in," I say. "So if you say, 'I'm going to fence you in with elf costumes,' might that be an issue?"

"Absolutely," says Doug. "But let me show you something."

We climb into Doug's pickup truck. He drives me around town.

"Some people," Doug says, "think North Pole looks like a truck stop. And that's unconscionable."

We drive past the extremely festive Dalman's Family Restaurant, but then past the utterly non-Christmassy computer shop–cum–video game arcade, where I see teenagers playing violent shooting games. We stop and enter. Half a dozen teenage boys are shooting the hell out of the SAS (the British army's Special Forces). British soldiers' heads are exploding. Blood sprays from their backs as they lie convulsing in the desert dirt.

Doug walks purposefully past the boys and toward the owner. He produces an elf costume from his bag. Doug doesn't have to say anything. The owner instinctively knows where this is heading.

"No," he says.

"Will you at least try the hat on?" Doug asks.

"No," he says.

Doug tries to appeal to him entrepreneur to entrepreneur. Apparently North Pole has recently lost a big Alaska Airlines promotion. For the past two years, the airline flew tourists into North Pole and took them dogsledding, Christmas-ornament making, and so on. But this year, Alaska Airlines has decided that North Pole just doesn't look Christmassy enough.

"If we want to capture that Christmassy tourist," Doug says

unapologetically, "then, yeah, for at least six weeks out of the year, people ought to wear elf suits."

The computer-shop owner says he'll think about it.

I drift away and get talking to one of the teenage boys. He's spraying an SAS officer up the back with a machine gun.

"Do you ever get an overdose of Christmas, living here?" I ask him.

"Pretty much all summer," he says.

"What do you do to redress the balance?" I ask.

"I come here and shoot people all day," he shrugs.

"Doug," I say as we leave the computer shop, "do you think that if the town had been more Christmassy back in April, those kids at the middle school wouldn't have wanted to plot their Columbine-style massacre?"

"Let's just say that if the spirit of Christmas were permeating the entire soul of this community, no child would be feeling that despondent," Doug replies. "What is the spirit of Christmas? Isn't it peace on earth? Good will to men?"

WEDNESDAY LUNCHTIME. I call Jessie Desmond, my North Pole Myspace friend who hates Christmas.

"I'm going to the middle school to watch the sixth graders open their first-ever batch of Santa letters," I say. "Do you remember your first batch of Santa letters?"

"It was one of my first moments of real disappointment," she says.

"Sorry?" I say.

"You learn really fast that Santa doesn't exist," says Jessie.

"You're kidding," I say.

"Most of the kids say they're OK with it," she says, "but you know they're not. Because there we were, thinking something was up there, but in sixth grade we realize there's nothing. It's just us up there."

She says the children have no idea that they'll one day be obliged to become letter-writing elves. So that class can come as a real shock to them. Although it isn't as bad as it could be. The school has rules: "If someone writes something like 'Dear Santa, my mom has cancer. Can you make it go away?' we don't deal with those. We give them back to the teacher." Jessie pauses. "I had written letters to Santa with really personal things in them. I told Santa I wanted a baby sister. The idea that some sixth-grade kids had read that. And suddenly you're in sixth grade, and you have this batch of letters on your desk and you're writing back: 'Yes, Santa's happy with you. Yes, you're going to get what you asked for.' It really ruined it for me. I felt like I was doing Santa's dirty work."

"Are you telling me that I'm about to go to middle school to watch a bunch of children be confronted, for the first time in their lives, with the idea that Santa doesn't exist?" I ask.

"Yes," Jessie says. "You'll probably see it in their faces. They prepare you for a few weeks before, but there's always that one person who's, like, 'Wait. What are we doing?' And that's the person you should be looking out for. The person who wasn't paying attention in class until the letters are right in front of them. And then they're shattered. It's a weird experience."

I DRIVE to the middle school. In the classroom Jeff hands out Christmas hats. He asks the children to think up elf names for themselves. Then he distributes the Santa letters. Of course I'm doing what Jessie told me to. I'm scrutinizing the children's faces. But they all seem quite excited.

Jeff instructs his elves not to write "Santa is going to give you everything you asked for." Instead he tells them to be more vague: "I'm sure you'll like whatever surprises you find under your tree. From all the elves at North Pole, and from Santa, Merry Christmas, and remember it's always better to be good than bad."

A dark cloud settles over the room only once, when one little boy reads out a letter that says, "Dear Santa, this year I would like to wear a lot of clothes and shoes, but my mom can't buy us a lot of clothes because she gets paid a little bit and she pays a lot of rent. Santa, that is my wish for Christmas. I know it may seem a lot for you but that is all I want for Christmas. To wear a lot of clothes."

LATER, after the children go home, I ask Jeff, "Do you ever get a kid saying, 'Hang on. If we're opening the letters, what does that say about . . . ?'"

"Santa?" says Jeff. "Well, at eleven and twelve they're pretty savvy. They all know that Santa is basically Mom and Dad."

I give Jeff a quizzical look. Jeff gives me a look back that says, "Don't be silly."

Still, I can't help wondering if Jeff has inadvertently made a mistake getting his sixth graders to be letter-opening elves. My week in North Pole has made me suspect that the job can mess you up. There's poor Twinkle in the Lotto shop, constantly in tears, powerless to help. Then there's Jessie, realizing that if she was the magic, then the magic was rubbish.

.   .   .

THAT NIGHT, back at the hotel, the telephone rings. It's a man's voice. He says his name is Joe.

"My son was one of the ringleaders," he says.

Joe says he's willing to talk to me, but not at his house. I call Jeff. He says we can use the middle school.

And so that's where I meet Joe, on Saturday morning, in the deserted cafeteria in the deserted middle school.

Joe's a soldier. "I was in Iraq when I got the word," he says.

"Where were you?" I ask.

"South of Basra," Joe says. "I'd been there quite a few months."

Joe says he was in the habit of chatting with his wife online early each morning, and one morning in April she typed into the chat box, "I've got to tell you something. We need to talk about Jack."

Jack isn't the boy's real name. He had just turned thirteen in April.

"He's OK," typed Joe's wife. "There's nothing physically wrong."

"I thought maybe he skipped a few days of school or something," says Joe.

But, instead, Joe's wife typed the news that Jack had got involved with a group of boys, and they had made a list, and Jack was "highly involved" with this, and their plan was to kill the kids on the list, and to do it in the cafeteria.

As Joe relays this to me, I look up with a start. This is where we're sitting: in the school cafeteria.

"Were they serious?" I ask.

"I've asked my son that point-blank," Joe replies. "I said,

'Would you have done this?' He said, 'Yes. I would have.' And he maintains that to this day. He says they would have done it." Joe pauses. "They were going to fire some warning shots," he says. "There were other kids that were indirectly involved—they'd been told about the plan: They were to get certain other kids out of the cafeteria when the warning shots were fired. My son was to go to the office with a rifle and disable the communications equipment, and then they were going to start shooting the kids from the list."

"How many kids were on the list?" I ask.

"Fifteen or twenty," Joe says. "And there was a comment on there: 'And all the other cool kids.' Who knows what that means? That's kind of open-ended, right? That's kind of subjective."

After Joe's wife told Joe the news of the plot, via the chat box, Joe sought emergency leave. He says it was hard to leave Iraq.

"I had a sense of responsibility to my comrades," he says. "You want to come home with your unit."

Sometimes, during our interview, Joe sounds like a soldier making a report to his commanding officer. He says things like "My son stated to me . . ." and so on. But there are other occasions when he's doing all he can to stop himself from breaking down. I think he thinks he can conceal his broken heart better than he actually can.

Jack was in custody when Joe returned from Iraq. The charge was conspiracy to commit first-degree murder.

"I really didn't know how to react," he says. "Part of me wanted to grab him and shake him and say, 'What is your problem?' And the other part wanted to hug him and say, 'We'll protect you from this.'"

"What did you do?" I ask.

"I gave him a hug," Joe says. "I said, 'I love you,' and then I said, 'Sit down.' I could tell he was kind of scared. I asked him, 'Why would you do this?' He said, 'I don't know.'"

Joe says he doesn't know, either. It's not like Jack's a Goth, he says. Contrary to rumor, he's no Goth. "He likes to fish," says Joe. "He likes to go camping. He likes to make up his own jokes. The counselor is trying to figure out why they'd do this. These kids don't fit the mold. He doesn't come from a dysfunctional family. I mean, we have our dysfunctions, but he's not abused. I don't use drugs. I don't consider myself an alcoholic. I spend time with him. I coached baseball for him when he was younger."

Joe pauses. "We have rules. He doesn't dress Goth. He's not allowed to dress Goth. He's not allowed to have baggy pants that hang down. He's not allowed to wear his hat cocked to the side and walk around looking like a little punk. We never let him have violent posters on his walls. He's not allowed to play violent video games. He's never been to the mall by himself. He doesn't have any CDs, like rap CDs, with violent themes. That kind of stuff just doesn't fit in with our lives."

As Joe says this, I think about my eight-year-old son, Joel. I always let him wear his baseball cap cocked to one side. He has a *Kill Bill* poster on his wall. He listens to Eminem.

"My God," I think in a panic. "If Jack was going to kill everyone in his school *without* all those violent influences, what the hell is Joel going to grow up to be? Or maybe it was the absence of all those violent influences that led Jack to want to commit mass murder. Or could it have been the town's Christmas theme? The elf business?"

"I guess that theory is as good as any theory." Joe shrugs. "The doctors and the counselors have no answers. *I* have no answers. *The boy himself* has no answers."

Then there's the other possibility: that Joe's months away fighting in Iraq did something to his son's psyche.

Joe sighs.

"Maybe," he says.

North Pole has been hit hard by Iraq. At the end of September, two soldiers in full-dress uniform arrived at the home of one of Joe's neighbors, Donna Thornton, to tell her that her twenty-four-year-old son, James, had recently died from cardiac arrest in Baghdad.

James had been at the middle school, a year or two ahead of Jessie.

And there have been others. Joseph Love-Fowler—who was twenty-two and in the same year as Jessie—was blown up by a roadside bomb in Balad in April. North Pole has a smallish military base, Fort Wainwright, on its borders. Fort Wainwright has so far lost twenty-six soldiers in Iraq.

Or maybe being thirteen, and being picked on, was reason enough. Everyone behaves irrationally when they reach thirteen. I suppose it is a statistical inevitability that some bullied thirteen-year-olds, somewhere, will be plotting a school shooting. (Although I don't have much sympathy for the bullying motive. There were six ringleaders, and nine others with knowledge of the plot. That makes fifteen. So they can hardly call themselves bullied outcast loners. Fifteen is more friends than *I* ever had.)

Joe often wonders what might have happened had the guns reached the school. This is the only reason why the plot failed: The boy who was supposed to bring the guns didn't turn up.

Apparently, Jack behaved perfectly normally over breakfast

that Monday morning. He was joking around as usual, even though he believed that within a few hours he was to commit mass murder.

Joe looks around the cafeteria.

"His sister goes here," he says. "I said to him, 'Did you tell her, so she could get out when the shooting started?' And he said, 'No.' I said, 'What if your sister heard the shooting, worried about you, ran to see what you were doing, and one of the kids shot her?' And I could see from the look on his face that those thoughts had never crossed his mind. He said to me, 'We were just going to shoot the bad kids.' And I said, 'Bullets don't care who they hit or who they kill. They go through people. They tear flesh and they go through. It doesn't matter who's on the other side.' He had not thought about that. It was not in his thought process."

Then Joe mentions the ill-thought-out escape plan—how the kids were going to start new lives in Anchorage.

"To even think they were going to get out of the school without being killed by the police . . ." he says.

IN THE END, Jack got off lightly: two years' probation, a five-thousand-word essay on the effects of school shootings across America, a hundred hours of community service, some anger-management therapy.

Joe says he's pleased and relieved nobody has thrown a brick through their window.

"I don't want people taking the law into their own hands," he says, "because I have an obligation to protect my son and the rest of my family. So if they push, I'm going to have to push back. And if that happens, it's not going to be pretty."

But he's sending his son back to school next year: "I told him, 'You have to face this. You have to face the kids on that list.'"

Joe takes his son out running each morning. Back in April, Jack could barely run half a mile. Now he's running a mile and a half.

Joe looks proud when he tells me this.

There's a school for excluded children on the edge of North Pole. The kids who—for whatever reason—don't fit into the middle school end up studying here. It's quite possible that some of the plotters will join the school next April, when their year's expulsion from the public school system is up. It seems a great place: small, bright, open-plan classrooms and lovely teachers, like Suze, who shows me around. Suze is another rare liberal in a town full of staunch Republicans. I notice that this is one of the very few buildings in town that hasn't any Christmas decorations whatsoever.

"We're a respite from Christmas, I guess," Suze explains. "Our kids are all Christmassed out."

Then I ask Suze a question I've been asking everyone this week. "Do you happen to know," I ask, "where Kris Kringle is?"

BEFORE I ARRIVED IN TOWN, I kept hearing stories of an amazing North Pole resident who looks just like Santa and has changed his name by deed poll to Kris Kringle. I heard he was in permanent residence as the in-house Santa at the local Santa Claus House gift shop. But when I visited the place on Monday, I saw that his chair was empty. Since then, I've been asking everyone: Where is Kris Kringle?

Jeff Jacobson said he thought Kris Kringle had had some recent falling-out with Santa Claus House—"I think he was de-manding more hot chocolate and cookies," he said—and he is now a kind of roving Santa around town, surprising children in diners and so on with cries of "Ho! Ho! Ho!"

Gaby, who runs the Lotto scratch-card and cigarette shop, said, "He comes in occasionally, so he might surprise us. He could pop in at any time."

"Does he gamble?" I asked.

"Yes," said Gaby.

James at the Pizza Hut said, "He was up working at the hot springs last time I heard."

But the people at the Chena Hot Springs Resort said they hadn't seen him.

Charlie Livingston, the taxidermist, told me he got hit by a car but he's fine now.

My hunt for Kris Kringle was proving fruitless. People kept telling me they'd just seen him, and he was a wonderful man, but I never saw him. I began to wonder if he even existed. And then I visit the school for excluded children on the edge of town.

"Do you know where Kris Kringle is?" I ask Suze, the teacher.

She looks a little awkward and shuffles uneasily on her feet.

"Have you looked him up on the Internet?" she says.

"No?" I say.

"I think he—uh—died," says Suze.

"No," I say. "That's impossible. People keep telling me they just saw him."

"I'm sorry to break it to you," Suze says, "and it might be the absence of Christmas decorations that allows me to say this, but I think Santa is dead. He passed away this summer."

There is a silence.

"Well, the taxidermist did say he was hit by a car," I say. "But he also said he recovered fine." I pause. "Does everyone know and they're not saying?"

"They might know and they don't want to say," Suze says, nodding.

"Like a town-wide conspiracy?" I say.

"Maybe," says Suze. She looks a little embarrassed.

"I am amazed," I say. "All this week people I've become good friends with have been looking me in the eye and saying, 'I'm sure I saw him a couple of days ago.'"

"I can't believe I'm the only person to have owned up to it," says Suze. She sighs. "The one that burst the bubble. I hope they don't ride me out of town."

In the end I go to the library and find conflicting reports from the local paper. One report says Kris Kringle survived a car crash this summer and moved south. The other report says he died in the car crash. I never do find out for certain whether Kris Kringle is alive or not.

IT IS SUNDAY, my last day in North Pole. Today, finally, a new Santa will be occupying the vacant seat at Santa Claus House. He is a fantastic Santa. He looks just as Santa should. The setting is perfect: a red velvet chair, presents piled up under the tree, etc. Santa's helper Cerys the elf is here, too, in a pink elf suit, with pink circles painted on her cheeks.

I introduce myself to Cerys. My plane home is in a few hours, and so Cerys is my last chance of finding out whether Kris Kringle is alive or dead. She'd know, because she would have been his elf when he used to work here.

"Cerys," I say. "Do you know where Kris Kringle is?"

"I do," she says, a big smile on her face.

"Oh!" I say.

"He's right here in Santa Claus House," says Cerys.

"Oh?" I say, looking around. "Where?"

"He's right on that chair over there," says Cerys.

She points at the new Santa.

"That's Kris Kringle," says Cerys. "That's Santa. They're one and the same. OK?"

"I understand," I say.

She introduces me to the new Santa. "Do you remember Jon when he was a little boy?" she asks him.

"Oh yes," Santa says. "I remember Jon. He took a little convincing that I was real."

"That's *true*!" I say. "Very early on, when I was four, I told the rest of my class that you didn't exist."

Santa gasps. "Come here," he says. "Pull my beard."

I do. "It's real," I say.

"And what town are you in?" Santa asks.

"North Pole," I say.

"And this particular building is . . . ?"

"Santa Claus House," I say.

"So," says Santa. "If you're in a *real* North Pole, in a *real* Santa Claus House, and Santa has a *real* beard, that must make me . . . real."

Most of the children here are very young, but there are two older girls in the crowd. I ask them how old they are.

"Thirteen," they say.

That's the same age as the plotters. I remember what Jessie said about how being a letter-writing elf at the age of twelve ruined her belief in Santa, and then I remember what Jeff Jacobson said about how kids of that age are savvy, and they know fact from fantasy.

So I decide to put it to the test.

"Do you believe in Santa?" I ask them.

There is a long silence.

"Half and half," says one.

"Yes," says the other.

Phoning a Friend

n November 2001, when Major Charles Ingram, his wife, Diana, and another man, Tecwen Whittock, were arrested attempting to cheat the TV show *Who Wants to Be a Millionaire?* out of a million pounds using an elaborate system of audience-based coughs, my mother called me to say, "You know them! You were at school with them!"

"With who?" I asked.

"Diana Ingram's brothers, Adrian and Marcus Pollock," she said. "You must remember Diana Pollock. Their cousin Julian lived around the corner from us. You must remember them."

"No," I said.

The next day it dawned on me that this was an in that money couldn't buy, so I wrote to the Ingrams, reminding them of our halcyon days together.

"My family and I are experiencing a very real nightmare," Charles wrote back. "I have no doubt that there is a case to prove against media manipulation after consideration of the content, its cyclical nature, the care taken to quickly undermine expressions of support, the outrageous leaking of privileged information, and so on."

Charles wrote that perhaps I was the journalist to prove that case. I reread the letter. Its cyclical nature? It seemed curiously over-erudite, as if Charles wanted to prove that he was the sort of person clever enough to legitimately win a million pounds. I had no idea what he meant.

Still, it was odd. Diana, Adrian, and Marcus Pollock attended the same synagogue I did. They were well-to-do in an ordinary way. What happened to them? I did, in fact, have some vague memory, some Pollock-related to-do that rocked the local Jewish community when I was about ten. It was something to do with a car with the number plate APOLLO G and the manufacture of watch straps. But I couldn't remember anything more than that, and neither could my mother.

THURSDAY AFTERNOON, March 20, 2003, Southwark Crown Court, is when it all goes wrong for Charles Ingram. He's being cross-examined by prosecuting barrister Nicholas Hilliard about Particular Coughs 12 to 14. Those of us who've attended this long, slow trial from the beginning know the coughs so well we can mouth them: The tape of Charles's appearance on *Millionaire* has been played nearly a dozen times. During Charles's tenure in the hot seat, 192 coughs rang out from the audience: 173 were, experts agree, innocent clearings of throats, etc. But nineteen have been termed Particular Coughs.

Perhaps the most devastating of all is Particular Cough 12. It arose during Chris Tarrant's £500,000 question: "Baron Haussmann is best known for his planning of which city? Rome, Paris, Berlin, Athens."

"I think it's Berlin," Charles immediately, and confidently, replied. "Haussmann is a more German name than Italian or Parisian or Athens. I'd be saying Berlin if I was at home watching this on TV."

This is when Cough 12 occurred. It sounds, from the tape, like a cough born from terrible frustration. If the prosecution case is true, the plan was for Charles to chew over the answers out loud and for Tecwen Whittock—sitting behind him in a Fastest Finger First seat—to cough after the correct one. But now it seemed that Charles was going to plump straight for Berlin.

"Cough. *No!*"

(The first time this "No!" was played in court, every journalist and member of the public burst out laughing. Judge Rivlin threatened to clear the court.)

"I don't think it's Paris," he said.

"Cough."

"I don't think it's Athens."

No cough.

"I'm sure it's not Rome."

No cough.

"I would have thought it's Berlin but there's a chance it's Paris," said Charles. "Think, think! I think it's Berlin. It could be Paris. I think it's Paris."

"Cough."

"Yes," said Charles. "I am going to play . . ."

Now Nicholas Hilliard asks Charles why he changed his mind and opted for Paris.

"I knew that Paris was a planned city," explains Charles. "The center of Paris was cleared of slums during the nineteenth century, and it was rebuilt into districts and boulevards. Prominent in my mind was the economic reason. In the middle of the nine-teenth century France was coming out of the Revolutionary pe-riod and it was decided, I think by Napoleon III, that he would concentrate on Paris and thereby the remainder of France would flourish."

Charles looks hopefully at the jury. "But at the time," sighs Hilliard, "you said you thought it was Berlin because he had a German-sounding name."

There is a silence.

"Oh, Mr. Ingram," says Hilliard. "Surely you can help us a lit-tle bit better than that."

Judge Rivlin calls for a break. We all file out to the corridor. Charles looks shaken. He lights a cigarillo. I notice he's wearing a Mensa badge. He put it on as a special touch, but it is so tiny—just a little *M* on his lapel—that the jury surely can't spot it.

"Hilliard has got me all tied up in knots," he says. "I just don't want to say anything stupid." I do an upbeat smile, even though I believe that only a miracle can save them now.

"How does it feel to have to keep watching that tape?" I ask. I imagine it must be embarrassing. From the tape they look quite extraordinarily guilty, albeit in a sweet and funny way. It seems such a slapstick-type crime—a half-baked plot executed badly.

"I still get a thrill," Charles replies, "when it gets to the part where I win a million."

Corridors outside courtrooms are exciting places. The players all stand together smoking cigarettes—defendants, barristers, clerks, ushers, solicitors, journalists, police, and victims—as if there's a victim in this crime! Celador, the makers of *Millionaire*, has signed up almost every witness for a documentary to be shown across the world after the verdict. This will, of course, earn them far more than the million pounds they say Charles almost cheated out of them. Sometimes I think that whoever masterminded this harebrained plot should be given a cut of Celador's documentary profits. I wonder who the criminal genius was. I don't think it was Charles.

The only major players who've not been signed up by Celador are the defendants. Three thousand journalists have approached the Ingrams for interviews. Although I am way ahead, being a close family friend, I note that many other reporters have their own ingratiating tactics, and I'm not resting on my laurels. On Day One, for example, Charles entered court and gave his solicitors a kind of victory salute: a punch in the air. Half a dozen journalists, me included, thought he was punching the air at us, so we performed slightly awkward victory salutes back. It was a little embarrassing.

A few feet down the corridor, the reporters gather in a circle, comparing notes. "I liked it when Charles said the charges were 'absolute rot,'" says one journalist. "Do you think we can get away with having him say 'tommyrot'?" says another. Everyone laughs.

It is agreed that Hilliard is a brilliantly scathing cross-examiner. A passing barrister on his way to Court 5 tells me that Hilliard "trounced me in a murder trial once." I didn't think to ask him whether the convicted murderer did it or not.

Tecwen Whittock sits far down the corridor, sometimes alone, sometimes with his son, Rhys. He's so unassuming that I never once see him enter the dock. He just seems to materialize. I wander over to him.

"I'm from Cardiff too," I say.

"That's a coincidence," he says.

"And my mother went to Howell's," I say.

Howell's is the private school Tecwen sent his daughter to, running up a £20,000 bill. This debt, say the prosecutors, was Tecwen's motive.

"See?" says Tecwen. "That's another coincidence. Coincidences do happen!"

"I was at prep school with Adrian and Marcus Pollock," I say.

"That's another coincidence!" says Tecwen. "I'd like to see what Hilliard would do to you, with all those coincidences, if he got you on the stand."

I don't tell Tecwen the fourth coincidence—that Judge Rivlin is a distant cousin of my mother's.

I wander down the corridor to talk to the arresting officers. "Is this trial really worth it?" I ask Detective Sergeant Ian Williamson. "I mean, come on, in the end, what exactly did they do? Why didn't Celador just settle their differences with the Ingrams in a civil court?"

This is the worst question you can ask an arresting officer. They hate ambiguities. The police have a lot to lose if this trial goes badly for them. Some of the arresting officers were Paul Burrell's arresting officers. They really need a success after that fiasco.

"This trial," Williamson replies, crisply, "is about protecting the integrity of the *Millionaire* format. *Millionaire* is the most popular quiz show in the history of television. Celador has sold it to a hundred countries. Thousands of jobs depend on its success. . . ."

This is true. In fact, a BBC reporter down the corridor has just returned from Jordan, where she was meeting Palestinian leaders. They asked her why she was going back to Britain. "It's to do with a quiz show called *Who Wants to Be a Millionaire?*" she said. The Palestinian leaders got really excited and said, "The Coughing Major! You're going to that trial?"

So I understand what Williamson means, but another thought occurs to me. The prize money Charles allegedly tried to cheat out of Celador came from the revenue generated from the premium-rate phone lines—the calls the viewers make in their frequently fruitless attempts to get on to the show. So it is revenue generated from the far-fetched hopes and dreams of the viewing public, which seems like a cheat in itself. And how much is this trial costing? The answer is around a million pounds. If there's a guilty verdict, we the viewing public stand to lose a million pounds. If there's a not-guilty verdict, Celador will be forced to give Charles his check back.

"Watching that cross-examination has taught me," I say to Detective Sergeant Williamson, "if I'm ever in a situation like that, I'm going to plead guilty."

There is a small silence.

"Proper criminals do," he replies.

Every morning sees a scrum for the public-gallery seats. I secure my place each day because I arrive an hour early and I don't budge, even though I often very much need the toilet. Charles's father, himself an army man, sits next to me. He wears a tiepin shaped like a steam train. Unyielding pensioners with flasks of coffee mercilessly nab most of the other seats. One regular keeps passing me notes. I tend to open them with great anticipation. It is exciting to be handed a note in a courtroom. Today's note reads: "Is your suit made out of corduroy?"

The pensioners spend much of the day noisily unwrapping

packets of Lockets and readjusting their screeching hearing aids. A young man behind me cracks his knuckles from 10:00 a.m. to 4:00 p.m. Each time the barristers mention the word "cough"—and the word "cough" is mentioned very frequently— many people sitting around me involuntarily cough. We are like a comedy-club audience, determined to enjoy ourselves even if the comedian isn't very funny. Even Chris Tarrant's reading of the oath gets a loud chuckle from a man behind me.

Chris Tarrant may not be the world's greatest superstar, but within the context of this grubby building we've come to call home, the wallpaper peeling, the soap in the toilets as hard as rock, the evidence dragging on and on, he is a vision of paradise entering Court 4.

"Has anyone ever got the first question wrong?" asks one defense barrister.

"It's happened in America," replies Tarrant, to huge laughter around the court. Tarrant looks surprised. He was just giving a factual response. During all the merriment, the fact that Tarrant heard no coughing, suspected no foul play, and even said to the show's producers, "Don't be stupid," when he was told of their suspicions, seems to have got lost.

Rod Taylor, Celador's head of marketing, gets a big laugh, too, during his evidence about how he frisked Charles shortly after he'd "won" the million. Taylor offers to frisk one of the barristers to show him how he did it. That gets a laugh. In the dock, Charles begins to cry.

"Why then?" I ask him at Starbucks the next day. "Why did you cry at that moment?"

I often meet Charles and Diana at Starbucks. I discovered

early on that if I happen to be there at 9:05 a.m., this is exactly when Charles queues up. We make small talk. Five minutes a day. That adds up, in my reckoning, to a substantial exclusive interview.

"It was when Mr. Aubrey [Tecwen Whittock's barrister] was cross-examining Rod Taylor and he said something and everyone laughed," replies Charles.

"What did he say?" I ask.

"He made a joke," says Charles. "Here I am, this cataclysmic event, my family on the line, and everyone is laughing. And you know how I feel about not wanting to look stupid."

"What was the joke?" I ask. "What was the exact thing he said that made you cry?"

Charles pauses. Then he says, "It was when Mr. Aubrey said to Rod Taylor, 'Did you search his privates?'"

THIS STORY BEGINS in 2000. Tecwen Whittock was watching *Who Wants to Be a Millionaire?* one night when he recognized a contestant but couldn't remember where from. I could have told him. It was my old school pal, Diana's brother, Adrian Pollock.

"That's the same guy," Tecwen realized, "who was on a few weeks ago. He's been on four times now! I think I'll track him down and ask him what his secret is."

Tecwen is a quiz-show veteran. He keeps a journal of trivia, of random facts and figures accrued over the years. He's been on *Fifteen to One*, although he was eliminated in the first round. He didn't fare much better on *The People Versus*. He managed to Beat the Bong, whatever that means, but still only won £500. *Sale of the Century* was another disaster. "I convinced my wife I'd win a car, but in fact I won the booby prize of a world atlas," he later tells the court. He had, however, once made it to the semifinal of *Brain of Britain*.

Tecwen hoped to buy a silk bed for his dog, Bouncer, and a Reliant Robin for his son, Rhys, who was a member of the *Only Fools and Horses* fan club and wanted to drive the same car as the Trotters. Plus, he had credit-card debts from his children's private education. He wondered if Adrian Pollock might give him tips on becoming a contestant, so he tracked him down to St. Hilary, a village near Cardiff, and staked out his home.

"He seemed normal," Tecwen later told the police. "A couple of kids. A dog." When he later read that he and Marcus were supposedly involved in some Internet scam, he thought, "Uh-oh. Suspicious."

Tecwen introduced himself to Adrian, who was flattered by his curiosity. They went to the pub, where Adrian took on the role of Tecwen's mentor, imparting his secrets. First, Adrian told Tecwen, keep calling Celador's premium-rate phone line. Adrian had himself phoned 1,700 times. Second, when the random selector asks you a trivia question, try and answer it in a computer voice. Adrian had come to believe that Celador had programmed the selector to weed out certain regional accents.

He took his mentoring of Tecwen very seriously. He and Marcus visited Tecwen's home. They spoke on the phone twenty-seven times. Adrian even asked Diana to become Tecwen's co-mentor.

"What did you talk to him about?" asks Hilliard, when he cross-examines Diana about her relationship with Tecwen.

"The closest-to question," replies Diana.

The "closest-to" is the question the *Millionaire* researchers ask you over the phone if you've been randomly selected and are now down to the last hundred possible contestants. It is always a numerical question: "How many radio stations are there in North America?" for example.

"They can be quite hard," explains Diana. "They've always got a numerical answer that could be anything, really."

"And that's the kind of insight you were offering Tecwen Whittock, was it?" asks Hilliard. "That they're quite hard and could be anything really?"

In fact, shortly before the arrests, Adrian and Diana delivered a manuscript of a book to John Brown Publishing, offering tips on how to get on to *Millionaire.* Both Diana and Adrian had won £32,000 in the hot seat. John Brown was ready to publish, but the arrests changed all that.

Meanwhile, over in Devizes, Wiltshire, Adrian had loaned his brother-in-law, Charles, his pretend mock-up Fastest Finger First console. Charles practiced being fast-fingered on it. He phoned and phoned the random selector. He didn't, however, imitate a staccato computer voice. He thought Adrian's conspiracy theory about that was far-fetched. In fact, he later tells the court, he really doesn't like Adrian and Marcus.

"I don't like Diana getting involved in whatever it is they do," he says, adding that Adrian and Marcus have a history of hare-brained get-rich-quick schemes.

Back in Cardiff, Tecwen repeatedly called the *Millionaire* random selector in a staccato voice. "Before I knew it," he tells the court, "it worked. I was on."

Tecwen was booked to appear on September 10, 2001. Charles got on too—on September 9. Even though the prosecution says that some other plot was probably in operation that evening, involving buzzing pagers strapped to Charles's body—or perhaps to Marcus's body as he sat in the audience—Charles didn't do well. He made it to £4,000 but lost two of his lifelines before the recording ended. Still, he survived to carry on the following night. Chris Tarrant announced the names of the Fastest Finger contestants who'd be joining Charles in the studio. Second on the list was Tecwen Whittock.

Charles told the police that the first he'd heard of Tecwen Whittock was two weeks later, on September 25, when the *Sun* named him as the mysterious cougher. He says the first time he met him was just a few weeks ago, right here at Southwark Crown Court. Certainly, in the dock, they studiously behave as if they are strangers. However, Diana's mobile telephone bill shows that at 11:02 p.m. on the night of September 9—as the Ingrams were driving home from the studio down the M4—she phoned Tecwen for just over five minutes. Diana says the call was simply to congratulate her fellow *Millionaire* devotee on getting on to the show, and that Charles was asleep at the time. The prosecution says the call was for the three of them to put the coughing plot into action, a plot that must have been vaguely hatched during the "mentoring" conversations of the previous weeks.

When Detective Sergeant Williamson told me a few days ago that "proper criminals" plead guilty, I asked him what made the Ingrams and Tecwen not proper criminals. He said, "They may have engaged in a criminal act, but they don't have criminal minds. They made too many stupid mistakes."

One stupid mistake, he said, was that they called each other on their own phones. Another was that, at the *Millionaire* studio on September 10, neither Charles nor Diana said a word to Tecwen. How suspicious for Diana "the mentor" not to say hello to her student, especially when they'd been on the phone with each other just hours earlier. Diana says she didn't talk to Tecwen because she didn't know what he looked like. The most stupid mistake of all—say the police—was that they made it so bloody obvious.

The audience gave Charles a standing ovation after he correctly answered the million-pound question. Diana ran down the studio stairs to hug her husband. Her radio microphone picked up her saying, "How the hell did you do it? You must be mad!" As they walked to their dressing room, another Fastest Finger contestant congratulated them and said, "How did you get the Holbein question?" Diana turned to Charles, "Oh, that was one you knew, wasn't it, darling?"

CHRIS TARRANT: "*The Ambassadors* in the National Gallery is a painting by which artist: Van Eyck? Holbein? Michelangelo? Rembrandt?"

CHARLES: "I think it was either Holbein or Rembrandt. I've seen it. I think it was Holbein."

"Cough."

CHARLES: "I'm sure it was Holbein."

"Cough."

CHARLES: "I'm sure it was Holbein. I'm sure of it. I think I'm going to go for it."

"Cough."

CHARLES: "Yeah, Holbein."

CHRIS TARRANT: "You're fantastic, just fantastic."

IT IS WEEK THREE of the trial, and the Ingrams' case has been effortlessly torn apart by Nicholas Hilliard.

"It's not nice to watch, is it?" says one arresting officer to me out in the corridor. I'm starting to think it may be driving Charles toward some sort of breakdown. He's already told the court about his year on medication since the arrest, how passersby yell, "Cheat!" when he's in his garden having a picnic and how someone recently tried to shoot his cat, though this may have been unconnected. Personally, I think being cross-examined by Hilliard is punishment enough for a bit of cheeky deception on *Millionaire*.

My relationship with Charles is becoming awkward. My upbeat smiles have involuntarily turned into pitying grimaces. Charles seems compelled to behave in a fake-laddish manner in front of me.

"Oh," he laughs throatily in the corridor during a break after performing particularly badly on cross-examination, "I knew I shouldn't have gone out on the piss last night!"

I play along. "Did you?" I ask.

"Well," he adds, theatrically massaging his forehead, "it was a supper party, but it was much the same thing!"

"Charles!" calls Diana from down the corridor. "Come here!"

"Sorry, sorry," he calls back.

Diana has gone off me. Yesterday I was staring into space for a long time near Starbucks, thinking about other things, when I realized that I was staring straight at Diana, who was looking back at me, horrified, as if I was an obsessed stalker glaring at her from afar.

Today an incongruously suave stranger sits next to me in the public gallery. He is Robert Brydges, and he was in the *Millionaire* audience on September 10.

"I kept looking round for where Charles was getting help from," Robert says. "I knew the process was bogus—he was just so erratic—but I didn't hear the coughs."

Robert thinks Charles should have stuck on £500,000. Celador might have been suspicious, but it would have probably honored the check. Even though Robert himself was suspicious, he was also inspired by Charles's success. Over the next two days, while Britain reeled from the World Trade Center attacks, Robert repeatedly called the *Millionaire* random selector.

"I worked out," he says, "that if you call three hundred and fifty times you have a fifty-fifty chance of getting onto a particular show."

He phoned more than a thousand times.

"I read that Charles had been practicing the Fastest Finger First on a mock-up console, so I built one, too, on my laptop."

Robert's plan worked. On September 25 he found himself in the same place Charles had been a fortnight earlier—in the *Millionaire* hot seat.

The next day's *Sun* headline read: MILLIONAIRE WORTH FEW BOB MORE.

Super-rich Robert Brydges beamed with joy last night as he returned home after winning a million on Who Wants to Be a Millionaire? Banker Robert could not contain his excitement, even though he was a millionaire twice over before appearing on the quiz show. He declared with a grin: "Believe me I'm happy. I'm very happy."

Robert is writing a book called *The Third Millionaire* about his and Charles's parallel lives. What is it about the human condition that one good man can win a million pounds legitimately, when another has to resort to fraud? In the corridor, Robert introduces himself to Charles and mentions the name of his book.

"If you don't mind, I like to think of you as the fourth millionaire," says Charles.

"Can we agree on 3A and 3B?" says Robert.

"Charles!" calls Diana, from down the corridor.

"OK, sorry!" Charles calls back, and scuttles off.

"I don't care how many Mensa badges he's wearing," mutters Robert. "On the eight-thousand-pound question he could hardly remember that Emmental cheese was from Switzerland."

I laugh.

"Does all this remind you of Macbeth?" says Robert. "The bluff soldier, with the pale, mysterious woman behind him?"

We regulars spend much of our time psychoanalyzing the Ingrams. This is because their demeanors are so uncriminal. Even the police get involved in the speculation.

"The major is a strange character," says one arresting officer during a press briefing. "Puzzling. I can't figure him out. There have been some comments in court about Diana being stronger . . ." He pauses. "I don't understand that sort of relationship. I'm not part of a relationship like that."

"You're a lucky man!" shouts a journalist.

At 2:15 p.m. on March 23, a miracle occurs that might just save the defendants. Tecwen Whittock takes the stand, and he is brilliant. He begins with a tour of his harrowing childhood: born in a psychiatric hospital to a mother with behavioral problems, whom he never saw again, and an alcoholic father he never knew.

"I have a recollection of seeing him once when I was seven," he says.

He was raised in foster care, and pulled himself up through hard work to become head of business studies at Pontypridd Polytechnic, now known as the University of Glamorgan.

"Would you jeopardize all you've worked for to get involved in something like this?" asks his barrister, David Aubrey.

"Of course not," says Tecwen. "I wouldn't do that. It's against all my morals, all I do. I wouldn't put my family on the line for this. I know I'd land up in jail." It is a convincing moment. And then comes the bombshell. "Look closely at the photograph," says David Aubrey—it was a long-lens photograph of Tecwen on his way to work, head bowed, that appeared in the *Sun* on September 25.

"What have you got in your hand in that photograph?" asks David Aubrey.

"Some work files," replies Tecwen.

"And in your other hand?"

"Two five-hundred-milliliter bottles."

"Bottles of what?"

"Water. Tap water."

"Why?"

Tecwen has his entire life suffered from a persistent cough. Water helps. He carries some everywhere, and fruit juice, and inhalers and cough medicine. It's a ticklish cough, like a frog in his throat, very phlegmy. A stream of doctors and friends take the stand, attesting to Tecwen's irritating cough.

Aubrey sums up by saying, "So, when was this plan supposedly hatched? During a late-night telephone call, on 9 September, lasting less than five minutes. Is it really likely that Mr. Whittock would take part in such a hastily conceived scheme? Wouldn't he have said, 'You can't count on me. I'm liable to cough at any time!'"

MY RELATIONSHIP WITH the Ingrams has suffered a dreadful blow. Not only does Diana think I glower at her with a crazed expression, but the Ingrams have now appointed a media agent called David Thomas. These days, every time I bump into them at Starbucks or in the corridor outside Court 4, Thomas is there, saying "Hello, Jon" in a snarly manner. The rumor is that Thomas is going to handpick one journalist, and the rest of us will get nothing.

"Can I have just five minutes with the Ingrams?" I ask him.

"I'm mentally logging your request," says Thomas.

"All I want is for them to be able to tell their side of the story," I say.

"So your pitch is 'I'm Honest Jon,'" he replies.

"Yes."

"It's mentally logged," says Thomas. "You've batted your corner very well."

I tell him my one question: "What was that thing that happened back in our childhoods with the watch straps and the number plate APOLLO G?"

"Your question is logged up here," he says, pointing at his head. I spend the next three days sitting in the corridor, waiting for him to come back with an answer.

The jury retire to consider its verdict, and the corridor outside Court 4 becomes a frenzied bazaar. While everyone else crowds around Thomas, telling him how much they love dogs too (Thomas is a dog lover) and explaining that all they want to do is let the Ingrams tell their side of the story (he tells them they batted their corners well), I sidle up to Diana.

"I'll tell you the one thing I really want to know . . ." I begin breezily.

"Have you met David Thomas?" she replies, looking frantically around for him.

Robert Brydges hears that John Brown Publishing—the company that had once planned to publish Diana and Adrian's book—is now interested in reading the manuscript of *The Third Millionaire*.

Suddenly, there is drama. Judge Rivlin calls us all back in. "A very serious matter has arisen that does not concern the defendants," he says. The jury is temporarily discharged. We file back out into the corridor, bewildered. It turns out that a juror was overheard holding court in a pub, saying how fantastic it was to be on the *Millionaire* trial jury. For a day and a half, the various parties debate whether to start the trial again with a new jury. In the end, Judge Rivlin decides to allow the eleven remaining jurors to continue.

"Well, that," Charles mutters to himself, "amounted to the square root of fuck-all."

So this trial, which was all about entertainment, is almost chucked out because one of the jurors found it too entertaining.

When the guilty verdict comes in, after nearly fourteen hours of deliberations over three days, Diana closes her eyes and looks down. Charles holds her hand and kisses her on the cheek. Tecwen doesn't respond in any way. The only noises in court are tuts—the kind of tuts that mean "It's all a bit of a shame."

Charles and Diana have three daughters, two with special needs.

Judge Rivlin has the reputation of being tough when sentencing, but says, "I'm going to put you out of your misery. There's no way I'm going to deprive these children of their parents."

The defense barristers stand up to make their mitigation pleas. In the public gallery the defendants' family members strain to hear what's being said. We can just make out, "His career in the army is at an end. . . . Their home was provided by the army, so they've lost their home. . . . The children are suffering from panic attacks. . . . All three will have to leave their schools. . . ."

The reason why we can only barely hear this is because three pensioners in the public gallery are coughing uncontrollably.

Judge Rivlin says it was all just a shabby schoolboy trick. He says he doesn't think this crime was about greed, it was about wanting to look good on a TV quiz show. He says the fact that their reputations have been so publicly ruined is appropriate punishment—and I remember what Charles said about how he hates to be thought of as stupid. Judge Rivlin hands out suspended sentences and fines totaling £60,000. On the courthouse steps, the paparazzi cough theatrically when Tecwen and his quiet son, Rhys, walk out.

The scrum is even more dramatic for Charles and Diana. Cameras and tripods and photographers crash to the floor in the violent scuffle to get pictures. "I've seen child murderers get more respect than that," says one journalist. Other journalists and some nearby builders scream with laughter at Charles and Diana and chant, "Cheat! Cheat! Cheat!"

(An Indian diplomat named Vikas Swarup is at home watching the news reports on TV. Suddenly he has an idea for a novel. He will call it *Q & A*. The movie adaptation will be called *Slum-*

dog Millionaire. Later Swarup will explain his moment of inspiration to the *Guardian*: "If a British army major can be accused
of cheating, then an ignorant tiffin boy [urchin] from the world's
biggest slum can definitely be accused of cheating," he'll say.)

I phone David Thomas to ask if Diana can give me the answer
to my question. He says, "You've not fallen off my mental list." I
never hear from him again.

Instead I phone childhood friends to ask if they can remember
anything about it. Most of them can. There were two Pollock
brothers, they tell me. Bill and Arthur. They were in a family
business together, making leather watch straps. There was a big
falling-out in the family, and Arthur left the company. Bill became rich, driving around in a fancy car with the personalized
number plate APOLLO G. His family were the ones who lived
near me, in a big house in Lisvane. They had a son called Julian.
Arthur Pollock never really recovered. He was left penniless and
in ill health. His children vowed to pull themselves back up and
never suffer the indignity their father endured. They would make
something of their lives, they promised themselves. So Adrian
and Marcus set up an estate agency together, and Diana married
an army major. The estate agency failed. In fact, the whole thing
failed.

Who Killed Richard Cullen?

(This story was published in the *Guardian* on July 16, 2005,
two years before the global financial crash that began with
the subprime mortgage crisis of July 2007.)

t is a wet February day in a very smoky room in a terraced cottage in Trowbridge, Wiltshire. A portable TV in an alcove plays the news. Everything in here is quite old. No spending spree has taken place in this house. There are wedding and baby and school photographs scattered around. Six children, now all grown up, were raised here. There's a framed child's painting in the toilet, a picture of Wendy Cullen. It reads "Supergran." When I phoned Wendy a week ago she said I was welcome to visit, "Just as long as you don't mind cigarette smoke. I'm smoking myself to death here."

The *"Congratulations! You have been pre-approved for a loan"*–type junk mail is still pouring through their letter box. Wendy has just thrown another batch in the bin.

"You know what the post is like," she says.

"I don't get all that much credit-card junk mail," I say. "I get some, I suppose, but not nearly as much as you do."

"Really?" says Wendy. "I assumed everyone was constantly bombarded."

"Not me," I say.

We both shrug as if to say, "That's a mystery."

IT WAS A MONTH AGO today that Wendy's husband, Richard, committed suicide. It was the end of what had been an ordinary twenty-five-year marriage. They met when Wendy owned a B and B on the other side of Trowbridge. He turned up one day and rented a room. Richard had trained to be an electrical engineer but he ended up as a mechanic.

"He loved repairing people's cars," Wendy says. Then she narrows her eyes at my line of questioning and makes me promise that I am not here to write "a slushy horrible mawky love story."

"I'm really not," I say. So Wendy continues. Everything was normal until six years ago, when she needed an operation. "I couldn't face the Royal United Hospital in Bath," she says, "so I went private. I took out a four-thousand-pound loan."

She says she remembers a time when it was hard for people like them to get loans, but this was easy. Companies were practically throwing money at them.

"Richard handled all the finances. He said, 'I can get you one with nought percent interest and after six months we'll switch you to another one.'"

But then, a few months after the first operation, Wendy was diagnosed with breast cancer and Richard had to take six weeks off to drive her to radiotherapy. The bills needed paying and so, once again, he did that peculiarly modern British thing. He began signing up for credit cards, behaving like a company, thinking he could beat the lenders at their own game by cleverly rolling the debts over from account to account.

There are currently eight million more credit cards in circulation in Britain than there are people: sixty-seven million credit cards, fifty-nine million people.

He signed up with MINT: "Apply for your MINT Card. You'd need a seriously good reason not to. What's stopping you?"

And Frizzell: "A name you can trust."

And Barclaycard: "Wake up to a fresh start."

And Morgan Stanley: "Choose from our Flags of Great Britain range of card designs."

And American Express: "Go on, treat yourself."

And so on.

Right now nobody knows how Richard Cullen's shrewd acumen fell apart.

"He wasn't a man that talked a great deal," says Wendy, "and he never, ever discussed finances with me." But somehow it all spiraled out of control.

Wendy first got the inkling that something was wrong just before Christmas 2004, when the debt-collection departments of various credit-card companies began phoning. Richard called them back out of his wife's hearing.

"You know how men will walk around with their mobiles," says Wendy. "He used to go out into the garden."

She looks over to the garden behind the conservatory extension and says, "He was a very proud man. He must have been going through hell. They were very, very persistent. I don't think he was even phoning them back in the end."

Finally, he admitted it to his wife. He said he didn't seek out

all of the twenty-two credit cards he had somehow ended up ac-
quiring between 1998 and 2004. On many occasions they just arrived through the letter box in the form of *"Congratulations! You
have been pre-approved . . ."* junk. He said he thought he owed
about £30,000. There had been no spending spree, he said, no
secret vices. He had just tied himself up in knots, using each card
to pay off the interest and the charges on the others. The fog of
late-payment fees and so on had somehow crept up and engulfed
him. He got a pair of scissors from the kitchen and cut up ten
credit cards in front of her.

On January 10, 2005, Richard visited his ex-wife, Jennifer,
who later told the police that he seemed "very quiet, like he'd retreated into himself, like his mind was gone."

She asked him how his weekend was. He replied, "Not very
good."

Then he went missing for two days.

"Nobody knows where he went," says Wendy.

On the morning of January 12, Wendy's son Christopher
looked in the garage. It was padlocked, so he broke in with a
screwdriver. There was an old Vauxhall Nova covered with
a sheet.

"I don't know why," Christopher later told the police, "but I
decided to look under the sheet."

Richard Cullen had gassed himself in his car. He left his wife
a note: "I just can't take this any more and you'll be better off
without me."

WHO KILLED RICHARD CULLEN?

For instance: Why did so many credit-card companies choose
to swamp the Cullens with junk when they don't swamp me?

How did they even get their address? How can I even begin to find something complicated like that out?

And then I have a brainstorm. I'll devise an experiment. I'll create a number of personas. Their surnames will all be Ronson, and they'll all live at my address, but they'll have different first names. Each Ronson will be poles apart, personality-wise. Each will have a unique set of hopes, desires, predilections, vices, and spending habits, reflected in the various mailing lists they'll sign up for—from Porsche down to hard-core pornography. The one thing that'll unite them is that they won't be at all interested in credit cards. They will not seek loans or any financial services as they wander around, filling out lifestyle surveys and entering competitions and purchasing things by mail order. Whenever they're invited to tick a box forbidding whichever company from passing their details to other companies, they'll neglect to tick the box.

Which, if any, of my personas will end up getting sent credit-card junk mail? Which personality type will be most attractive to the credit-card companies?

I name my personas John, Paul, George, Ringo, Dave Dee, Dozy, Beaky, Mick, Titch, Willy, Biff, Happy, and Bernard. And I begin.

HAPPY RONSON

Happy is delightfully ethical. He cares about everything all the time. He has a surfeit of caring. He subscribes to the magazines *Going Green*, *Natural Parenting*, and *Vegetarians International Voice for Animals*. He shops at Ecozone and donates to PETA—People for the Ethical Treatment of Animals.

"Happy! What a lovely name!" says the man in the Body Shop on Oxford Street as Happy fills out a Loyalty Card application form.

"Thank you!" I say.

Happy is happy for the Body Shop to pass his details to whoever they see fit. He doesn't tick the box.

Happy fills out many lifestyle surveys, like the one published by the International Fund for Animal Welfare that asks which animals he especially cares about. Happy especially cares about dogs, cats, elephants, gorillas, tigers, whales, seals, dolphins, and all other animals in distress from oil spills. So he ticks everything.

Then I get worried that if anyone is really paying attention to Happy's predilections, they might become wary of his wholesale compassion and suspect him of being an imaginary character, created by a journalist, to trick businesses into inadvertently revealing their data-trafficking practices. So I untick tigers.

PAUL RONSON

I imagine Paul looks like the kind of guy you see in credit-card adverts, the kind of guy you used to see in cigarette adverts—staggeringly handsome and healthy, fooling around in swimming pools on sunny days with equally beautiful friends.

Paul is an entrepreneur, a suave millionaire, the director of Paul Ronson Enterprises. Being a narcissistic aesthete who can't bear being around ordinary people, he subscribes to *Porsche Design* ("Porsche: The Engineers of Purism"), Priority Pass ("The ultimate privilege for frequent travelers: Escape the crowds to a

VIP oasis of calm. Your key to over 450 airport VIP lounges worldwide"), and so on.

GEORGE RONSON

George Ronson is a charming older gentleman. George orders from the *Daily Express* the CD set *Sentimental Journey*: "Take a sentimental journey with these 60 everlasting love songs on 4 fabulous CDs . . . Henry Mancini ('Moon River') * Glenn Miller ('Moonlight Serenade') * Perry Como ('Don't Let the Stars Get in Your Eyes') . . ."

"If you do not wish to receive offers from other companies carefully selected by us, please tick this box," reads the tiniest of letters at the bottom of the order form.

I imagine that George's eyes still have quite the twinkle, but his eyesight isn't what it once was. He is absentminded and cannot find his glasses, and so he doesn't notice this infinitesimal print.

For this reason, he doesn't tick the box.

George has also entered the Specsavers Spectacle Wearer of the Year competition ("Have You Got Specs Appeal? Our first-prize winner will be awarded a fantastic two-week all-inclusive holiday for two in the Maldives. Send a recent color photograph of yourself wearing specs to . . .").

I am, unlike George, an embittered cynic, ground down by the travails of life, and so I consequently wonder if this whole spectacle-wearing beauty pageant is an excuse for the company to gather our names and addresses for their database, and to sell them on to other databases.

TITCH RONSON

Titch is the least favorite of my personas. He is venal. He is a gullible sex maniac. He thinks about nothing but pornography, his virility, Nazi memorabilia, and extreme martial arts. Today Titch takes up an offer in the *News of the World*: "The original BLUE PILL. Something for the weekend, sir?"

In this newspaper advert, a topless woman wearing a policeman's helmet has a speech bubble that reads, "Allo, Allo, Allo. What have we here—is it a lethal weapon I see before me?" A warning covers her breasts: "IMPORTANT NOTICE. Some customers find the 100 mg Blue Pill we supply TOO EFFECTIVE. If this happens to you simply reduce usage to half a tablet."

I assume the Blue Pill is some kind of herbal Viagra. Titch is taken in hook, line and sinker, because he does in fact see his penis as a lethal weapon.

He barely notices a tiny sentence at the bottom of the order form: "If you don't wish to receive further mailings of exciting offers from us, or associated companies, please tick this box."

Titch spends his every waking hour seeking depraved gratification and is therefore tantalized by the promise of exciting offers, so he doesn't tick the box. Then he reads the rest of the *News of the World* and is saddened to discover that Kate Moss has got back together with Peter Doherty.

Titch also subscribes to *Fighters Only*, a magazine dedicated to photographs of frequently blood-splattered boxers, with captions like "Psycho Steve Tetley. Lightweight. Hyper aggressive. He's called Psycho for a reason!"

There is no end to Titch's troubles. He's also, I decide, a hopeless gambling addict, and has signed up to William Hill and the Loopy Lotto free daily Internet draw.

Midway through my experiment I fill in a consumer lifestyle survey on Titch's behalf, attached to a "Win a Day on a *Playboy* Shoot" competition. ("Get to hang out with girls like this in the flesh! There'll be naked girls! It's a once in an adulthood experience!")

The consumer-lifestyle survey is quite detailed, and so it gives me the opportunity to really flesh out Titch's character and circumstances:

Is Titch in employment?

No. He is an unemployed, single, thirty-eight-year-old homeowner.

His annual earnings are what?

I tick the "less than £10,000" box.

What are his annual outgoings?

I think for a moment, then tick the "£10,000–£24,000" box. So every year Titch somehow manages to spend approximately £14,000 more than he earns. How frequently does Titch pay off his credit-card balance in full?

Funny question, I think. Titch answers: Rarely.

Then Titch tires of these relentless questions and instead scuttles away to order the PABO Sizzling Adult Mail Order Catalogue from their online sex shop. Titch, who thought he had seen it all, is startled by the voluminous choice on offer by PABO. Many of the items for sale involve pumps and studs and—mysteriously— "tracts" that even the grotesque Titch can't picture aiding a sexual situation.

I put all the things Titch subscribes to in an old picnic hamper, which I keep on a shelf in my office. Rifling through the contents of this picnic hamper is a disturbing experience. Red blood, pink flesh, green baize. Although I have to say that when I troop around the betting offices looking for loyalty schemes for Titch to add his name to, I always stop to play video roulette. It is terribly moreish.

EVERY MORNING for three weeks I walk the streets of London in the guise of one or other of my personas. I inevitably spend slightly less time being Titch because I find the prospect of being spotted slouching into sex shops incredibly embarrassing. But by the time three weeks are up, I believe I've been fair and signed each Ronson up to a similar number of lists. And then I wait.

It takes three months for the first unsolicited-loan offer to arrive. And then, suddenly, I am bombarded. And which Ronson is inundated more than any other? Which Ronson receives the first and, in fact, all the credit-card junk mail?

It's Paul: the handsome, high-achieving, aesthetic, sagacious millionaire Paul. No, I'm joking. Paul doesn't receive any credit-card junk mail at all.

It's Titch: stupid, superstitious, venal Titch.

Titch has so far been offered loans by Ocean Finance, Shakespeare Finance, Blair Endersby, e-loanshop.com, TML Mortgage Solutions, loans.co.uk, and easy-loans.co.uk, and an MBNA Platinum card, and an American Express Red card.

What—I wonder—is Titch's most attractive personality trait for the lenders? Is it his sex addiction, his gambling addiction, his—surely not—interest in bare-knuckle boxing and Nazism? It has to be something. And then I find the culprits! They are in Shoreditch, East London. And they are called Loopy Lotto.

IN A SPLURGE of gambling addiction back in April, Titch signed up for the Loopy Lotto free daily Internet draw (top prize £1 million). I remember the occasion well because I had to pick six numbers for him, and so I became—on Titch's behalf—a superstitious fool, choosing numbers that intuitively felt special to me. Last night, as I examined the e-mails offering Titch "up to £75,000 for almost any purpose" (loans.co.uk) and "We will consider all applications, no matter what your credit rating" (Ocean Finance), I noticed the small print explaining that they came via Loopy Lotto.

And so I telephone them.

Dan Bannister, the company's director, sounds lovely and very surprised to hear from me. He says journalists usually have no interest in what people like him do, because it's terribly boring. But I'm welcome to come over if I like.

The whitewashed loft-style offices of Loopy Lotto could belong to an advertising agency or a TV production company. Boho-yuppies with wire-framed glasses beaver glamorously away as Dan and I sit in the lounge area.

"Who is the average Loopy Lotto subscriber?" I ask him.

"People who are looking for something for nothing and are into instant gratification," Dan replies. "It's not a massively upmarket list."

Dan says they have six hundred thousand registered players. I say one of them is Titch Ronson.

I tell Dan about my experiment. I explain that my fancy, upmarket personas received no junk mail at all, yet Titch was bombarded, primarily through Loopy Lotto.

Dan nods, pleased and unsurprised. He explains that Titch sounds classically, enticingly "subprime."

"Subprime is the golden egg," Dan says. "If, as a direct marketer, you can identify subprime characteristics, you can do very well."

Dan says the vast majority of all junk mail—be it loans or otherwise—is directed at the subprime market: "The best thing you can tell a client is that you can accurately identify subprime individuals. Which is why, when people are asked to fill in lifestyle surveys, they'll often see questions like 'Have you ever experienced difficulty getting credit?' or 'Have you ever missed a mortgage payment?' Those are the sorts of triggers that will identify you as potentially subprime. It's valuable information."

It is slightly chilling to realize there are rational, functional people up there employed to spot, nurture, and exploit those down here among us who are irrational and can barely cope. If you want to know how stupid you're perceived to be by the people up there, count the unsolicited junk mail you receive. If you get a lot, you're perceived to be alluringly stupid.

THIS DOESN'T SOLVE the Richard Cullen mystery. In the weeks before his death, he insisted to his wife that there had been no secret vices, nothing like that at all. If that was true—if there was nothing Titch Ronson–like about him—why was he, in particular, bombarded?

I have coffee at Portcullis House with the Labour MP Chris Bryant. He's a member of the Treasury Select Committee, a group of MPs who are trying to investigate the credit-card industry.

"We all know they target the people who are just bumping along," he says, "who don't read the small print and don't realize the extortionate interest rates they're paying. We know they use aggressive marketing techniques to persuade those people to take out loans that they often don't understand and simply can't afford."

"Do any credit-card companies ever admit to this?" I ask.

"Of course not," says Chris. Then he pauses and says, "Have you heard of this thing called Mosaic?"

Chris says he doesn't know much about Mosaic, only that it is some computer program. He says he's heard that the credit-card junk-mail departments have grown to rely on Mosaic when determining whom to shower. Apparently, he says, if you type a postcode into Mosaic, it'll tell you if the person living at that house wears Burberry, or drinks Coke or white wine, or whatever.

Then Chris moves his chair slightly closer to mine.

"The Tories have Mosaic," he says. "They're using it to decide who to target with *their* junk."

"Are they?" I reply darkly. What Chris doesn't tell me—and I only find out later—is that Labour has Mosaic too.

TORIES USE CONSUMER HABITS TO TARGET VOTERS

The contents of voters' shopping baskets are being studied by both main political parties to help them prepare "bespoke" campaigns in the coming election. The program was developed in the US where the Republicans' more skillful use of consumer information to target voters is credited with helping George Bush win.

Drinkers of Coors beer, for example, were more likely to vote Republican, as were bourbon drinkers. Those with a taste for brandy, on the other hand, were found to be Democrats. One senior Labour strategist was dismissive of attempts to "fetishise" marketing tools, while admitting that the party was also using Mosaic.

—*Independent on Sunday,* February 6, 2005

The article goes on to explain how Mosaic is even influencing the Tories' dissemination of their message. For instance, they intend to post their anti-immigration leaflets to households deemed, via Mosaic, to be intolerant of outsiders, but they won't bother sending those leaflets to the more cosmopolitan Tory voters. I wonder: If Chris Bryant was right about Mosaic's influence on the credit-card junk mailers, what was it about Richard Cullen's lifestyle that made him seem a suitable target?

I LEAVE A MESSAGE with the Mosaic people, who turn out to be a company called Experian. Their press officer, Bruno, calls me back. Over the phone he eulogizes Mosaic. He says it is incredibly accurate and used by everyone, more than fifty thousand businesses, including many credit-card companies.

I tell him I still don't quite understand what it does.

"I'll give you a demonstration," Bruno replies. "Give me a postcode."

"Ah," I say. I scrabble frantically around my notes until I find Richard Cullen's postcode—the postcode shared by the twenty or so households on the Cullens' street.

"Uh . . . BA14 . . ." I begin, making it sound like I've just invented a postcode at random.

I hear him type it into his computer.

The Cullens, it turns out, belong to Mosaic's Group B 11: "Happy Families: Families Making Good." These are "older people on middle incomes . . . not highfliers up career ladders of large conglomerates." Neighborhoods like this are "hardly centers of intellectual or aesthetic style." Happy Families are "likely to be interested in adverts for financial products."

"This is a culture," concludes Mosaic, "that is keen to take advantage of easy credit."

I later discover that a fledgling incarnation of Mosaic called ACORN (A Classification of Residential Neighbourhoods), which is also used by some credit-card companies, says of Richard Cullen's postcode: "The interest in current affairs is low. They are educated to a low degree." (ACORN was invented by the creator of Mosaic—Professor Richard Webber—but it is owned and operated by a company called CACI, and not by Experian.)

Then Bruno types my postcode into Mosaic.

"Wow!" he says. "You're a Global Connector. Roman Abramovich is a Global Connector too."

Bruno is clearly impressed.

"We bought before the boom," I explain, slightly embarrassed.

"Not many *Guardian* journalists are Global Connectors," says Bruno.

"My street isn't *that* nice," I say.

"Well, if we've got it wrong, you're the exception that proves the rule," says Bruno, a little defensively.

He reads out my profile. Nowhere does it say that we Global Connectors are likely to take advantage of easy credit, nor will we be interested in adverts for financial products.

The reason neither I nor my horrendous alter ego Titch don't get nearly as much credit-card junk mail as Richard Cullen did is that our postcode, N1, suggests affluence. If I lived in a down-market postal area, one more befitting Titch's characteristics, he wouldn't have been filtered out by Mosaic. He'd have been deluged.

Bruno invites me to Experian's London offices. I've never heard of them. It turns out that they're not only the power behind Mosaic, they are also Britain's biggest credit-reference agency, with files on forty million people in Britain. Bruno gives me directions. I should walk down Park Lane, he says, turn onto Curzon Street, and after 150 yards I'll see Leconfield House.

"Apparently it used to be MI5 headquarters," says Bruno, "which is very appropriate, I suppose."

"You've taken over MI5's old building?" I repeat.

He laughs. "Yes," he says.

LECONFIELD HOUSE was indeed MI5 HQ—between 1945 and 1976. And you can tell. It has no street number. Leconfield House is not number anything, Curzon Street. Inside, Experian's offices are all beige and pine, like an airport hotel. Bruno arrives with another man—Professor Richard Webber, "the father of geo-demographics." This is the man who invented both Mosaic and ACORN.

It isn't my imagination. As we walk to Conference Room A, Professor Webber is looking me up and down, categorizing me on the spot.

"You're wearing training shoes," he says, slightly baffled, because they don't quite fit with the rest of my clothes.

"I walked here," I explain. "I need comfortable shoes for walking."

"Hm," says Professor Webber.

PROFESSOR WEBBER'S WORK—profiling and categorizing the lifestyles of the nation—began in the 1970s when he was commissioned by Liverpool City Council to design a computer program that might explain certain nuances of geographical deprivation. Why were some poor areas prone to rioting when others weren't? It turned out that some Liverpool ghettos had preponderances of "ethnics, drug issues, single parents, low levels of education," whereas others had "high fertility, high church attendance," and so on. Beefeater gin was shown to be particularly popular in certain areas.

"Until then," Professor Webber says, "nobody knew the connection between neighborhoods and consumption. It wasn't long before the private sector saw the potential."

Ever since, the professor has been tallying and perfecting, buying up databases from the DVLA (Driver and Vehicle Licensing Agency), the electoral roll, the British Crime Survey, and so on, and augmenting this data with Experian's own lifestyle surveys.

"Which Mosaic category do you fall into?" I ask the professor.

"Cultural Leadership," he says.

"Are you a typical Cultural Leader?" I ask him.

"Yes," he says.

> Cultural Leadership: "These [highly fastidious] people are assured, secure and very discriminating. They spend their

abundant wealth very carefully. They value the privacy of their homes and home life.

It doesn't sound like any credit-card companies will be bombarding Professor Webber's home with junk. Mosaic's lifestyle data (Professor Webber writes the text himself) is often really quite impolite. For instance, when people within the category known as "Welfare Borderlines" purchase cosmetics, they are "likely to be striking accessories rather than means for displaying natural beauty." The professor has, however, been most glowing about his own people, the Cultural Leaders.

I TELL BRUNO and Professor Webber about Richard Cullen's suicide. I suggest that families like the Cullens are bombarded with junk because the direct-marketing departments of the lenders are guided by Mosaic pointers such as: "likely to be interested in adverts for financial products . . . keen to take advantage of easy credit," and ACORN pointers like "educated to a low degree." In the mathematical world of the credit industry's computer lifestyle calculations, it strikes me that a consensus had been formed about the Cullens. The family needed the money, but because they owned their own home, there was something to seize if need be. And they weren't smart enough to read the small print and spot the trap they were being beckoned into.

For a moment Bruno seems unsure how to respond to this. My impression is that he doesn't want to downplay Mosaic's significance, but neither does he want to admit that his company's computer program played a role—however peripheral—in a suicide. So he shrugs and says, yes, some credit-card companies use Mosaic, but they use their own files too.

Before I met Professor Webber, I fancifully imagined him as a Caractacus Potts, a madcap inventor filled with sorrow at how the private sector had hijacked his brilliant machine. But when I ask him if he's alarmed by any of Mosaic's current uses, he says the opposite is true. He wishes the public sector were efficient enough to use Mosaic more.

"Our country," he says, "would be better organized if they did."

But this is beginning to change, says Bruno. For example, TV Licensing are using Mosaic to choose which areas to target with their vans.

MY LASTING MEMORY of my afternoon at Experian is Professor Webber and I, a Cultural Leader and a Global Connector, sitting inside these mysterious former MI5 headquarters in the heart of Mayfair, imperiously scrutinizing, via a computer slideshow, Welfare Borderlines.

As we looked at the slides I asked Professor Webber if he considered himself an academic, but he laughed scornfully and said he was a taxonomist. He said, "I like putting things into categories. Taxonomy is less authoritarian than academia."

But Mosaic is packed with the professor's opinions and judgments—a subjective mind-set that is guiding countless credit-card companies and leading to Happy Families being swamped with offers of easy credit.

Of course, Bruno was right that no company will rely solely on Mosaic—but the computer program is surely indicative of the way things are done inside the whirring, mathematical, computer world of credit-card marketing.

"You've probably got enough for a book," said Bruno as I left that afternoon, which I presume was his way of saying, "Don't call me again."

ACCORDING TO THE National Consumer Council, one in five people are borrowing money just to pay household bills, and one in four are struggling to meet their repayments. Half a million people in Britain have "crippling debts on their credit cards."

Advice services such as Debt Free Direct—who try to help people like Richard Cullen—say they received 275 percent more calls per day in December 2004 than they did a year earlier. A quarter of those in debt are receiving treatment for stress, depression, and anxiety. Britain's bailiffs are enjoying 70 percent more work than they did two years ago.

Wendy Cullen is annoyed with Debt Free Direct. In the weeks before her husband's suicide, he phoned them countless times for help; but, she says, "They did sod all, excuse my language. They'd phone back and say, 'He hasn't sent us the right information.' And I'd reply, 'I *saw* him send the right information.'"

Wendy says that had Debt Free Direct been more helpful, her husband would be alive today.

I CALL ANDREW REDMOND of Debt Free Direct. He says they're required by law "to get all this verification. The creditors want proof that the person in question cannot afford to pay more than they say they can afford." Andrew says they've been fighting this for years.

"This," he says, "is a classic example of a case when a simplifi

cation of the process might have averted a tragedy. We had several conversations with Richard Cullen, and we offered the best
advice that we could, but it was too little too late."

Debt Free Direct have transcripts of all the conversations
between them and Richard Cullen. In these transcripts—they
say—you can read his continual pleas for help. And then you can
read the advisers' responses—that they can only help if he can
provide this verification, and then that verification, and then the
last transcript is the phone call from Christopher Cullen saying
that Richard has been found dead.

These days, only 40 percent of calls made to debt-advice centers are answered. Sixty percent of the time the centers are so
busy, the phone just rings and rings.

I PHONE BARCLAYS to see if someone will talk to me about
Richard Cullen.

"I don't think anyone will comment on this at all," says the first
press officer I speak to. "Someone will get back to you but I really
don't think this is something we'll be able to help you with."

I ask the second press officer if there's anything to be learned
from Richard Cullen's suicide. He says, "We did lend to Richard Cullen. That was clearly a poor decision. We should have
shared data better within the bank. We did get it wrong with
Richard Cullen. But we have learned from this. We are now
sharing data better within the bank."

Is Mosaic used within Barclays as a way to target certain people with junk?

"It is true to say that Mosaic and systems like Mosaic are used
by the direct-marketing departments to make our marketing as
efficient as possible," he replies. "We want to get as few pieces of

paper out as possible with the most number of responses. That is the very specific area in which we do use Mosaic—to target people who are likely to respond to direct mail."

"And Mosaic pointers like 'keen to take advantage of easy credit'?" I say.

"Yeah, we would see those as pointers," he says. "However, this doesn't mean that the credit-card companies will be willing to lend to that customer. Because we mail to someone in no way suggests that we are willing to lend to that person."

The third Barclays press officer I speak to says the problem with Richard Cullen was that at the time he didn't *seem* to be in trouble. He was making his repayments. What nobody knew— he says—was he was achieving this by borrowing on other cards.

"Richard Cullen should have asked for help," he says.

Of course, he asked for help, repeatedly, with Debt Free Direct. But they were required by the creditors to make Richard Cullen jump through such complex hoops that they just couldn't help him in time.

I CALL WENDY CULLEN to see if there's any news. She says things are bad. Some credit-card companies have written off the debts, for the sake of good public relations, but others haven't. Morgan Stanley and the RBS, in particular, are being worryingly silent, she says. Wendy's house, and her £500 car, and the trailer, remain at risk.

Just before I phoned, Wendy opened a letter from the credit-card company MBNA. She assumed it was about the debts. Richard had three MBNA cards and sheets of MBNA credit-card checks, which he used to pay his Goldfish minimum repayments. Wendy knows this because she found the stubs stuffed behind the washing machine a few days ago when it was pulled out for repairs. There they were, in Richard Cullen's neat handwriting: "G/Fish £172.53." And so on.

But the letter she received from MBNA today was something different. It read:

> Dear Mr. Cullen
>   Let's face it most of us encounter financial problems at some stage in our lives. All it takes sometimes is a little bit of bad luck.

The letter goes on to offer Richard Cullen, who has now been dead for three months, a £15,000 loan. ("10.9 percent APR variable. Loans are secured on residential property.")

"Just imagine," the letter concludes, "this could give you a much needed light at the end of that dark tunnel."

In 2004, MBNA's profits were one and a half times that of McDonald's.

THE CULLENS are beginning to piece together the minutiae of the mess Richard got himself into. They've found credit-card statements stuffed in drawers and behind wardrobes all over the house. Wendy says I can come down and look at them.

While I'm sitting there, I hear a key in the front door. It is Christopher.

"Did you hear the radio?" he says. "Barclays has just announced its highest-ever profits. Four point five billion pounds. Seven hundred and sixty-one million pounds from Barclaycard."

Wendy lights another cigarette.

"Did your father have a Barclaycard?" I ask.

"Three," says Christopher.

"You'd think that would have triggered something off in Barclays' computers," says Wendy.

"And on top of that," says Christopher, "Barclays gave him a six-thousand-pound loan."

"Oh my God!" says Wendy. "I didn't know that."

"Which they upped to thirteen thousand pounds," says Christopher. "That's twenty thousand pounds in repayments over sixty months. That's just that one loan."

"How did they let him do that?" says Wendy. "He must have been crazy!" She pauses. "Barclays shouldn't have done that," she says.

Christopher drives me to his house to look at the statements. There are half a dozen files thick with them. There's a Jiffy bag, too, filled with sliced-up credit cards, cut in half when Richard Cullen finally admitted the problem to his wife. MBNA, Goldfish, Tesco, Amex, Frizzell, etc., all sliced up.

A typical page of a Richard Cullen credit-card statement reads like this:

> Alliance and Leicester
> Interest charged: £71.07
> Late fee: £25
> Overlimit fee: £25

There are thousands and thousands of pounds' worth of these £25s. Then there are letters, too, like this from Barclaycard:

> According to our records your Barclaycard history has been excellent and we have consequently enrolled you in

our Guaranteed Acceptance Masterloan Programme. This means we have set aside £7,000 for your immediate access without an application or any questions whatsoever.

And then, later, another letter from Barclays:

Dear Mr. Cullen,
  We regret that we have been unable to pay the following, as there were insufficient funds in your account:
  Payment in favor of Frizzell for £554.09
  Payment in favor of Barclaycard for £339.06
  Your account has been debited £30 which is the fee charged when we are unable to make payments due to insufficient funds.

This letter did not come from a human being. A computer, with the printed signature J Smith, churned it out. There are a number of identical ones—signed by J Smith—dating back to 2002. How can Barclays say Richard Cullen didn't seem to be in trouble, when payments were being declined from one corner of Barclays to another? At one point, Richard Cullen went 17p over his Lloyds limit. He was charged £20 for this, and then the interest on that £20.17, and so on.

And then, finally, in the last weeks of his life, scores of letters like this:

Your failure to pay your arrears of £166.04, despite our reminders and offers of assistance, has forced us to withdraw your credit line and take steps to inform the credit reference agency.

The statements tell the story of a man who thought he could beat the credit-card companies at their own game but discovered that he couldn't. He'd been telling the truth about his absence of secret vices. In the last year of his life, almost every payment on every page of every statement was to a different credit-card company. The odd exception was nothing: a £13 subscription to a gardening magazine, and so on.

But he had lied about one thing. Richard Cullen, at the time of his death, didn't owe £30,000. He owed £130,000.

I CALL KEITH TONDEUR of Credit Action, which monitors our spiraling debt problem. I tell him what Wendy had said about how hard it used to be for people like them to get loans.

"That's right," he says. "Thirty years ago you'd go to your local bank manager. He'd say, 'A thousand pounds? You must be joking. I'll give you three hundred.' We go into banks looking for the best advice, but I know one chief executive who describes his branches as 'shops.' We treat our bank managers like we treat our doctors. They say, 'Ah, you'll need to buy some insurance with that, sir.' And we believe them. But in fact we're just being sold things. And this is an industry that's self-regulating. Why is that?"

LATER I HEAR the story of why it takes three days for an electronic transfer to clear. Transfers used to *really* take three days to clear, in the days they were delivered by carrier pigeon, or whatever. But now, in this computer age, they take an instant to clear, but they keep the three-day rule going so they can accrue three days of interest. The banks make tens of millions from these wheezes.

. . .

IN OCTOBER 2003 Matthew Barrett, the CEO of Barclays, was called before the Treasury Select Committee. He was asked about the small print. Even though the base interest rate had gone down to 3.5 percent, buried away in the small print was the revelation that Barclaycard was charging 17.9 percent interest.

"The small print," Matthew Barrett admitted to the committee, "is an eye test for sure." Then he added, "I do not borrow on credit cards. It is too expensive."

I PHONE BARCLAYS again and speak with a press officer. I quote him his CEO's statement, that the "small print is an eye test for sure." He laughs and says, "That sounds like Matthew."

Then he turns serious and says, in terms of the small print, they have made "huge steps forward in the past twelve to eighteen months. All the credit-card companies have taken out the really important bits from the small print and put them in big letters in the summary box."

This sounded comforting. Or at least, it did until the day I attend the International Direct Marketing Fair at Earls Court, West London. This is the junk-mail industry's annual convention.

Even though a sign near the door at Earls Court reads "62 percent of consumers agree with the statement 'I enjoy going through my post,'" the mood here is undeniably panicky. Sue Baker, the PR lady in charge of the event, had told me over the phone, "People are really worried." More and more consumers are ticking the no box. They don't want their details passed to third parties.

"The list is severely compromised," said Sue.

An article in today's *Direct Marketing International* magazine doomily predicts, "In a couple of years there will be no cold telemarketing industry in Norway. Could this happen here? Well, wake up! It *is* happening."

Six point eight million British people, the article continues, have so far signed up to the telephone preference service, which filters out cold calls.

Everyone is here, from the brokers and profilers, like Mosaic and Baby Marketing, to the myriad businesses that provide the free gifts contained within junk. There's a stand displaying sticks of seaside rock that say "First Direct—The Time Has Come to Suck It and See."

The idea is that if someone is sent a sweet, they will be more likely to take out a loan.

LIKE A CHILD, I am drawn to the bright colors of the Post-it note stand, where Post-it notes of all the colors of the rainbow are displayed within glass cabinets like rare jewels.

(It is, by the way, possible that Stanley Kubrick may have influenced 3M's decision to diversify from their original yellowy-green into other colors. As a great fan of stationery, he once telephoned the head of 3M to suggest they branch out into blues and reds and so on. The man ostentatiously sighed. "If we did, there'd be no end to it," he said. But it was only a year or two later that the other colors began to appear.)

"Ever thought about using a Post-it note on a direct mail piece?" asks their publicity material. "Studies show that machine-applying a printed Post-it note can increase your response rate by 18 percent."

I ask Peter, who runs the stand, how it works. He shows me a recent piece of junk mail from Capital One. It consists of an offer letter from the credit-card company outlining all the terms and technicalities, the APRs, and the extra charges. Stuck on the front is a bright-yellow Post-it note, which reads:

> This week I will . . .
> Exercise.
> Eat Healthily.
> Sort out my finances. Call Capital One on 0800 . . .

"See?" says Peter. "The letter has all the technical details. You throw the letter away and keep the Post-it note!"

I CALL RICHARD HOLMES, a spokesperson for Capital One. He says, "By using a Post-it note, we are attempting to highlight the key issue for potential customers, which is to contact Capital One. This initiative in no way seeks to detract from the importance of the terms and conditions which have to be read and signed by anyone applying for a card."

AN IMAGE KEEPS POPPING into my head. It's the old days. A customer in need sits down with their bank manager, who says, "A thousand pounds? You must be crazy! I'll give you three hundred."

I wonder: Is there some economic sage out there who effectively invented the new way—someone who drew up a utopian image where banks would fall over one another to loan money to whoever wanted it?

And so I call Lord Brian Griffiths of Fforestfach. He's the vice chairman of Goldman Sachs International, a former director of the Bank of England, and once the head of Margaret Thatcher's

Policy Unit. I'd been told that if anyone could answer that question, he could.

I ask him if this whole mess can be traced back to one man. I expect him to say something like "Oh, no, it's far more complicated than that. It is a gradual shift. Nobody is to blame."

But he doesn't. Instead, he says, "I hate to say it, but I was one of the people who argued strongly in favor of it."

"When was this?" I ask.

"December 1970," he says. "At that time the banks were a classic cartel, very much a middle-class preserve, and I believed that the democratization of credit had to be a good thing. Everyone in principle should have access to credit."

So in December 1970, he says, he wrote a paper for the Institute of Economic Affairs advocating a revolution in banking. The report, *Competition in Banking,* concluded: "The only way in which to make banking a competitive industry is to remove *all* obstacles to potential new entrants into the industry."

It was, by all accounts, a key factor in the subsequent deregulation of UK banking.

IT BECOMES OBVIOUS during my conversation with Lord Griffiths that he's come to believe he's unleashed some kind of monster. He says he never could have predicted "the dynamism" with which the lenders would pursue his ideas.

"The dynamism," he says. "The innovation."

I've never heard these words uttered with such sadness.

"I don't think anyone would have foreseen how innovative and aggressive and competitive the financial services would become in their techniques," he says. "The whole lot of them are to blame." He pauses. "I'm not advocating a return to the status quo. But the pendulum has swung much too far."

Now Lord Griffiths has just published a new report—*What Price Credit?*—which has this somewhat apocalyptic conclusion: "The sheer scale of consumer debt [£1 trillion] has made millions of households extremely vulnerable to shocks to the economy . . . such as oil price rises, acts of terrorism and wars . . . Debt is a time-bomb . . . for the fifteen million people who struggle with repayments."

I tell Lord Griffiths about Richard Cullen's suicide and he sighs.

"I had a friend," he replies. "A clergyman. I met him for dinner one night. He was suffering from cancer. He broke down over dinner and confessed to me that he had thirty-two credit cards. He said he was using each card to pay off the charges on the others. He told me about the shame he felt. You could just sense the emotional pressure. I'm no doctor . . ." Lord Griffiths pauses and says, "He died soon afterward."

Then he says that a friend of his recently compared the credit-card industry to slavery—that the lenders are the new slave masters, and the borrowers are the slaves.

I ask Lord Griffiths if he's bombarded with credit-card junk mail and he says, "Oh yes. I probably get one every fortnight."

I say that the Cullens were sometimes getting three or four a day. "Hm," he says. "I would call one a fortnight bombardment."

AS I WRITE THIS, in mid-April 2006, the homeless charity Centrepoint has published a report revealing that almost a quarter of homeless youngsters surveyed have been sent letters from credit-card companies urging them to apply for loans, with interest rates as high as 29 percent. Somehow, it seems, the list brokers have been able to buy up the names of young people living in hostels and halfway houses.

Since I began writing this article, in January, I have paid Visa about £300 in interest and minimum repayments. I keep thinking I should pay my Visa debts off in full and slice the card up. But I haven't bothered. This is because—like millions of us—I am lazy and stupid.

ON APRIL 26, Wendy and two of her children arrive at Salisbury coroner's court to hear the verdict. The coroner says the cause of death was carbon monoxide poisoning: an 85.7 percent saturation.

"I can tell you, Mrs. Cullen, that is very high," he says. "That concludes the postmortem evidence. I am satisfied that his intention was to take his own life. Can I also say, Mrs. Cullen . . ."

Wendy is hoping he's about to say something critical of the credit-card companies. But instead he says, "Thank you for coming. By gathering here together we do right by your husband. I formally close the inquest."

There is one piece of good news. The credit-card companies have all written off the debts now.

"It makes me sad how easy it was for them to write it off," one of Richard's daughters tells me in the corridor outside.

The Sociopath Mind Guru
and the TV Hypnotist

t is a Friday in April and you'd think some evangelical faith-healing show was occurring in the big brown conference room of the Ibis Hotel in Earls Court, West London. The music is pumping and the six hundred delegates are ecstatic. And it's true that there are lots of damaged people here who've come to be healed. But this is no faith-healing show. The speakers are atheists. And the audience is full of people from British Airways, Virgin Atlantic, British Gas, BT, Bupa, Dixons, the Department for Work and Pensions, Ladbrokes, and Transport for London. These people have come to learn how to be better in the workplace. Now the audience jumps, cheering, to its feet. I look behind me. And I see him passing through the crowd looking like Don Corleone, square-jawed and inscrutable: Richard Bandler.

Of all the gurus who thrived during the Californian New Age gold rush of the 1970s, Bandler nowadays has by far the biggest influence, on millions of people, most of whom know nothing about him or his extraordinary past. These days nobody bothers much with naked hot-tub encounter sessions, or primal screaming, or whatever. But Bandler's invention—NLP, Neuro-Linguistic Programming (he's actually the coinventor with the linguistics professor John Grinder)—is everywhere.

The training manual we delegates have been handed describes NLP as "a methodology based on the presupposition that all behavior has a structure that can be modeled, learned, taught, and changed."

The rest of the manual is a confusing mix of psychobabble and diagrams marked "submodalities" and "kinesthetics," etc. But from what I can gather, NLP is a way of "repatterning" the human brain to turn us into superbeings—confident, nonphobic, thin superbeings who can sell coals to Newcastle and know what people are thinking just by their eye movements. It is the theory that we are computers and can be reprogrammed as easily as computers can. You were abused as a child? That makes you a badly programmed computer who needs a spot of instant reprogramming. Forget therapy: Just turn off the bit of the brain that remembers the abuse. You aren't selling enough houses? NLP can instantly reprogram you to become a great salesperson, or public speaker, or whatever. NLP teaches that, like computers, we are a tapestry of telltale visual and auditory clues to what's going on inside our brains. Our winks, our tics, our seemingly insignificant choice of words—it is all a map of our innermost desires and doubts. It is the secret language of the subconscious. NLP can teach the salesperson how to read that map and act accordingly.

Some people hail the way NLP has seeped into training programs in businesses across the world. Other people say terrible things about NLP. They say it is a cult invented by a crazy man.

. . .

I FIRST HEARD of Richard Bandler, NLP's inventor (he actually coinvented the technique, with John Grinder), in 2002 when
a former U.S. Special Forces soldier told me he'd watched him,
two decades earlier, bring a tiny little girl into Special Forces and
reprogram her to be a world-class sniper in seconds. Intrigued, I
tried to learn more. This is when I heard about the good times,
how Bandler's theories were greeted with high praise in the
1970s and 1980s, how Al Gore and Bill Clinton and practically
every Fortune 500 corporate chief declared themselves fans, and
then there was the descent into the dark side. Reportedly, during
the 1980s, the coked-up Bandler had a habit of telling people he
could dial a number and have them killed just like that. Then
came the murder trial. In 1988 Bandler was tried and acquitted
of murdering a prostitute, Corine Christensen. She'd been found
slumped over a dining table, a bullet in her head. Her blood was
found sprayed on Bandler's shirt. And then there was the renais-
sance in the form of Bandler's unexpected partnership with the
TV hypnotist Paul McKenna, and the fact that they were going
to be teaching a course together this week at the Ibis Hotel.

In the end I will get to meet Richard Bandler and Paul Mc-
Kenna, and extraordinary things will occur when I do, but the
road to those meetings will prove to be a rocky one.

EARLIER TODAY I had coffee with Sue Crowley. She's been
friendly with Paul McKenna for years, since back in the days
when he was touring regional theaters, hypnotizing people into
believing they were kangaroos. Before that he was a DJ—at Top-
shop, then Radio Caroline, and finally Capital FM radio. Back

then the idea that he'd one day hook up with Richard Bandler would have seemed as likely as David Copperfield becoming business partners with L. Ron Hubbard. But, Sue said, "Paul was like a dog with a bone when he first learned of Richard. He studied him at seminars. He modeled Richard like nobody's ever modeled anyone before."

Modeling is a practice at the heart of NLP. This is how McKenna has described Bandler's invention of modeling: "If someone's got a skill that you want to master, you 'model' that skill so that you can learn to do what they do in a fraction of the time it took them. Say someone's a master salesperson. They'll be doing certain things with their body, and certain things with their language. So you 'model' that. Study it, break it down, work out the thinking behind it."

Sue said Paul McKenna was incredibly nervous about approaching Richard Bandler before he finally did, in 1994, to suggest they go into business together. Since then, NLP has—thanks to McKenna's skills—become bigger than ever, a vast empire that's making everyone millions.

"Paul is an unexpected protégé of Richard's," Sue said. "The squeaky-clean DJ and the . . . uh . . ." She paused, not knowing which bits of the Richard Bandler life history to mention, in case I didn't know the full extent of the horror. "The . . . uh . . . Hells Angel, up for God knows what, CIA . . . But Richard Bandler is a Leonardo of our times. He is one of our living greats."

(Much later, by the way, after this story appears in the *Guardian*, I'll chance upon a flier advertising a Richard Bandler seminar. It'll read: "Richard Bandler is a Leonardo of our times. He is one of our living greats—The Guardian.")

Now "Purple Haze" booms through the speakers and Richard

Bandler climbs onto the stage. He hushes the crowd. They sit down. I am momentarily lost in my thoughts and I remain standing.

"ARE—YOU—GOING—TO—SIT—DOWN—NOW?" hisses a voice in my ear. I jump. It is one of Paul McKenna's assistants. I hurriedly sit down.

"I marched up the Amazon," Bandler tells the audience. "I threatened gurus to get them to tell me their secrets. They're pretty cooperative when you hold them over the edge of a cliff."

There is laughter.

"There was one Indian guru," Bandler continues, "I was holding him over the edge of a cliff. I said to him, 'My hand is getting tired. You have seven seconds to tell me your secrets.' Well, he told me them fast and in perfect English!"

I have to say that had I been tried for murder, I would be less forthcoming with the murder gags. Practically every one of Richard Bandler's jokes is murder- or at least violent-crime related. I hope—when I finally get to meet him—to ask him about the murder trial, although I'm nervous at the prospect of this.

Suddenly, we hear a loud noise from somewhere outside.

"A ghost," Bandler says. "I do have ghosts that follow me around. And they're angry ghosts. But I don't care. The truth is, the ghosts are more afraid of me than I am of them."

He is mesmerizing. Two hours pass in a flash. He talks about childhood trauma. He puts on a whiny voice: "When I was five I wanted a pony . . . my parents told me I was ugly . . . 'Shut the fuck up!'"

He gets the audience to chant it: "Shut the fuck up! Shut the fuck up! Shut the fuck up!" If you hear voices in your head, he says, tell the voices to shut the fuck up. "If you suffered childhood abuse, don't go back and relive it in your mind. Once is enough!"

He says psychotherapy is nonsense and a racket: Therapists are rewarded for failure. The longer a problem lasts, the more the therapist is paid. Who cares about the roots of the trauma?

"Don't think about bad things!" Bandler says. "There's a machine inside your brain that gets rid of shit that doesn't need to be there. Use it! I can give myself amnesia. I can just forget." He clicks his fingers. "Just like that."

This seven-day training course is costing delegates £1,500 each. Which means Paul McKenna's company will rake in almost a million pounds for this one week's work. The tea and biscuits may be free but we have to buy our own lunch. For all the hero-worship of McKenna and Bandler, there's still a lot of grumbling about this, especially because whenever we traipse out into the rain to try and find somewhere to eat in this crappy part of town, we're compelled to traipse past Paul McKenna's immaculate chauffeur-driven silver Bentley, number plate 75PM, parked up in the ugly forecourt, waiting to swish Richard Bandler off somewhere unimaginably fancier.

IT IS LUNCHTIME NOW. I walk past the Bentley. A delegate sidles up to me. "You're a very naughty boy!" she says. "Richard will be very cross with you!"

"What?" I practically yell.

"You kept writing when Richard was talking even though you *know* you weren't supposed to!" she says. "And you didn't have a smile on your face. Everyone was laughing, but you were scowling."

I missed yesterday's session, which is perhaps why everyone is so far ahead of me in the frenzied-adoration stakes. In fact, earlier today Richard Bandler said he had no unhappy clients. His exact words were "The reason why all my clients are a success is that I killed all the ones who weren't."

Lots of delegates have told me they signed up because of the TV star Paul McKenna but the great revelation has been the man they hadn't heard of: Richard Bandler.

THREE OF PAUL MCKENNA'S NLP-inspired self-help books (*Change Your Life in 7 Days, Instant Confidence*—which is dedicated to Bandler—and *I Can Make You Thin*) are currently in the WHSmith Top 10. So that's the therapy side. The NLP-can-do-wonders-for-your-business side is thriving too. In fact when I meet Iain Aitken, the managing director of McKenna's company, he says the phobic delegates are becoming the minority now that NLP has become so widespread in the business world. I ask Iain what is it about NLP that attracts the salespeople. Bandler, he replies, teaches that everyone has a dominant way of perceiving the world through seeing, hearing, or feeling. If a customer says, "I see what you mean," that makes them a visual person. The NLP-trained salesperson will spot the clue and establish rapport by mirroring the language.

"I get the picture," the NLP-trained salesperson can reply, rather than "That rings a bell" or "That feels good to me."

AFTER LUNCH, we split into small groups to practice NLP techniques on one another. I pair up with Vish, who runs a property company in the Midlands.

"What did I miss yesterday?" I ask him.

"It was great," he says. "We did anchoring. Let me show you how it works."

Vish moves his chair closer to mine.

"How are you enjoying your time here?" he asks me.

"OK," I say.

Vish pokes my elbow.

"Brilliant!" he says. "Did you have a good lunch?"

"It was all right," I say.

Vish prods my elbow again.

"Fantastic!" he says. "Have you got kids?"

"A son," I say.

"Did you have fun with him last weekend?" he asks.

"Yes, I did," I say.

Vish pokes my elbow.

"Brilliant!" he says. "Now. Did you notice what I was doing?"

"You were poking my elbow every time I expressed positive feeling," I say.

"Exactly!" says Vish, although he looks peeved that I spotted the poking, which is supposed to be so subtle as to exist only on the unconscious level.

"Now," says Vish. "When I want to sell you something, I'll touch your elbow and you'll associate that touch with a good feeling, and you'll want to buy. That's deep psychology." Vish pauses. "What I really like about NLP is how it can hypnotize and manipulate people. But in a good way."

I STAND UP to stretch my legs and I spot Paul McKenna at the front, near the stage. Even though I'm still supposed to be doing the small-group workshop, I decide to introduce myself. I take a few steps toward McKenna. Instantly, one of his assistants swoops down on me. There are about forty assistants in all, scattered around the room.

"Do you need help?" she asks me.

"No," I say.

"Have you *finished* the workshop already?" she asks sarcastically.

"Yes," I say.

"Well, you must have finished quicker than everyone else because everyone else is still doing it," she says.

"I'm a journalist and I'm going to talk to Paul McKenna," I say.

I walk on. Ten steps later, two more assistants appear from nowhere.

"Aren't you joining in?" asks one.

"You're going to miss all the benefits," says the other.

"I'm OK, honestly," I say.

Another assistant appears.

"Didn't you understand your instruction?" he says. "Paul explained *three times* that you're supposed to do the workshop for fifteen minutes."

Finally, exhausted, I reach Paul McKenna. I introduce myself.

"How did you end up in business with Richard Bandler?" I ask him.

"I know!" he says. "It seems incredible from the outside. But he's one of my best friends . . ." Then he excuses himself to do a spot of speed-healing on an overeater.

AN HOUR LATER Paul McKenna's PR rep, Jaime, tells me in the corridor quite sternly that I am not to hang out with Paul or

Richard before, between, or after sessions because they're far too busy and tired. I can meet them next Wednesday, she says, when the course is over. I go home. I don't think I have ever, in all my life, had so many people try to control me in one single day. Advocates and critics alike say attaining a mastery of NLP can be an excellent way of controlling people, so I suppose the training courses attract that sort of person. Ross Jeffries, author of *How to Get the Women You Desire into Bed*, is a great NLP fan, as is Duane Lakin, author of *The Unfair Advantage: Sell with NLP!* (Both books advocate the "That *feels* good to me" style of mirroring/rapport-building invented by Bandler.)

But still, the controlling didn't work on me. Nobody successfully got inside my head and changed—for their benefit—the way I saw NLP. In fact, quite the opposite happened. This makes me wonder if NLP even works.

E-mails and telephone calls fly back and forth. I tell Jaime the PR rep that I don't want to be kept away from Richard Bandler during the sessions. Finally it is agreed I can meet him before he goes onstage on Monday.

THINGS IMPROVE. There's a nice, normal delegate here called Nick who teaches executives how to be good public speakers.

"These group things are always a bit creepy," he says, "but that isn't the point. The point is that NLP isn't bogus."

I tell Nick about Vish noticeably prodding me in the elbow.

"Well, he was just doing it badly," says Nick. "Honestly. NLP is the most sensible thing out there."

I corner Paul McKenna and tell him his assistants are driving me crazy.

"You *have* to make them leave me alone," I say.

He looks mortified and says they're just overexcited and trying too hard. But, he adds, the course would be a lot worse without them energizing the stragglers into practicing NLP techniques on one another.

Onstage, Bandler and McKenna cure a stream of delegates of their phobias and compulsions. There's a woman who's barely left her home for years, convinced the heater will turn itself on when she's out and burn the house down.

"Do they pay you to think like this?" asks Bandler. "It seems like an awful lot of work. Aren't you fucking sick of it?"

The woman says a bossy voice in her head tells her the heater will do this.

Bandler gets her to turn down the knob in her brain that controls the volume of the bossy voice.

Then he gets the bossy voice to tell her, "If you keep worrying about this heater, you're going to miss out on everything good in your life."

This, Bandler explains, is an invention of his called the Swish technique: You take a bad thought, turn it into a radio or TV image, and then swish it away, replacing it with a good thought.

"I don't care about you anymore, heater, because I want to get my life back," the woman says, and the audience cheers.

I still don't quite understand the Swish technique, and so I make a mental note to get Paul McKenna to do it on me when I meet him at his house on Wednesday. I have a whole potpourri of bad thoughts I wouldn't mind swishing away.

YESTERDAY RICHARD BANDLER cured someone who had a fear of doctors. Now he gets him to stand up.

"Are you scared of going to the doctor?" he asks.

"I . . . uh . . . hope not," the man quietly replies.

"BOO!" shouts the audience, only half-good-naturedly.

Suddenly, I feel a poke in my elbow. I spin around. It is Vish. I catch him in the act of giving my elbow a second poke.

"Did that make you feel good?" he asks me.

"It made me feel confused," I say.

When someone appears cured, Bandler and McKenna seem quietly, sincerely thrilled. I'm sure they derive real pleasure from helping damaged people improve their lives. And the room truly is scattered with NLP success stories. There are the shy salespeople who aren't shy anymore, the arachnophobes who swish away their spider phobias and stroke the tarantulas Paul McKenna provides one afternoon.

Onstage each day, McKenna is a mix of entertainer and college lecturer. He tells a joke and then he says, "What was I just doing?"

"REFRAMING!" the audience yells as one. (Reframing is NLP's way of putting a miserable person in a good mood. If someone says, "My wife's always nagging me," the NLP-trained therapist will "reframe" by replying, "She must really care about you to tell you what she thinks.") I sit in the audience and watch all this, and back at home in the evenings I talk to friends who, it transpires, secretly listen to Paul McKenna's CDs and get cured.

There's another speaker here: the life coach Michael Neill, author of *You Can Have What You Want*. One day Michael asks me if I can spot the covert intelligence officers in the audience.

"I'm not joking," he says. "There's always one or two."

"Why?" I ask.

"Most people who want to get inside your brain," says Michael, moving closer to me, "have negative reasons."

Michael tells me about an oil-executive friend who only ever uses NLP for bad, to "mess people up." In busy bars his friend frantically "mismatches." He sits at a crowded table, uses NLP to establish rapport with strangers, and then behaves in the exact opposite way to what he knows would make them feel comfortable. Before long he has the table to himself. Then Michael adds, "Anyone who knows NLP will have an advantage over anyone who doesn't. My dream is for everyone in the world to know NLP. Then there'd be an even playing field."

Paul McKenna, standing nearby, comes over. He scans the room. When the six hundred delegates graduate in a few days, they'll be given Licensed NLP Practitioner certificates. Some will set up their own NLP training schools. He says he cannot guard against what happens next.

"Some people teach NLP in a way that makes it sound highly manipulative and coercive," McKenna says. "You know, 'I will give you power over others.' And the people who end up going to those are people with very small penises, frankly. People who think, 'Oh my God! I'm not enough! I'm so out of control! Maybe if I learned how to have power over others, I'd be a better person!' So you see that criticizing NLP is like criticizing a hammer."

I tell him I've read terrible things about NLP on the Internet—how some scientists call it nonsense—and he says, "I *know* it's not scientific. Some of the techniques will not always work in the same way in a laboratory every time!" He laughs. "But Louis Pasteur was accused of being in league with the Devil. The Wright brothers were called fraudsters. . . ."

MONDAY. I spot Richard Bandler by the stage, surrounded by fans.

"Wow," he says as a woman hands him a rare copy of his book *Trance-formations*. "That goes for, like, six hundred dollars on eBay."

"That's where I got it," the woman replies. He autographs it.

Everything is going fine until someone hands Bandler a blank piece of paper to sign.

"What's this?" he says. "I just don't sign blank paper." He pauses. "I have a thing about it."

Misunderstanding, the woman hands him different blank paper.

"No, no," he says. "I just can't sign blank paper."

Some of the fans laugh as if to say, "How can you hand him blank paper after he's just *told* you he doesn't sign blank paper? Are you *nuts* to expect him to sign blank paper?"

But really it is a strange moment: Richard Bandler has just spent the last few days effortlessly convincing us that phobias are nonsense, and here he is, phobic about signing blank paper.

The moment passes. A woman kisses him and says, "From one child of the sixties to another." Bandler laughs and replies, "They called us the fringe. We're fucking *mainstream* now!" Then I introduce myself, and we go upstairs.

RICHARD BANDLER was born in 1950. He grew up in a rough part of New Jersey. I don't expect him to talk much about his childhood because several profiles say he never does. The one thing known for sure is that he had language problems and he barely spoke until he was a teenager. So I'm surprised when he says, "I was a compulsive kid."

I'm sitting down on a low sofa. He's standing above me.

"When I was a kid I took up archery," he says. "I can remember sitting out by the side of the house, until three a.m., with just a little lightbulb, shooting at a fucking target, over and over, until I got it exactly the way it was supposed to be."

"Where did your compulsiveness come from?" I ask him.

"From being alone most of the time," he says. "I had to be self-motivated. My mother was always out working, and my father was violent and dangerous." He pauses. "Well, my first father was gone by the time I was five, and he was very violent. My mother later married a guy who was a drunk and a prizefighter in the navy. He was very violent. Broke a lot of my bones. But in the end I won."

"How?" I ask, expecting him to say something like "Look at me now. I'm getting driven around in Paul McKenna's Bentley."

But instead he says, "I electrocuted him."

"Really?" I say.

"I didn't kill him," he says, "but I could have."

"How did you electrocute him?" I ask.

"I waited until it was raining," he says. "I got a wire-mesh doormat. I stripped a lamp cord, put it underneath the doormat, put the other end in the keyhole, and put my hand on the switch. When the key went in, I clicked the switch. There was a loud scream. He went over the railing. Six months in the hospital."

"How old were you?" I ask.

"Ten," he says.

The family moved to California, where Bandler became "a juvenile delinquent. Then I discovered it wasn't the Harley that was scaring people. It was the look in the eye."

He says he was diagnosed as a sociopath. "And, yeah, I am a little sociopathic. But it turns out I *am* right. And my illusions were so powerful they became real, and not just to me."

He says NLP came to him in a series of hallucinations while he was "sitting in a little cabin, with raindrops coming through the roof, typing on my manual typewriter."

This was 1975. By then he was a computer programmer, a twenty-five-year-old graduate of the University of California, Santa Cruz.

It's surprising to me that Bandler would cheerfully refer to NLP as a sociopathic hallucination that struck a chord with the business world. I'm not sure he's ever been that blunt about it before. But I suppose, when you think about it, there *is* something sociopathic about seeing people as machines—computers that store desires in one part of the brain and doubts in another.

"See, it's funny," he says. "When you get people to think about their doubts, notice where their eyes move. They look down! So when salespeople slide that contract in, suddenly people feel doubt, because that's where all the doubt stuff is."

"So where should a salesperson put the contract?" I ask.

"They've got to buy themselves a clipboard!" he says. "When you ask people to think about things that are absolutely right for them, they look up! So you put the contract on a clipboard and present it to them up here!"

These were the kinds of ideas Bandler was typing in Santa Cruz at the age of twenty-five. The book would eventually be cowritten with linguistics professor John Grinder and published under the title *The Structure of Magic*.

Throughout the interview, I'm sitting on a low, dark red leather sofa with Bandler standing above me. "If I was standing and you were sitting," I ask, "would I be forming different opinions of you?"

"Yeah," he says. "Of course."

"So are you deliberately positioning yourself in my hopes-and-desires eye line?" I ask.

There's a silence. Bandler smiles to himself.

"No," he says. "My leg hurts. That's why I'm standing up."

The Structure of Magic was a huge hit. "*Time* magazine, *Psychology Today*, all of these people started seeking me out in Santa Cruz," he says. "And I started getting interest from places I really didn't expect, like IBM."

He designed sales-training programs for businesses across America. They made him rich. He bought a home in Hawaii and a mansion in Santa Cruz. He was hailed as a genius. The CIA and military intelligence squirreled him in, which is how I first heard of him. Had he really smuggled a tiny girl into Special Forces and got her to "model" a world-class sniper?

"It wasn't a little girl," he says. "It was a ten-year-old boy. And that's not as great as it sounds. You can teach a ten-year-old boy to pretty much do anything."

But by the early 1980s, things were spiraling downward for him. His first wife filed for divorce, claiming he choked her. According to a 1989 *Mother Jones* profile, he began to warn associates, "All I need to do is dial seven digits and with my connections with the Mafia I could have you all wiped out without even batting an eye."

He struck up a friendship with his cocaine dealer, a fifty-four-year-old man named James Marino. By 1986 he was living in a house built by Marino. A few doors away lived Marino's girlfriend, Corine Christensen.

In early November 1986, James Marino was beaten up, and he got it into his head that Corine had organized the beating so she could take over his cocaine business. Marino was paranoid, and he infected his friend with the paranoia. Bandler phoned Corine up, recording the conversation: "Why is my friend hurt? I'll give you two more questions, and then I'll blow your brains out. . . ."

Eight hours later, Corine Christensen was shot in the head at her home, and twelve hours after that Bandler was arrested for the murder.

I've been worried about bringing this up with him. Bandler may be quite brilliant and charismatic but he also seems overbearing and frightening. And although Paul McKenna himself strikes me as likable, his team of overzealous (literally overzealous) assistants scattered around the hotel are forever eyeing me with suspicion if I appear anything less than completely thrilled. Plus, earlier Jaime the PR rep cornered me in the corridor and said, "A few people have reported to me that you've been asking about banking and finance. You aren't going to be writing about how NLP can be misused, are you?"

Then she looked me in the eye and added, "Some people are concerned."

And that's just because I was asking about banking! What'll happen if I ask about murder—not the pretend murders Bandler jokes about onstage, but a real one?

Still, they aren't in the room now.

"Tell me about the murder trial," I say.

He doesn't pause at all. He tells me what he told the jury— that James Marino did it. There were two men in the house when Corine was murdered—the famous Richard Bandler and the lowlife James Marino. Yes, he was there. He lifted her head, which is how her blood ended up on his shirt. Why do I think the police went after him?

"With me, the DA gets to make a big reputation," he says. "But if it's some thug drug dealer, you're not going to make any mileage."

The trial lasted three months. The jury acquitted Bandler after five hours of deliberation. On the stand, Bandler blamed Marino and Marino blamed Bandler. There was no way for the jury to know which of the two was telling the truth. Furthermore, James Marino was at times an unbelievable witness, frequently changing his story. Sometimes he was upstairs when Bandler shot her, sometimes he was downstairs. Plus, as the *Mother Jones* profile pointed out, who had the greater motive: the man who had been beaten up, or the man who was righteously indignant on behalf of a friend who had been beaten up?

"It took the jury longer to pick a foreman than to decide if I was guilty or innocent," Bandler says. "The guy was a convicted felon! We caught him lying, falsifying evidence. . . ."

It is at this exact moment that Paul McKenna and the entire upper echelons of his company troop cheerfully into the room.

"The other guy was their stool pigeon they used to bust dope dealers!" Bandler is now hollering at me. "I mean, *excuse me*! A lot of very dirty things went on through that trial."

Earlier today Paul McKenna got a compulsive blusher onstage and cured her of her blush. I am like the blush lady now, sitting on the chesterfield sofa, Bandler towering over me, yelling about the murder rap, while Paul McKenna and his managing director look anxiously on.

I change the subject. I say, half joking, that being an NLP genius must be awful: "To know in an instant what everyone's thinking by their winks and tics and barely perceptible sideways glances and eye movements," I say, "you must sometimes feel like one of those superheroes, ground down by their own super-powers."

"Yeah," Bandler replies, suddenly looking really quite upset. "It's called the supermarket."

He pauses.

"You walk into a supermarket and you hear someone say to their kid, 'You're never going to be as smart as other kids.' And I see the kid's eyes, pupils dilating, and I see the trance going on in that moment. . . . It became a burden to know as much as I did. I went through a lot of things to distract myself. I used to just sit and draw all the time. Just draw. Focus on drawing to keep my mind from thinking about this kind of stuff." And then he goes quiet, as if he is falling into himself.

I SUPPOSE PEOPLE shouldn't judge gurus until they need one. Luckily, I do, a bit. And so on Wednesday I use my ninety minutes with Paul McKenna to get him to cure me of my somewhat obsessive, debilitating conviction that something bad has happened to my wife and son when I can't get ahold of them on the phone. I've always suffered from this. If I am in America and I can't reach them on the phone, I become convinced that Elaine has fallen down the stairs and is lying at the bottom with a broken neck, and Joel is reaching up to grab the electrical cord of a newly boiled kettle. I have panicked unnecessarily about this all over the world.

Paul McKenna does Richard Bandler's Swish technique on me. He gets me to picture one of my horrific imaginary scenes. I choose my son stepping out in front of a car.

He spots, from my eye and hand movements, that the mental

image is situated in the top right hand of my vision, big, close to my eyes.

"Part of the neural coding where we get our feelings from, and ultimately our behavior, comes from the position of these pictures," he explains. "Pictures that are close and big and bright and bold have a greater emotional intensity than those that are dull and dim and farther away."

"And Richard Bandler was the first person to identify this?" I ask.

"Yes," he says.

He chats away to me, in his hypnotic baritone voice, about this and that: his own worries in life, etc. Suddenly, when I'm not expecting it, he grabs the space in the air where my vision was and mimes chucking it away.

"Let's shoot it off into the distance," he says. "Shrink the picture down, drain the color out of it, make it black-and-white. Make it transparent. . . ."

And, sure enough, as the image shoots away, far into the distance, the neurotic feelings associated with it fade too. This is Paul McKenna "repatterning" my brain. He says this isn't self-help. I don't have to do anything. This is reprogramming, he says, and I am fixed.

"Oh yeah," he says. "You don't have to do anything now. It's worked."

A year passes. I don't have a single paranoid fantasy about something bad happening to my wife and son. I really am cured.

And so I have to say, for all the weirdness, I become very grateful that Richard Bandler invented NLP and taught it to Paul McKenna.

Death at the Château

The Château de Fretay is a hundred-acre estate in the Brittany countryside, with chapels and cottages and a lake and forests. From a distance, the place looks like a dream. Some teenagers from the village tell me that until a few weeks ago they'd go up to hang out with the children of the English couple who lived there. The mother, Joanne, always had an open fire and English breakfasts on the go. The place was so big and overgrown that one time they found a chapel on the grounds that nobody, not even the English kids, knew existed.

I park my car. There are hundreds of seedlings in little plastic cups in rows on tables, ready to plant but all dead now; abandoned plastic garden furniture is strewn everywhere, as if a tornado had come through; a statue of the Madonna and Child stands in some builder's rubble; and a swimming pool is filled with rotten green water—two unopened bottles of Heineken sit there poolside.

I peer in through the window of the main house. It isn't, actually, a château. There's nothing castle-like about it. It's a big farmhouse. It is dark. The doors and windows are police-taped up, as they have been for the past seven weeks, since September 4, so the place is a time capsule of that weekend. There's a pack of playing cards on the living room table, a beer on the arm of a comfy-looking leather chair, next to a folder filled with complicated-looking business plans. In the kitchen, the dishwasher is still turned on. You get the eerie sensation that Mr. and Mrs. Hall have just gone into another room and will probably return any second and have a fright to see a journalist peering in through their window.

The village mayor, Pierre Sourdain, a farmer, says he liked Robert and Joanne Hall very much. All the villagers say the same: They were impressive, charming, self-possessed. (Saying that, the people in the village speak no English, and Robert Hall— despite living here for ten years—never learned French.) For years the Halls had been trying to get an ambitious golf project off the ground. They wanted to turn the château into an eighteen-hole golf resort with holiday cottages. That's presumably what the file resting on the chair was all about, Mayor Sourdain says.

"It would have happened too," he says. "They would have made it happen. That's the kind of man Robert Hall was. It would have been so good for the region." There's a short silence. Then he says, less confidently, "I'm sure it would have happened."

On the evening of September 4, Sourdain got a call from the gendarmes: Something had happened at the château. It is a French custom for the gendarmes to call the mayor, as the representative of the people, to the scene of a crime or a terrible accident. He arrived to see the oldest son, Christopher, twenty-two, with the gendarmes as they stood in protective suits, breaking up a big block of concrete. Robert Hall was inside the house, crying.

"After twenty-four hours, concrete is like biscuit," Sourdain explains. We're sitting in his office in the village of Le Châtellier, two miles from the château. "So the gendarmes were crumbling it with their hands. And after a while they discovered a ring. They asked Christopher, 'Is this your mother's ring?' He said, '*Oui*.'"

Robert Hall had told the gendarmes that twenty-four hours earlier he'd had a drunken argument with Joanne during which she accidentally fell, hit her head, and died. Then, during the hours that followed, he set her body on fire, put her remains into a builder's bag, poured in concrete, and hauled it onto the back of a lorry. All this happened behind the house, near the back gate, next to a row of half-built holiday cottages.

Then he stopped. He telephoned Christopher. He said he was going to commit suicide. Christopher called the ambulance, who called the gendarmes, who called the mayor.

Catherine Denis, from the prosecutor's office in Rennes, told a press conference later that week that when the gendarmes asked Robert why he burned Joanne's body and encased her remains in concrete, he explained that she'd always said she wanted to be cremated and laid to rest in a mausoleum and he was simply respecting her wishes, albeit in a somewhat informal way.

"What did the Halls do for money?" I ask Mayor Sourdain. "How were they living? How were they funding the golfing project?"

"He told me he was a big success in England," he replies. "He had lots of businesses there. And sometimes British tourists would rent the château for their holidays."

"Do you know if the tourists enjoyed staying there?" I ask.

"I wouldn't know anything about that," he replies. "It would have been between English people. You see?"

FABRICE FOUREL works in a bright office in the nearby village of Saint-Étienne-en-Coglès. Posters advertising successful Brittany tourist endeavors line the walls. I am sitting, he says, exactly where Robert and Joanne Hall sat when they came to him in a flap regarding their golf project, in September 2008.

"They were lost," he says.

Fabrice's job is to be the middleman between prospective tourist businesses and the labyrinthine French bureaucracy.

"What were the problems?" I ask.

Fabrice sighs as if to say, "Where do I begin?" "They wanted to clear some trees. French law says you have to plant three trees for each one you cut down, not necessarily on your property, but in the region." He pauses. "It was a big problem. In fact, the administration was angry with the Halls because they didn't follow the procedure. We had to calm everything."

"How many trees would they have needed to plant?" I ask.

"Around twenty thousand," Fabrice says.

Fabrice says people basically already have all the trees they want. If you go to people and offer them trees, they tend to say no. And that wasn't the only problem. The Halls needed sprinklers, enough electricity for thousands of visitors . . .

"We quickly noticed a gap between the financial needs for such a project and what they had," Fabrice says. "A project like that could cost twenty million euro." Twenty-seven million dollars.

"Was it a big gap?" I ask.

Fabrice indicates with his hands a very big gap.

"But they were really motivated," he says. "That's why we didn't want to say, 'You can't do it.' People have to be a bit crazy to lead these kinds of projects."

I ask Fabrice if he knows whether the Halls' business renting out the château to British tourists was a success.

"We know nothing about that," he says. "We know they welcomed people into their house. But we don't know the details."

IN AUGUST 2006, Laura Walsh was looking to rent a château for her family holiday when she chanced upon chateaudefretay .com. The site is gone now, but you can still find it on the Internet archive, with its photograph of horses grazing by the lake, plus a list of activities such as fishing, swimming, a games room, a go-karting stadium, cycling, and a weekly treasure hunt.

Laura phoned Joanne Hall, who told her, "We're not Center Parcs, but we do our best," which Laura took to mean they were something like Center Parcs.

And so, swept up in the lovely-sounding nature of the thing, she offered to pay the full amount up front—$4,000 for a fortnight's stay.

"The first thing we saw, as we walked into the bedroom, was what looked like mouse droppings on the bed," Laura says. "Robert Hall appeared in the doorway. I said, 'There are mouse droppings on the bed.' He said, 'Oh no, no, they're more likely to be bat droppings.'"

"How was he?" I ask.

"Friendly," Laura says.

She ran herself a bath and left the bathroom for a minute. When she came back, the bath was empty and the bathroom floor was flooded. They decided to persevere, and went looking for the go-karting stadium.

"We found it in a clearing in the forest," Laura says. "It was a mess. A shambles. An overgrown shambles. And in the middle of it was a dead goat."

And so on. There were live wires dangling in the outside toilet, the pool was leaking, there was rubble and broken glass everywhere, and so that evening they confronted the Halls.

"They seemed dazed," she says, "out of their depth. And drunk. They must have known on some level that this wasn't right, but instead of admitting it, there was a restrained crossness about them. Robert kept saying, 'You're just not getting it. You're not getting it. You don't get it.'"

"'Not getting it'?" I ask.

"He meant, 'You're not getting what this is about,'" she says. "'You're not getting how idyllic it is.'"

The saddest thing, Laura says, was that the most clearheaded family member was Christopher, the teenage son. He was the only one trying to make everything OK. Laura negotiated with him, and they agreed to stay a week and get a refund for the second. On day two they decided to try out the games room.

"In the hall right outside it," Laura says, "propped up against the wall, was a shotgun."

"Was it loaded?" I ask.

"There was live ammunition on the shelf next to it," she says.

When they left, Laura let the tourist office in nearby Fougères know what a mess the place was. They told her they'd had countless similar reports and had been trying to shut down the place for years. It was widely known in the area, she says, that Château de Fretay was a disaster.

From August 2006 onwards, anybody Googling the château would have straightaway come across Laura's startling reviews on TripAdvisor and Mumsnet: "BEWARE: CHÂTEAU DE FRETAY!!"

The Halls' neighbors—farmers who didn't want to be named—tell me that very few tourists, if any, came to stay at the château these past few years. The Halls' income seemed to dry up.

THE HALLS HAD BEEN in France for only a year when, in 2000, Robert Hall called on Yves Bourel, a local journalist. Yves knew him by reputation, he says, as there had been some excitement locally about the family's arrival. "English people with money usually go to the south of France," he tells me. "We tend to get the poor English people here, because living here is cheap."

Yves and I are having breakfast at my hotel in Fougères.

"Why did he come to see you?" I ask.

"He had a business proposal he wanted publicized," he says. "He wanted to create a hot-air balloon port from the grounds of the château."

"Oh?" I say.

"We have a lot of wind here," he says. "The balloons would have lifted off and . . . whoosh!" He waves his arm to indicate a hot-air balloon flying uncontrollably away.

We laugh. "Did anyone say anything to them about the wind?" I ask.

"Oh no!" he replies. "We don't see rich English people often. So we put the red carpet out for them!"

Yves asks if I've heard the news: The prosecutor has decided to charge Robert Hall with aggravated murder.

. . .

THERE'S A BEAUTIFUL double-fronted Georgian mill owner's house outside Holmfirth, West Yorkshire, with an oak-paneled dining room, low beams, marble fireplaces. The windows look out across the fields where they filmed *Last of the Summer Wine.*

In front of the big AGA-type stove in the kitchen, the owner, Richard Skelton, tells me a story about what happened shortly after they bought the place from the bank, who had repossessed it from the previous owner, Robert Hall. Late one night—this was in 1999—there was a knock on the door. Richard's wife, Loretta, answered. Two frightening-looking men were standing there.

"Is Robert in?" they asked.

"They didn't look like normal bailiffs," Richard says. "These were serious, hard men."

Loretta knew something like this might happen one day. They had heard stories from the neighbors. On one especially creepy occasion, the next-door neighbor had had a knock on the door in the middle of the night. The two men standing there wouldn't believe him when he said he wasn't Robert Hall. He had to get a utility bill to prove it.

"There was a trail of irresponsible behavior all over town," Richard says. "Not paying loans back . . . And you should have seen the state of this place when we moved in. The pattern over and over is that people would do work for him, he wouldn't pay them, so they'd walk away, leaving everything all rough and unfinished. Wiring, joinery . . ."

Loretta told the men at the door that Robert Hall didn't live there anymore, that he'd moved to France. Luckily, they took her word for it. As they left, one of them turned to her and said, quite cheerfully, "Oh, if you ever want someone beaten up, it's two hundred pounds."

Richard gives me a tour of the house. He shows me the en suite bathroom. "They had a corner bath in here," he says, "which was an utter disaster. It was cracked, leaking. The chap who put in the new toilet says it's amazing any waste got out of the old one."

He pauses. "Everyone says Robert was a very closed person," Richard says. "He was very sociable and charming, but after a conversation with him, you'd walk away realizing you'd learned nothing."

"What was Joanne like?" I ask.

"She was considered to be lovely and charming," he says. "A neighbor said that regular as clockwork she'd go blasting past the houses in a battered Porsche, taking the kids to school at five past nine. Everything was always chaotic."

I stop off at the local ironmonger's store, J W Kaye, to test Richard's story about Robert Hall leaving debts all over town.

"Yes, he owed me money," says Dave Earnshaw, who runs the place. "But it wasn't much, so I didn't think it was worth pursuing. He owed a lot of other people a lot more money than he owed me when he disappeared out of sight."

"To France?" I say.

Dave shrugs: "I suppose."

He reels off a list of failed Robert Hall businesses: a kitchen place in Dewsbury; a fitness center; an abandoned golf-resort project in Derbyshire; a company that imported cars from Europe and (illegally) adapted them from left-hand to right-hand drive; a disastrous Santa's grotto in the farmers' market in Hollowgate.

"He told Kirklees Council he was going to make it Christmassy and lovely, like a fair," Dave says, "but when it opened, it was just a stall selling cheap plastic crap."

When the council shut it down, Robert Hall smashed his way back in with a baseball bat.

MAN SELLING FESTIVE GIFTS
IS CLOSED DOWN

. . . Security guards are patrolling the former Castle garage in Hollowgate and Robert Hall has been given until the end of the month to remove his property. Mr. Hall admitted he broke in and continued to trade for two days after the locks were changed by the council. Councilor George Speight, who chairs the council's markets committee, said, "In our opinion this was a market and not a fair."

—*Huddersfield Examiner,* December 1993

"He always had big plans that were always . . ." Dave pauses. "Crumbling."

A FEW HUNDRED MILES south of the Château de Fretay, in the countryside near Cognac, Maria-Louise Sawyer runs a support group for British people who've moved to rural France to try to live the *Year in Provence*–type dream, only to find the whole thing spiraling out of control.

"It's the same story time and again," she says. And then—with a quite chilling fluidity—she tells me the "story":

"The French like to live in little tiny modern bungalows. When they inherit these big old properties, they don't want them. So they sell them cheap to the British. Back in Britain, the man was working, the lady was home. That was fine. They saw each other for only a couple of hours in the evening and at weekends. But then they move here. These are larger properties with grounds. So they're isolated. They can't speak the language. The man is possibly renovating an old property, but he doesn't know how to do it. Everything is different. You go to a government office, you don't speak French, you're an outsider. So he gets more and more isolated and resentful. He and his wife are together all the time. And they realize they don't like each other. They drive each other bonkers. They drink, because the drink over here is less expensive than water. And then . . . bang."

Maria-Louise pauses. "That's what happened with my husband. He buggered off back to Britain after shredding all my clothes, daubing food over the walls, and leaving a note that said, 'I've gone.'"

THE DAY JOANNE HALL DIED, some neighbors saw her in the garden. It was the last sighting of her. She was pruning the trees and gardening—starting to plant the hundreds of seedlings in the plastic cups on the table that are still there but all dead now. The neighbors say she looked up at them and, with a big smile, waved.

"I've Thought About Doing Myself in Loads of Times . . ."

Maesbrook, Shropshire, is a beautiful, well-to-do village on the Welsh border. The houses are vine-covered Georgian mansions. The cars parked in the driveways are Range Rovers and Porsches. The people of Maesbrook are, by and large, self-made millionaires from Birmingham and Wolverhampton, entrepreneurs who've made it big.

"I'd love to live somewhere like this if I could afford it," I think ruefully as I drive through the village, closely tailed by a police car. The police have been following me ever since they spotted me reading the condolence bouquets on the road outside the grand Osbaston House.

On August 26, the mansion's owner, Christopher Foster, returned from a neighbor's barbecue and meticulously destroyed everything he owned. At some point he made the decision to include his family in that. He shot his wife, Jill, in the back of her head in their bedroom. He did the same to his fifteen-year-old daughter, Kirstie, in her bedroom, interrupting her as she chatted with friends on Bebo. He shot the horses and the dogs, and he jammed a horse trailer against the gate and shot out the tires, presumably to stop potential Good Samaritans from intervening. He flooded the mansion with oil, set everything on fire, and then shot himself. A few hours later, the bailiffs arrived, unaware that the possessions they were supposed to impound that day no longer existed.

"From a neighbouring family—absolutely stunned," read one bouquet. "You were all such a lovely family," read another.

According to his friends, Foster adored his family in a very ordinary way. He was apparently forever seen laughing and joking and cuddling them while watching TV and so on, right up until the night he murdered them.

I read the condolence cards for a few minutes and then a policeman pulls up.

"Can I help you?" he asks.

I show him my press card.

"You look too scruffy to be a journalist," he says.

We both laugh. Then I bid him farewell and drive away. Now the police are following me, past the gated mansion belonging to John Hughes, the millionaire luxury car dealer whose barbecue and clay-pigeon shoot the Fosters attended a few hours before the murders; past their local pub, the Black Horse Inn; and toward my meeting with Foster's friend and blacksmith, Ian.

Had this been a working-class double murder-suicide, I don't think the police would have bothered following me all the way out of town, but Maesbrook is a rarefied, aspirational village, and they seem to want to make absolutely sure I've gone.

Once I'm out of the village limits, the police car turns around and I make the final part of the journey alone. Ian lives in Meifod, Powys. He's a friendly, welcoming, shaven-headed man with five horses and eleven acres. We sit in his kitchen. He makes me a cup of tea and says he keeps remembering a weird incident that occurred a month before the murders.

"Before I explain what it was," Ian says, "let me tell you something about Chris Foster. He was always busy, messing with the horse trailer, cleaning it, fixing this or that, taking out trees. He was always home. I did wonder why he wasn't at work. I knew he was something to do with oil, and everyone called him 'the Millionaire,' but he was always home. He kept his barn spotless."

"That's weird," I say, in a dark chuckle, "to keep a barn spotless."

"I keep mine spotless too," Ian says.

"Oh, well, not weird . . ." I say.

"Let me show you my barn," Ian says. "And then I'll tell you about the weird thing that happened a month before the fire."

On the way to the barn I tell him what I've learned about why Foster was always home. In 1997, he had a eureka moment. He invented, and patented, a new chemical formula.

"It came to him in a flash," said Terence Baines, who'd been his accountant back then. I had phoned Terence shortly before leaving for Shropshire. "Before then, he was just an ordinary bloke from Wolverhampton," Terence said, "a salesman living in Telford, working for some company that went bust. But one day he suddenly thought, 'Hang on. If I get a bit of this and a bit of that, a bit of special rubber and plastic, and put it all together, it'll make a new type of oil-rig insulation.'"

Foster called his invention Ulva Shield. It won an apparently fantastically rare AI fire-test rating. Where other oil-rig insulations burst into flames, Ulva Shield just formed a safe, crisp shell. The big oil companies began placing orders.

"The company went great guns," Terence continued. "Chris started dressing very smartly. He wanted to present himself well. He liked good holidays, a decent car . . ."

Actually, he bought a fleet of decent cars—two Porsches, an Aston Martin, a 4×4 for his wife (with the license plate JILL 40), and a tractor for the mansion, Osbaston House, that he'd bought in Maesbrook. He was doing an extreme version of what an awful lot of people were doing back then: living on credit, believing the boom would never bust. "He never planned on what things would be like when he was sixty-five or seventy," Terence said. "It was always 'What can I do now?'"

Along with the mansion and the cars, there were the affairs. Foster had at least eight mistresses, according to Jill's sister, Anne Giddings. "He had a big thing about blondes," Giddings later told the *Sunday People*. "Jill knew all about his affairs. There were lots of women on the scene. But she played the dutiful wife and kept quiet. He wasn't a good-looking guy, but money did the talking. He was always flashing the cash—it seemed to give him confidence."

But then it all went bust. In 2003 Foster contracted a supplier, DRC Distribution, to manufacture Ulva Shield exclusively. But by 2005 his liabilities were £2.8 million higher than his assets, presumably because he'd spent so much on mansions and Porsches and guns and membership to various fancy clay-pigeon-shooting clubs. In desperation, Foster sourced a California supplier who could manufacture Ulva Shield cheaper. DRC found itself lumbered with a warehouse full of Ulva Shield it couldn't sell because it was patented to Foster. DRC sued and won.

At the Royal Courts of Justice, on February 28, 2008, Lord Justice Rimer said Foster was "bereft of the basic instincts of commercial morality. He was not to be trusted." And so it all came crashing down. DRC took control of the Ulva Shield patent. Foster may have been lacking in commercial morality, but he certainly knew how to invent a good new fireproof chemical formula. Under DRC's less flashy stewardship, Ulva Shield has become a huge deal in the oil-rig world, supplying to Exxon, BP, Shell, and thirty-nine other giants. Foster, meanwhile, suddenly found he had nothing to do but stay home and look after the horses and the fifteen acres.

We reach Ian's barn. It really is spotless. The hay is as smooth as a freshly made bed at a posh hotel. "Our horses are our lives. They're everything to me and the children. I'm going through a divorce at the moment—"

"Anyway," I interrupt, "something weird happened a month before the murders . . . ?"

"Oh yes," Ian says. "I was at Osbaston House when there was an almighty crash. A massive branch, as big as a tree, had come off a willow and crashed onto the path. Chris came running up. He said his tractor had been parked exactly where the branch had landed, but he'd decided for absolutely no reason to reverse it forty yards out of the way a few minutes earlier. It was a lucky escape." Ian falls silent. Then he adds, "Although if it had hit him, it would have been a godsend for the other two."

"Is that the weird incident?" I ask.

"Yes," Ian says.

"It doesn't seem that weird," I say.

"Well, think about it," Ian says.

Ian says it didn't strike him as weird, either, at first, "but after the murders I was just so gutted, I started obsessively watching the news. . . . There was something about going to that place that was so nice. It was the welcome you had, from both of them, but especially Jill. She was bubbly, always had that same smile, always turned out very well, but not flash, just very well-groomed. Kirstie was very quiet but polite. And Chris would always give you a big handshake." Ian pauses. "So I was watching the news, and I saw those pictures of the burned-out tractor, and it hit me. Chris had had absolutely no reason whatsoever to move the tractor that day. He said it himself. He didn't chalk it up to anything. He just moved it. This was a man who invented a product. You have to be pretty active in your brain to invent something. And now he had so little in his life that he needed to fill his days by just moving a tractor up and down a path for no reason."

We head inside. Ian makes me another cup of tea. We sit in silence. Then Ian says, "What Chris did has put thoughts in my own head, I must admit."

"Sorry?" I ask.

"I empathize with Chris," Ian says. "And I feel guilty for empathizing."

"What do you mean?" I ask.

"Don't get me wrong," Ian says. "There's no way I could harm my children. But I'm going through a divorce at the moment. It's looming. I probably seem normal and relaxed to you, but inside I'm finding it very stressful. My chest is real tight. I get this pain down here." Ian points to his left side.

"What's the point of keeping all that stress hidden away?" I ask.

"We're supposed to be manly," Ian replies. "We're not supposed to get upset. We're supposed to be the breadwinners and the providers, especially in our children's eyes. We're supposed to do miracles."

As I sit in Ian's kitchen, it suddenly makes sense to me that Chris Foster would choose to shoot Jill and Kirstie in the back of their heads. It was as if he was too ashamed to look at them. Maybe the murders were a type of honor killing, as if Foster simply couldn't bear the idea of losing their respect and the respect of his friends. I ask Ian if he thinks Foster planned his night of mayhem or if it was a spur-of-the-moment thing. "Oh, he was meticulous that night," Ian says. "That's weeks of planning, isn't it?"

"When do you think he did the planning?" I ask.

"Probably in the middle of the night when he couldn't sleep. That's when people's brains start thinking about that kind of thing, isn't it?"

A FEW WEEKS LATER, I drive to Hodnet, near Maesbrook, to the West Midlands Shooting Ground, where I'm due to meet Graham Evans, an old friend and shooting partner of Foster's. Clay-pigeon shooting was one of Foster's great hobbies. He used to come to Hodnet every Tuesday night. It was, in fact, how he spent his last day on earth: clay-pigeon shooting at his neighbor's barbecue.

On the way, it starts to rain, and so, by the time I arrive, Graham Evans and the other shooters are crammed into the bar, passing the time until they can shoot by telling incredibly offensive jokes.

"What's the difference between a prostitute and crack cocaine?" says Bill (not his real name). "A prostitute can clean her crack and resell it."

Everyone laughs. There are an awful lot of tasteless jokes floating around here today. In fact, the minute I arrived at the club—practically before I was out of the car—someone asked if I knew the one about the black woman in the sauna. Then there was the sign on the gate of the pretty wisteria-covered farm next door to the shooting range: "Every third traveler [meaning 'Gypsy'] is shot. The second has just left." In the old days, I think, jokes such as these were intended to display superiority, but now they seem to do the opposite. Although this is a lovely, rustic, and quite posh shooting club, the men here seem a bit sad and ground down.

"I'm sure there are jokes we can do about Fossie," says a club member called Simon (not his real name). "Let's see. Did you hear the one about the barbecue that ran out of Fosters . . . ?" Everyone looks at Simon.

"Um . . ." he says. He falls silent. "That doesn't really work," he says.

"I can understand why Fossie might want to kill himself," Bill says. "I've thought about doing myself in loads of times. . . ."

Nobody seems at all surprised by this blunt admission, so casually made. Who knows: Maybe Bill is always going on about killing himself. Or maybe lots of the men here have considered the option. There are racks of rifles for sale all over the place—Berettas and Winchesters and so on. Perhaps being in proximity to so much weaponry invariably turns a man's mind to thoughts of suicide.

"I even know the place where I'd do it," Bill continues. "There's a lovely spot up over there on that hill near the satellite dish."

There are a few murmurs along the lines of "That is a nice spot."

"But to shoot your own daughter . . ." Bill says. He trails off.

"Anyway," Graham Evans says. "The rain's stopped. Do you want a go at shooting?"

"OK," I say.

We head outside. Graham hands me a shotgun. I aim, shout "Pull!" and proceed effortlessly to blow to pieces every clay pigeon that has the misfortune to fly past my magnificence. I'm a natural at this, and clay-pigeon shooting turns out to be an incredibly exciting thing to do.

Suddenly, lots of the other shooters start yelling, "Whoa! Whoa! Jon! Steady on!"

"What?" I say, perplexed.

"You're doing this," says Graham. He does an impersonation of a crazed person waving a gun terrifyingly around.

"I am not," I say.

"You are," half a dozen shooters say in unison.

Graham says it's great to see me so invigorated, and adds that if I want even more excitement, I should try shooting pheasants. "Pheasants have minds of their own," he says, "so that's rewarding. The best time to shoot them is at the end of October, a few weeks into the season, because they've already been shot at and survived. So they're wise then, you see?"

And then it starts raining again, so we rush back indoors and pass the time window-shopping the guns for sale. The conversation returns to Foster. Graham says he was a really impressive sight, turning up in his Porsche every Tuesday night. He says everyone knew he was loaded, "but around here people aren't prejudiced against that sort of thing. Fossie was a good guy. A good shot. He called me El Supremo." Graham pauses sadly. "He loved guns," he says. "He had hundreds of thousands of pounds' worth of them. He was a real collector."

On my way home, I drive once more through posh little Maes-brook. All the talk on the radio is of the credit crunch. They're interviewing Oliver Letwin and Harriet Harman. Both admit, quite sheepishly, that they have no savings, only overdrafts.

"I wish it weren't so," Letwin says, "and incidentally I wish people in Britain were all saving more. I know I ought to, but my wife and I are too extravagant and we should cut back."

The police followed me out of the village last time I was here, in part because I seemed too scruffy for these exclusive, nouveau-riche surroundings; but it dawns on me that perhaps—like Letwin—the people of Maesbrook actually have nothing but overdrafts and all these fancy cars and mansions are just an il-lusion. Maybe, with my meager savings, I'm the richest man in town.

LESS THAN A MONTH after the murders at Maesbrook, yet an-other father wiped out his family, this time in Southampton. His name was David Cass. He smothered his two daughters, tele-phoned his estranged partner, Kerrie Hughes, told her that the children had "gone to sleep forever," hung up, and hanged him-self. They were apparently going through a messy breakup. In the U.S., according to the Department of Justice, a parent—usually a man—wipes out his family, and then himself, about once every week.

It's startling to hear Foster's friends talk about how they em-pathize with his actions. I wouldn't have guessed how on the edge people in this Shropshire enclave can be, and how easy it is for the whole thing just to unravel.

PART FOUR

STEPPING OVER THE LINE

"I know it's bitter. Just keep drinking. Put your finger over your nose and chugalug it all down."

—*George Exoo*

Blood Sacrifice

On a Friday afternoon in January 2002, Susan Ellis sneaks past the security staff at Guy's Hospital, London. She's pretending to be a patient, although nobody asks. She catches the lift to the fourth floor, finds the kidney-dialysis waiting room, and whispers to me, "It's perfect."

And, for her purposes, it is. It's easily accessible from the corridor and security is not tight. It's almost empty of patients and staff. Most crucially, there's a table full of magazines. Susan pretends to read them. Nobody notices as she slips business cards inside the pages. She hopes patients will leaf through the magazines and see her card, which reads: "Need a kidney transplant? I can donate a kidney to you for free. Contact me at: kidney_for_free_from_me@yahoo.co.uk. This is a genuine free offer."

Donating kidneys to strangers is illegal in the UK. When I called the Department of Health to ask why, they said, "You mean, strangers selling kidneys?"

"No. Just giving them away."

There was a silence: "Giving them away?"

"Yes."

"You mean, when the donor is dead?"

"No, alive."

"We'll get back to you," they said. They did, with a prepared statement: "ULTRA [the Unrelated Live Transplant Regulatory Authority] insists on confirmation of an emotional relationship between a donor and a recipient."

The DH's view, they explained over the phone, is that anyone who wants to donate a kidney to a stranger must be in it for money. If they're not, they must have psychiatric problems, and so they need to be protected from themselves. No one would go through such a traumatic, invasive operation for sane, altruistic reasons. When I met ULTRA's chairman, Sir Roddy MacSween, he said he was sympathetic to altruistic donors in general, but added that the law's the law, and any infringement would result in three months in prison and a £2,000 fine.

Susan already knows about the illegality of strangers donating to strangers, so her plan is this: Once a recipient contacts her, they will together concoct a story about how they've been best friends for years. They will prove this long-standing friendship with faked photographs. Some of Susan's wedding photos, she says, could easily be doctored—a recipient's head superimposed onto a bridesmaid's body, etc. If this plan fails, Susan will try to donate abroad.

Susan is a Jesus Christian. She has long forsaken her possessions to live in a camper van currently parked next to a jogging track in Catford, South East London. Even though the Jesus Christians have been widely labeled as a sinister cult by the media and anticult groups, there is nothing externally odd about them—no unusual rituals or anything like that. They simply spend their days keeping fit, discussing theological matters, and hanging around shopping precincts, handing out cartoon books that look like *Simpsons* comics but, in fact, depict, among other parables, the persecution of the Jesus Christians by the courts, the media, and the anticult groups.

The lifestyle is the thing. The Jesus Christians alone, they believe, are obedient to the teachings of Jesus, particularly Luke 14:33: "Whosoever he be of you that forsaketh not all that he hath, he cannot be my disciple." They have forsaken everything: families, possessions, jobs, homes, their place in the outside world, and are now in the process of giving up their spare kidneys, too, en masse.

A year ago, their leader, Dave McKay, was flying home to Australia after visiting his followers in the UK, India, and the U.S. The in-flight entertainment was *A Gift of Love: The Daniel Huffman Story*, a TV movie about a boy who donates his kidney to his grandmother. Dave was profoundly moved, and that's when he had the idea. In a round-robin to his followers (there are around two dozen Jesus Christians worldwide; Dave's strict lifestyle criteria tend to keep the numbers down), he e-mailed his own intention to donate a kidney to a stranger. He also wrote, "If anyone else is interested in doing the same, let me know." The majority took him up on the offer.

Dave imagines that when the world learns of his mass kidney-donating plan, we'll regard it in one of two ways—either as a really lovely thing for the Jesus Christians to do, or as the self-destructive act of a religious cult acting under the spell of a notorious leader. I am surprised to learn later that he is not only expecting the latter response, he is hoping for it.

Susan has been researching and strategizing. As well as the

business cards, she's been posting messages in chat rooms where people with failing kidneys support one another emotionally while they queue, often in vain, for a transplant. At an Internet café in Sutton, she checks her account to see if anyone has responded to her latest messages. There are scores of e-mails for her. The first is from the chat-room host: "I do not wish to be associated with anything that could be construed as illicit as this would risk the group being shut down. I will discuss this matter with my son who's a police chief inspector and get back to you."

Susan laughs nervously. "Whoa!" she says.

She clicks on to the next e-mail, which reads: "You are probably using this opportunity to get into the USA. Sorry, but no black-market organs here. Stay in your own country."

"Why is everyone taking this the wrong way?" sighs Susan.

She clicks on to the next e-mail, from Portsmouth: "What are you? Some kind of sick moron? This is no fun. Don't mess around with us. We have a severe illness. Can't imagine anyone would donate a kidney to a stranger without any strings."

And then the next one: "You're sick. How can you give people false hope like that? A lot of these people are on dialysis, waiting for a kidney, and Mrs. Christianity has got two good ones! Whoopee for you! What are you going to do? Eenie, meeny, minie, mo, or a raffle? You're one sick attention-seeker. If you're for real, why be so desperate to send so many ads? You sound sad, lonely and unwanted. The gate you'll be touching when your number is up is bound to be hot."

There is a silence.

"Hasn't he got a point?" I ask.

She looks hurt.

"Not the going to hell," I clarify, "but the . . ."

"The eenie, meeny, minie, mo?" says Susan. "Sure. But that's like *Schindler's List*, right? He had an eenie, meeny, minie, mo situation, too, but what was he supposed to do—nothing? Just because there's a greater need than what you can give doesn't mean you shouldn't give."

And then she clicks on to the next e-mail: "Hi, I just received your e-mail about you giving away one of your kidneys for free. I'm curious why you would want to do such a thing, and for NOTHING? I'm sorry, but I find it hard to believe. I don't want to be rude but I'm 36 years old and I had a kidney transplant— my third—about five years ago, and have been told it's failing and will be needing dialysis shortly. I'm not looking to get your kidney. I'm just interested in hearing your reasons. Sincerely, C."

Susan is thrilled. "I'm jumping up and down. I'm so happy." She says she'll write back to C, who lives in Scotland, and perhaps strike up a friendship with her.

And then Susan returns to her camper van and her eight-year-old son, Danny, who is unaware that his mother wants to donate one of her kidneys to a stranger. Whenever I'm in their van, and we're talking about kidneys, and Danny runs in to ask his mother a question, we have to stop talking abruptly.

At the same time, in the U.S.—where altruistic kidney donors are welcomed at a handful of hospitals—two Jesus Christians in Dallas are ready to donate, in Minneapolis, on February 21. Robin is thirty-six and has been a Jesus Christian for twenty-one years. Casey is twenty-three and joined the group only in 2001. Like Susan, they decided to donate after Dave sent his e-mail. I telephone Casey in early February, three weeks before his scheduled operation. "Have you told your mother?" I ask him.

"No," he says.

"Why not?" I ask.

"If she's opposed to the idea, she's going to be opposed to it whenever I tell her. So I'd rather get the operation out of the way first and then tell her."

I e-mail Dave. I say I think Casey should tell his mother. Dave's response is this: "Although he's nearly 24 years old, and not a child, I can understand that it sounds cowardly, and maybe inconsiderate, not to tell her ahead of time. However, I'm the LEADER of this sinister little cult, and I am not telling relatives because they reacted so strongly when I first mentioned it. It's just a nuisance when people start raving and treating you like you've lost your mind. If it would make YOU feel better, I think he would probably agree to telling her. It's only three weeks now until he donates, so it'll have to be pretty soon. I personally would feel better if she DID know, so it won't be so much of a shock when she finds out afterward, as long as she does not try to make problems with the hospital where the transplant is taking place. See, in our case, she would only need to phone and say he's part of a religious 'cult'—the magic C word—and the operation would probably be off."

A few days later, Casey decides to test the water with a chatty e-mail to his mother. "It was full of mundane things," he tells me. "Small talk. How are her days going? And I just mentioned in the e-mail that I'm thinking of donating a kidney. I haven't heard anything yet."

"How do you think she'll respond?" I ask.

"She may have the impression that I'm being coerced," he says.

"Does she feel that way about the Jesus Christians, anyway?" I ask.

"She does feel conflicted by our unity."

"That you're a live-in group?"

"That we hold ourselves accountable to each other. We make group decisions. It isn't the kind of personal freedom she feels I should have, I guess."

During the pre-op psychological tests, the doctors soon realized that Robin and Casey's altruism was part of a group scheme. "Will your Christian friends think less of you if you don't donate?" they asked.

"No," said Robin.

"What if you have an accident in later life?" asked the doctors. "Maybe you'll need your spare kidney in the future."

"The Bible says we must step out in faith," replied Robin. "We must do the good we can do today and not wait until tomorrow."

They were given questionnaires. They had to tick the statements that they felt most applied to them: "I hear voices most of the time"; "I feel I have a tight band around my head most of the time"; "I've always wanted to be a girl." The doctors told them to answer honestly, because they had ways of telling if they were lying.

"I don't hear voices, but I do get stressed-out," Casey tells me. "But they don't provide little boxes where you can explain these things." Casey is feeling stressed-out, in part because he feels the process is taking too long. "I wish it would all go quicker, because I'm pretty committed," he says.

They passed the tests. The hospital warned that "even a hint of publicity" would result in the operations being abandoned. I send Casey and Robin a video camera, to film the trip to Minneapolis.

That night, I receive an anxious e-mail from Dave in Australia: "Jon, I am taking a big risk by sharing this with you before we have donated. Even the slightest leak could sabotage the entire project."

A flurry of e-mails follows from Dave, more than sixty in all. Sometimes they are chatty. Often they are tense: "You and I both know that the idea of a 'cult' donating kidneys en masse is a 'sensational' story. Susan said that you were talking like you still suspect that members are being coerced into donating, that they are getting paid for donations, and that the money is going to me. She said that she thought you were quite nervous about being seen with her placing the business cards in waiting rooms. You've asked us some hard questions, so I think it's time for us to ask you a few. ARE you thinking of writing something nasty about us?"

Sometimes Dave seems to regret letting me in on the secret and I begin to wonder why he did. Does he have a plan for me that I'm not aware of? Am I a pawn in some grander scheme of his? Yes, I soon discover, I am.

Dave McKay is a fifty-seven-year-old native of Rochester, New York. He was born into a family of Nazarene Christians. He married young, moved to Australia in 1968, and joined the Children of God sect that was famous for "flirty fishing" (dispatching attractive female members into the secular world to have sex with potential recruits). They preached the virtue and practice of pedophilia too. Dave was horrified by their sexual teachings, so he split from the Children of God and formed the Jesus Christians in 1982.

Dave has always admired martyrs who behave provocatively— the Buddhists who set themselves on fire to protest the war in Vietnam, and so on. In fact, he once considered setting himself on fire, in India, when a local orphanage was threatened with closure. More recently, when Abu Sayyaf guerrillas took twenty-five people hostage in the Philippines, Dave offered himself in their place, and tried to set up an international hostage-exchange program in which philanthropic Christians would swap places with hostages at a moment's notice. "I think they were just spiritual tests to ascertain whether I'd be willing to take such extreme steps," he tells me. "We don't want to sound a trumpet about how great we are, especially when we haven't actually done anything—at least, not yet."

Like most people, I first heard of the Jesus Christians on July 14, 2000, when they were splashed over the front page of the *Daily Express*—"Cult Kidnap Boy Aged 16." Susan and her husband, Roland, had apparently spirited away a sixteen-year-old boy called Bobby Kelly from Romford High Street, Essex. Bobby had picked up a Jesus Christians cartoon book outside Marks & Spencer. Within hours, he had forsaken his possessions and moved in with the group. The police were called. The airports and docks were put on the highest alert. The Jesus Christians were suddenly—in the eyes of the authorities and media, tabloids, broadsheets, and television news alike—a sinister, brainwashing, child-kidnapping religious cult, under the spell of their charismatic leader.

There was an emergency High Court action to "rescue" the boy, which led to Bobby's photo being circulated. That's when the Jesus Christians panicked and went on the run, with Bobby in tow. They became fugitives for two weeks. (It was a rather provincial run: They went to Hounslow because it has free parking, to Heston service station for nightly showers, and to a campsite on the Surrey–Hampshire border.) When the Jesus Christians tried to put their side of the story to Radio 4's *Today*, an injunction was taken out forbidding the BBC from broadcasting the interview.

"Isn't that classic!" wrote Dave at the time on his website. "Now that our critics have succeeded in slandering our name all over Britain, they want to gag us. And yet some people still tell us that we should have blind faith in the British system of justice! No, something is very wrong here."

The scandal ended peacefully. Bobby was found safe and well at the campsite and was made a ward of the court. I interviewed him soon after. He spoke highly of the Jesus Christians, and it became clear to me that some of the reporting was biased and verging on the hysterical. This is why Dave decided—a year later—to give me the story on the kidney endeavor.

IT IS MID-FEBRUARY 2002. Dave tells me that he has invented a woman called Anita Foster and has created an e-mail account for her. The fictitious Anita is writing to influential anticult groups in the UK, such as Reachout Trust and Catalyst. She says she's a concerned mother whose son has joined the Jesus Christians, and could they offer advice? Reachout Trust sends Anita their Jesus Christians fact file. Dave sends it on to me. Under "Obsession With Death," it quotes passages from Dave's pamphlets: "Fear of death is what gives the bosses their power! How long do you think you can survive without eating? Maybe a month or two! OK. Would you rather have one month of freedom or a lifetime of slavery? Anything that isn't worth dying for isn't worth living for. . . . If you'd like to be part of this army of martyrs, then please write to us today."

The e-mails between Anita and the anticult groups are getting chattier, Dave tells me. She's a likable, concerned mother. He says Anita will soon take on a pivotal role in this story—she will be the one to leak the kidney scandal to the anticult groups. This is Dave's plan: The fictitious Anita's fictitious son will donate a fictitious kidney; Anita will inform the anticult groups and imply that Dave is coercing his followers to sell their kidneys on the black market, and that the money will go to him. They will tell the tabloids, and the tabloids will go into a weeklong frenzy about the self-mutilating kidney cult. Then—and here's my role in the grand scheme—I'll arrive on the scene with the true story of the Jesus Christians' remarkable philanthropy.

It seems a funny scheme, and one that has the capacity to backfire in myriad ways. What if the anticult groups don't believe "Anita"? What if the tabloids decide that mass kidney-donating is a noble and heroic thing? What if I write unkindly about the group? Why does Dave want to make himself seem more sinister than he actually is?

"Your article will be like the resurrection," says Dave. "But the crucifixion is the key thing. If we have to get crucified for the message to get out, that's fine. And you'll be the resurrection."

Dave begins e-mailing me stern directives: "You DON'T HAVE TO BE THE DEVIL'S ADVOCATE on this one. We can let the tabloids do that for us. We want them to have egg on their faces."

I e-mail back. I tell Dave that I don't feel comfortable with his plan. I feel as if I'm being controlled. Our relationship descends into an irascible silence. I'm sure there's something philanthropic about his intention to donate a kidney. I'm certain that Robin, Casey, Susan, and the others have charitable motives. But when Dave e-mails me the details of his Machiavellian plot for media control—the Anita Foster leak, the ensuing tabloid frenzy, and then me cleaning it all up—I realize he's also seeking revenge for his treatment over the Bobby Kelly incident.

And, it occurs to me, Dave has scheduled the leak for mid-March, after Robin and Casey's operations, but before he, Susan, and the other Jesus Christians will have time to give their kidneys. Will the tabloid frenzy—if it occurs—scupper these plans?

"What if you become known as such a sinister cult that nobody wants your kidneys anymore?" I ask him.

"Yeah, we've considered that," he replies. "I think the biggest concern, as Christians, is that we get the message out. Donating kidneys, for us, is really a minor thing. If we can't do it, we can't."

"It's a big deal for the recipients," I snap.

There is a short silence.

"Yeah," says Dave. "Um. I'm sure we could, uh, still find ways. We could go to another hospital. We could give false names. . . ."

At the Internet café in Sutton, Susan is checking her e-mails again. There are a few from C in Scotland, with whom Susan now corresponds on an almost daily basis. C has told Susan that she doesn't need a kidney immediately and has suggested that if someone comes along with a more urgent need, Susan should give her kidney to them instead.

"I think that's excellent," says Susan. "A really good attitude."

She reads from C's latest: "Hey, never mind, I'm sure I'll survive, and even if I don't, that's no big deal, either. You might think it seems a bit flippant on my part not to value my life, and I'm not getting all morbid on you—smiley face—it's just that I believe if your time is up, it's up, and there's nothing you can do about it. Anyway, I hope you are well and continue to feel the way you do about donation of organs. I find your attitude most interesting and refreshing."

"That's very touching," says Susan. "'If your time is up, it's up.' She seems to have faced that reality and has a good attitude about it. I really like her."

The problem is that Susan has also become friends with another potential recipient: Larry, in Aspen, Colorado. "I would gladly pay for your transportation to the US, all expenses," he e-mailed her. "It is not legal to sell a kidney, but a good-Samaritan donation might be acceptable. Your gift would be a miracle. God bless you."

Susan says she's over the moon, but how to choose?

"They both seem so nice," she says.

So she decides to write a list of questions to both C and Larry—"How long have you been on dialysis?" "What does your doctor think about the chances of you surviving a transplant operation?" And other questions, too: "Do you drink?" "Do you smoke?" She sends off the questions.

It is, of course, the DH's ruling about altruistic kidney donations that has forced her into playing the role of the regulatory authority—or playing the role of an even higher authority than that. But I can't help thinking that, whichever way this story unfolds, some people are going to get hurt.

I begin to think of the story that was handed to me as a poisoned chalice. I am, in part, supportive of the Jesus Christians' scheme. But I feel queasy about the decision Susan has to make, and I feel queasy about Casey. He may be saving a life, but he's only twenty-three, has been a follower for just a year, and still hasn't told his mother. I e-mail Dave to suggest Casey should be given a cooling-off period—perhaps two months away from the group—before the operation.

I'm surprised to receive a friendly response.

"Thanks for being so frank," writes Dave. "How about we give Casey a couple of months away from the group to cool off?"

I e-mail back to ask if he's serious about this. He responds a few days later. Events have moved on, he says. Casey has now told his mother everything, and she has fully endorsed his decision: "Now that Casey's mother is in agreement, there really should be no objection from anyone else. Like, he's almost 24, has lived on his own for several years, has covered his body with tattoos and body-piercings without objections from his parents, and now that he has finally got his life together, he wants to do something really good with it by offering a kidney. If his parents are happy with it, then I don't see any reason why we should tell him to run away and think about it."

At the end of February, the video diary I asked Robin and Casey to film arrives. It is extraordinarily moving and vivid. It begins with them running at a track in Dallas. They run each morning. This is the day before they fly to Minneapolis. The thing that strikes me most is their smiles. Robin, especially, is always smiling.

Now Robin and Casey are having a snowball fight outside the hospital. Now they're in twin beds at a Days Inn next to the hospital. Robin addresses the camera: "I'm two days away from donating a kidney to someone I've never met before. The reason I'm doing this comes from my personal belief in God. I guess there are a few hard questions—you're probably wondering if I've thought about them. What happens if I donate a kidney to someone and it gets rejected? Obviously, I wouldn't feel very happy about that. However, part of the idea of being an altruistic donor is that it's a pure act of love. It's like a donation to the human race."

The camera clicks off.

It clicks back on again. Robin is still smiling. "Most kidney donations come from cadavers," he says. "The recipient has to race in as quickly as possible. They all wear beepers. As soon as they're beeped, they race to the hospital. The working life expectancy of a kidney harvested from a dead person is ten years, whereas a kidney from a live donor lasts at least twenty years. Twenty years is a long time. That's a lease on life."

Now they are at the hospital, having last-minute electrocardiograms and chest X-rays. Casey strips to his waist. "What's this 777 mean?" asks the nurse, pointing to one of Casey's many tattoos.

"It's supposed to be the Lord's number," says Casey. "The opposite of 666." He laughs. "I was too young to think about what I was doing."

The nurse says, "You're a brave man, Casey."

Now, suddenly, it is the night before the operation. Robin and Casey are back at the hotel, preparing their superlaxative. "So when the surgeons get in there and move our guts around, there won't be any accidents," Robin explains. The superlaxative is called GoLYTELY ("Go Lightly").

They need to drink half a gallon, one glass every ten minutes, "until our watery stool is clear and free of solid matter," says Robin. It's pineapple-flavored. They say "Cheers!" and start drinking.

Casey screws up his face. "It's really bad," he says.

"We'll get there, buddy," says Robin. He pats Casey lightly on the knee.

Casey takes another sip. "I feel like I'm defiling myself," he says.

Now it's 5:20 a.m. on February 21, 2002. "We should be leaving," says Robin. "Sounds like Casey's still in the shower. I'm feeling a bit dehydrated from the diarrhea. I guess they could put me on an IV or something. I got a call last night from the doctor. He said I have an unusual structure. He said there's a chance they'll have to go in through the back, which means it's a longer and more difficult recovery. They may have to remove one of the ribs for access."

"How do you feel about that?" asks Christine, Robin's wife, from behind the camera. Christine is also a Jesus Christian.

"OK, I guess," replies Robin.

Casey pops his head around the bathroom door and grins. Now they head off, in the snow and the dawn, toward their operations. Now they are in the pre-op room.

"I'm debating whether to keep my eyes open when they put the knockout drug into me," says Casey.

He's sitting on a chair, his body covered in a tight stocking, like a leotard. "I keep trying to focus on the spiritual side of this," says Casey. "The motivation behind the donation. The benefits of it. Yeah. I'm trying to stay in touch with the One who's making it all possible."

"Do you have any doubts?" asks Christine.

"I'm just, uh, trying to stay open to what God wants," says Casey.

Now, from his bed in the pre-op room, Casey tries to phone

his mother to tell her that he's about to go into surgery. But she's not there. The phone just rings out. Casey hangs up.

Now the hospital porters arrive. There are hugs from Christine. Robin and Casey are wheeled away toward the operating room. The camera clicks off. When it comes back on again, Casey and Robin are just beginning to stir from the anesthetic. Casey is mumbling. Christine is stroking his arm. There are drips, and bandages cover their stomachs. The camera clicks off.

"I'm feeling very dizzy and nauseous," says Casey—his voice is hazy, as if he's still in a dream. It is the next morning. "I just vomited up some gastric juice or something. You wanna come and have a look at my wound? The pain medication is making it really itchy. I keep scratching. You want to see me press my morphine button? Ah!"

"That's my buddy," says Robin. The camera clicks off.

The days progress. Casey tries walking, but he has to sit down again. His colon is twisted from the operation. For a while he lies under the duvet cover. He says he doesn't want to talk to anyone, and he wants Christine to stop filming him. He says he wishes he hadn't done it.

"I keep asking myself, 'Why did I donate?'" he says. "I was trying to do something good and this pain is what I get for it. Maybe God is having me go through this trial to make me feel more sensitive to other people who are uncomfortable and in pain. I have to be careful not to become hateful or bitter. That's what I'm working on now."

The next day, Casey and Robin are wheeled out into the sunshine. "We heard a little bit about the recipients today," says Robin. "My kidney went to a fifty-nine-year-old man who's been a diabetic all his life. So the fact that he's fifty-nine and he hasn't needed a transplant until now is an indication that he's been looking after himself. Apparently, it's going really well for him. The kidney began producing urine straightaway. Tell them about your recipient, Casey."

Casey seems happier today.

"My recipient was a fifty-three-year-old woman who had been on dialysis for five years," he says. "Her time was nearly up. Hopefully, she doesn't have to worry about that anymore." Then he adds, "A lot of people pray to God for a miracle specifically relating to kidney failure, and all it takes is someone to step forward and say, 'I'll do it.' That's the miracle. That willingness to step forward. That's God's miracle. We don't have to sit around waiting for God to do all the work. He's waiting for us to do something."

"We can make a miracle happen," says Robin.

ON MARCH 15, I receive an e-mail from Dave McKay. He's decided to kill off Anita. He realized that attempting to control the tabloids and the anticult groups was bound to backfire.

"I know we're going to cop to it sometime. We just wanted to have control over when we cop to it. I just wanted to show how adept the media is at turning something good into something evil."

Dave says that Casey and Robin are recovering well. Casey's had regrets, but now he's pulling out of it and is glad of his decision again. Susan's relationships with C in Scotland and Larry in Colorado continue to flourish. She hopes to donate to one or the other of them as soon as she can. Dave hopes to donate within a few weeks, at a hospital in Australia.

He says the hospital in Minneapolis gave Robin and Casey's address to their two recipients, but neither has written to thank them.

AFTERWORD

Dave McKay hated the story I wrote. He *hated* it. I'd been filming the group for a Channel 4 documentary and the moment Dave read the article he pulled the plug on the filming.

He said he wanted me to think about what I had done.

I didn't know what he meant. I thought the story was fine. I'd spent about £40,000 of Channel 4's money, and now Dave had pulled the plug on the filming.

For the next three months or so, Dave consumed my life. He kept saying I had to think about what I'd done. I needed to find a way to continue filming, so I began to suggest things I had possibly done wrong. "Mentioning the whole Anita Foster thing?" I e-mailed to ask.

Dave's mysterious, cold antipathy turned into rage. He began e-mailing long, furious explanations of what I had done wrong. Scores of e-mails arrived, containing line-by-line analyses of all that was bad about my story.

How I was always looking for cheap laughs or scandal. How I was more insidious than a tabloid cult-buster. At least you knew where you stood with the tabloids. I buried my attacks in clever, sneaky little phrases like "There is a silence."

The Jesus Christians were saving lives. I was attacking them with nasty sarcasm and underhanded, belittling tactics. Why, Dave asked, did I go on about Casey's brief regrets when he was recovering from the operation? "A woman in labor probably regrets ever getting pregnant," he e-mailed.

These e-mails from Dave arrived almost every day for months. I began to wish he would donate both his kidneys. I'd open my in-box each morning with a knot in my stomach. The e-mails read like admonishments from a teacher, like I should feel grateful that even though Dave was at the end of his tether he was still taking the time and trouble to point out my faults to me. He hated the line about the poisoned chalice, and read it out sarcastically in a video message he sent me: "'I begin to think of the story that has been handed to me as a poisoned chalice. I feel queasy about the decision Susan has to make and I feel queasy about Casey.' So why did you write the story, Jon? It was your poisoned chalice and you drank from it with gusto."

No tabloid frenzy ensued as a result of my story appearing, only an article in a local paper called the *Catford News Shopper.*

"You are only reaping what you have sown," Dave e-mailed, referring to the trouble I was in now that he'd canceled the filming. "Welcome to the real world. Love, Dave."

After a few months of this I began to agree with Dave's criticisms of me.

I agreed especially with his criticism that the line "'It's a big deal for the recipients,' I snap" was intensely annoying, as it was erroneously presenting me as some kind of journalistic knight in shining armor. Eventually Dave and I agreed that if I pledged to publicly apologize in the documentary for what I had written in the *Guardian,* I would be allowed to continue filming.

"An apology is a GREAT idea!" Dave e-mailed to say.

I met up with Roland, one of the London-based leaders of the Jesus Christians and Susan's husband. He drafted an impromptu apology for me to read out in the documentary.

"It would be great," Roland said, "if you could say something like, 'Hello, I'm Jon Ronson. I really must apologize for my article. I said this . . . Blah blah blah . . . It was wrong. And I guess

I've been doing it for many years—reading into things or trying to make them more exciting—and in my zeal I misrepresented a few things. And I apologize.'"

"Many years?" I thought.

I didn't say anything. I had been admonished into submission. Roland said he thought Dave was "extremely patient" with me when it came to pointing out my faults. "I was marveling at the amount of time he took over it," he said.

"It certainly took many e-mails from Dave for me to see the error of my ways," I said.

"It was worth it," Roland said.

A month or so earlier, Roland's wife, Susan, had gone to visit C in Scotland, and I went with her. This was the woman with kidney failure Susan had been corresponding with by e-mail, along with Larry in Aspen.

C turned out to be a young woman called Christine.

"When I first read the e-mail," Christine told me when Susan was out of earshot, "I thought, 'Nutter.' A part of me still thinks there has to be some catch. But as yet I've not sussed it out. And maybe there isn't one. Maybe it's just my untrusting nature. She doesn't seem like a crazy, off-her-head person. She seems like a normal, sane person. So she obviously knows what she's doing. She hasn't been brainwashed, as far as you can make out. It's what she believes. And everyone's entitled to their own beliefs, right? What's the group called?"

"The Jesus Christians," I said.

"I've not heard of them," she said.

"They've never been that successful," I said, "because they aren't the most fun religious cult to be in."

"It doesn't sound like it if you have to give a bit of your body away to join," Christine said, shrugging. We laughed.

Now, Roland told me, Susan had decided to donate her kidney not to Christine but to Larry in Aspen. The decision came to her in a dream. In the dream, she met a sixty-year-old man with gray hair, a little overweight, and he was happy to see her because she was about to give him her kidney. That's exactly what Larry looked like, which is why she took this dream to be a message from God.

A few weeks passed. Then I received an e-mail from Dave in Australia. He wrote that Christine from Scotland was dying. He said he *could* instruct one of his members to give her a kidney, but if he did I would only accuse him of manipulation. So instead, he wrote, he had decided to let Christine die and let her death be on my conscience.

He posted me a video message. It was him, sitting on a sofa, speaking directly into the camera.

"It's one thirty in the morning here in Australia," he said, "and I've just received an urgent telephone call from the UK. It seems that Christine in Scotland has had a turn for the worse and I have to make a decision immediately if we're going to help her at all. At the moment the only person in the community available to help Christine is Reinhart, and he's booked to fly to India tomorrow morning. The problem with Reinhart is that although he's willing to donate, he's not very keen. I could push him into it. I have to make a decision, and there's a life dependent on it."

Dave paused. The bags under his eyes practically reached down to the end of his nose. His beard looked stragglier than ever.

"The decision I make," he said, "is going to have to take into consideration repercussions from the media—people like yourself. As you know, we stopped the filming after your article appeared in the *Guardian*. Among other things, I was upset about the fact that you portrayed me as a manipulator, forcing or coercing Casey into doing something he might later regret. I think that was terribly unfair both to Casey and myself. No way did I push him into doing it. I didn't even approach him. It was his idea and he ran with it. And that's why we decided not to cooperate with you. But after this phone call tonight I've had a rethink. I'm prepared to go ahead with the documentary, but on one condition: You use this video. You see, I'm not going to say anything to Reinhart. I'll let him fly out tomorrow. And I'll let Christine's blood be on your head, Jon, and on the heads of the authorities there in England, those people who felt that because a group of Christians wanted to donate their kidneys to strangers, there was something wrong with us. So go ahead. Make your documentary. But don't forget to tell them about the recipients. That's the big picture, Jon, and that's been overlooked. These recipients are real people. People like Christine."

Dave bowed his head and said: "Thank you."

"You stupid fucking idiot," I thought.

I'd entered Dave's world convinced that the cult-busters were the crazy ones, comparing Dave to *Invasion of the Body Snatchers*, etc. But now *I* thought of him that way. Why? Because I really didn't like him. I began to dislike Dave hugely, in the way that former members of sects hate their former leaders after they rejoin the real world.

Dave had especially hated the implication in my article that he was personally hoping to get out of donating a kidney. And, as it transpired, Dave did indeed donate one, in January 2003, to a man from California.

Susan donated a kidney to Larry from Aspen. I don't know what happened to Christine from Scotland. Three years later, on April 26, 2006, the Department of Health announced plans to legalize altruistic kidney donations—donations from a stranger to a stranger—as long as they were assured no money was changing hands, and no coercion was taking place.

"I Make It Look Like They Died
in Their Sleep"

n January 2002 the Irish television news reports that a woman's
body has been found in a rented house in Donnybrook, Dublin. Her name is Rosemary Toole Gilhooly. The police say
it was suicide. She'd been suffering from depression. The story
would probably have gone unreported were it not for the fact
that she'd been spotted at Dublin Airport a day earlier, picking
up two jolly-seeming Americans at arrivals. The three of them
were then seen drinking Jack Daniel's and Coke at the Atlantic Coast Hotel in Westport, County Mayo. At one point, other
drinkers later testified to the police, Rosemary Toole Gilhooly
stood up to go to the toilet and did a jig at the table. The next day
she was dead and that night the two mysterious Americans, one
dressed as a reverend, left Dublin.

The Irish police release the names of their suspects. They're
seeking the arrest and extradition of the Reverend George Exoo
and his partner, Thomas McGurrin, of Beckley, West Virginia,
for the crime of assisting a suicide, which, under Irish law, carries a maximum prison sentence of fourteen years.

Radio phone-in shows across Ireland are ablaze with callers supporting Rosemary Toole Gilhooly's right to kill herself with a reverend at her side if that was what she wanted. I feel the same way. I contact George Exoo to ask if I can follow him around. He agrees.

And so, at dawn on a Monday in 2003, he and I set off in his old Mercedes on a five-hour drive to Baltimore to visit a new prospective client, Pam Acre, who has told him she's been suffering from chronic fatigue syndrome since the 1970s and is considering killing herself. George is paying for the petrol himself even though he's broke. He says he asks for donations from his clients but often doesn't get them, but he doesn't care because this is his calling.

"I've never done anything as important as this in my ministry," he tells me during the drive. "I think it's the reason I'm placed on this planet. I'm a midwife to the dying—for those who want to hasten their deaths."

George is cheerful, giggly, a gay, liberal, libertarian Unitarian preacher. He says he often carries around a large inflatable alligator to his suicides in case the police stop him en route. Should this happen he'll pretend he's a children's entertainer. The alligator will explain the canister of helium in the trunk. Helium is one of his methods.

But lately he's begun phasing the alligator out.

"It's been making me feel conspicuous," he says. "I want to not be noticed. If I'm carrying a big alligator, people are going to notice me."

"Plus," I say, "surely the last thing your clients would want to see in the minutes before their death is a large inflatable alligator coming through the door."

"Exactly," says George. "Anyway, I'm always careful and I always work quietly, like the Lone Ranger. I do so generally at night and for the most part I make it look like they just died in their sleep. I'll prop a book up on their lap so it looks like they just expired."

There's something Laurel and Hardy–ish about George. Earlier he had demonstrated the helium method for me by attaching a hose to the end of a tank, but he did something wrong and the gas tank practically exploded, shooting the hose across the room and whiplashing his stomach. He shrieked.

"Does this kind of thing happen when you're helping people kill themselves?" I asked.

"This has never happened before," George replied, looking sheepish.

Pam lives in a decrepit old country cottage on the outskirts of Baltimore. She looks as crumbling as her house. She's fifty-nine but looks far older. We sit on her sofa.

"Tell me about your illness," George asks her.

"This is a difficult disease to cope with," Pam replies, "because they run all the tests and they come back negative. Then they decide that . . ."

"It's all in your head," says George.

"Right," says Pam.

They smile at each other.

"They start wanting you to go to psychiatrists," says Pam. "But of course that's totally useless."

"Sure," says George softly. "Sure."

George says nothing to Pam that might make her reconsider suicide. Instead they talk about the "mechanics of the dying" (what pills and gas and apparatus Pam will need) and she seems delighted to have someone there who isn't questioning her symptoms or intentions at all. Then she turns to me.

"I've learned what I can from this," she says. "I don't judge much of anybody for anything. Because until you walk in somebody else's shoes, you do not know."

George says he drifted into assisting suicides in the early nineties when he was a Unitarian minister in Pittsburgh. Unitarianism is a middle-class, liberal religion and Pittsburgh is a tough, working-class town, so he had barely any parishioners. He'd look at his tiny congregation and wonder if he was wasting his life.

One day a parishioner approached him and said, "My husband has got ALS [amyotrophic lateral sclerosis, a form of motor neuron disease] and your name has been given to me as someone who might help."

"It was that vague," George says. "But I knew what she meant. Two weeks later he said to his wife, 'It's time. Call George Exoo.'"

That's how George found his calling. He says he's assisted 102 people, including Pam, who killed herself, with George at her side, a few months after our visit.

It didn't go smoothly. "We [George and his partner, Thomas] began chanting the Heart Sutra," George tells me later, "which we did for half an hour. Then she got up and said she wanted to have a bagel. So she proceeded to get up and toast a bagel. And put cream cheese on it. And sat there munching very slowly on the bagel. And proceeded to tell us that this woman who lives in the same house as her was expected to return about eleven-thirty p.m. Well, by then it was eleven-fifteen p.m. Sheesh! And she's still munching on the bagel. I said, 'I can't stay here! I will not leave until I'm finished here but I simply can't stay here and run the risk of all this audience coming in.'"

"It sounds like she'd changed her mind," I said.

"No, she was very much decided," said George. "Very much decided. I was thinking, there was one other time this happened. I was in Pittsburgh. And the woman didn't follow my instructions. She was sitting around eating stuff in some kind of crazy way, too, I remember. At one point somebody came into the house and I had to hide in the basement. It was horrible. I was scared to death. So I didn't want to repeat that circumstance. So that's what happened." So George left without helping her to die. "She had enough pills to sleep soundly but not enough pills to zap her," he said.

And then he returned to her house a few nights later, and was more successful.

In early 2004, the Irish police formally instigate extradition proceedings against George. They ask the FBI to arrest him. George telephones me. Can I come to Seattle? He has something he wants to tell me, he says. Something very important.

I meet him in the lobby of a Seattle airport hotel.

"So?" I say. "What's the news?"

There's a strange, almost coy smile on his face.

"I've ordered a magic potion because I certainly don't intend to travel to Dublin," he replies. "So I may be the first right-to-die martyr. Maybe I should call you over to Beckley for the big event."

"I don't want to sit there watching you die," I say.

He looks disappointed.

"Sorry but no way," I say. "That's the last thing I want to see."

George is in Seattle for a private meeting of international

right-to-die activists. The biggest names in the movement are here, such as Derek Humphry, a former British *Sunday Times* journalist who wrote a best-selling memoir, *Jean's Way*, about helping his terminally ill wife commit suicide in 1975. *Jean's Way* pretty much began the movement: A network of right-to-die groups inspired by it sprang up across the world in the late 1970s. These activists meet once a year in an anonymous hotel somewhere to discuss advances in suicide technologies.

"It's very hush-hush," George says. "I'm surprised they're letting you in."

The delegates sit around a table in a conference room. George begins by announcing, with a somewhat dramatic flourish, his intention to kill himself rather than face extradition. When he finishes he falls silent and awaits the outpouring of shock and sympathy, or whatever. But there's none. The other right-to-die activists look unimpressed and unemotional. In fact, they seem much more interested in discovering which method he's intending to go for. George says liquid Nembutal.

"My curiosity is why would you go with a drug approach?" one delegate asks. The others lean forward, paying attention.

George's reply is that when one uses helium, the person killing themselves often tries to involuntarily remove the bag once they're unconscious, and he consequently has to forcibly hold their hands down.

"I don't want to involve anyone else in my passing," he says.

He changes the subject. He says Rosemary Toole Gilhooly in Dublin had promised to send him a message from beyond the grave. The message would somehow take the form of roses. And she fulfilled the promise the day after she died.

"What happened was Thomas and I flew out the next morning to Amsterdam," he says, "and a man brushed by us on the street. He had roses flung over his shoulder. I've never seen anybody with so many roses. There must have been ten dozen roses! And Thomas said, 'There she is! There she is!'"

There's a silence. Then Dr. Pieter Admiraal, a pioneering Dutch advocate of euthanasia, coughs. "Oh, dear George," he says. "To meet somebody with roses in the Netherlands is not so extreme, because we are growing them to export to the world." There's muted laughter from the others. "And now you are in trouble," Dr. Admiraal continues. "Maybe God can help you."

"Maybe so," snaps George.

That evening I get to talking with Dr. Admiraal about George's idealism.

"He's too good for this world," Admiraal says. Then he adds, "I've been observing him for a long time, and I've asked our psychiatrists to observe him. He is, in my opinion, enjoying the death of another person. And that's dangerous. I have the strong impression that he wants to be there and see something dying. Well, he cannot help that. It's his character. It's a kind of phobia to enjoy death. And that's why he says, 'I will commit suicide.' Because he will want to die at that moment."

(Later, Admiraal clarifies this. He says he doesn't mean George derives psychopathic pleasure from being around death. Instead he thinks George is too in love with the afterlife. He believes in it too much and the pleasure he gets is from clapping and cheering his clients to a better place.)

I'm beginning to feel the same way about George. I've noticed that very few of his clients are terminally ill. Most are depressed or suffering from psychosomatic diseases. When I ask him about his client list, he says, "Many of my colleagues will avoid such persons like the plague, but I feel a very strong identity with the story of the Good Samaritan. I stop while others walk by and ignore their pleas."

How, I wonder, do George and his clients find each other?

After the conference I visit Derek Humphry, author of *Jean's Way* and the father of the modern right-to-die movement. He's from Wiltshire but now lives in Oregon, where we sit in his cabin in the forest.

"Once or twice a week," he tells me, "I get very strange people on the telephone who are anxious to commit suicide because of their depression or sad lives. When they get your number they want to talk and talk. And they call again and again. And they also call all the other right-to-die groups, who say, 'We can't help you. It's not within our parameters because you aren't terminally ill.' But they pursue you. They call and call. And eventually someone will say, 'George Exoo will probably help you.' And that gets them off the phone and on to George."

"Isn't that terrible?" I ask.

"Oh, yes," he says.

So George is like the backstreet abortionist of the assisted suicide world, getting under-the-counter referrals from the more respectable mainstream.

Three years pass. Even though the Irish government has been pressing the FBI to arrest George, they don't. Meanwhile he's traveling around America, helping nonterminally ill people die.

In the spring of 2007 a package arrives at my house. Inside is a videocassette. The postmark on the envelope is Beckley, West Virginia. I close my office door. I put it into the VCR and I press Play.

.   .   .

IT IS AN EMPTY ROOM. It's a mess. It's overflowing with detritus—paperweights, books, novelty ornaments, papers, coffee cups. Then George appears in the shot from behind the camera. He looks like he's been awake for days.

He says to the camera, to me, "Now. What I'm going to do is call my friend Shirley, who is out in a western state in a motel."

He picks up the phone and dials. He says, "Hey, Shirley. This is George. The hour has come that we've been planning." He hasn't bugged the phone, so I can only hear his end of the conversation. "I know you're nervous," George says. "You've never done this before. But that's all right. We're going to get through this. It's time for you to"—he sighs—"drink the potion that's in front of you. It's bitter and horrible-tasting, so it's important that you chugalug it right down. I ask you to raise that glass and I want you to know how honored I am to be with you at this moment."

There's a silence of perhaps ten seconds. Then George's voice hardens impatiently: "I know it's bitter. Just keep drinking. Put your finger over your nose and chugalug it all down."

He's talking to Shirley like someone would talk to a child who had disobeyed them. Then he chants a Buddhist chant: *"Gate, Gate, Paragate, Parasamgate..."*

(Gone. Gone. Gone completely beyond.)

Then: "Shirley? Can you hear me?"

He looks into the camera. "I think I heard the phone drop. Which would mean she is probably now gone."

He shrugs slightly. "And that's it. That's the way it's done."

He turns off the camera.

In May 2007 George begins teaching a friend, Cassandra

Mae, the ropes. He says he needs an assistant in case he's arrested or kills himself. I arrange to meet him at Cassandra's
house in North Carolina. I arrive before George. Cassandra lives
alone. Her house is filled with plastic lizards. She's in her forties.
While we wait, I ask her how they met.

"I was bitten by a brown recluse spider in 1993," she says. "It
was so painful I wanted to die."

She says she called the official right-to-die groups, "but they
wouldn't help me."

"Because you weren't terminally ill?"

"Yeah, they rejected me. But then somebody said, 'You might
want to call George.' Kind of like under the counter."

Cassandra says she would have killed herself with George's
help—he was perfectly willing—but she couldn't find anyone
to look after her pet snake. Eventually, they got to talking. If she
wasn't going to be his client, perhaps she should be his assistant.

GEORGE ARRIVES. He has a second job now, buying up houses
that have been seized by the banks, and then selling them on for
a quick profit, although he hasn't managed to sell any yet.

"You could provide the full service," I say. "You could sell
them a house, and when the banks foreclose, you could help
them kill themselves."

We laugh. I say to him, "In the Arizona tape, Shirley said, 'It's
bitter,' and you snapped, 'Drink it!'"

"Absolutely," he replies. "Because I'd been through that argument with her before."

"She'd tasted it before?" I ask.

"Yeah," he says. He's getting annoyed with me. "I'd been with her twice before in person. What kind of bull twaddle is that? If you're serious, you're going to drink it and not whine about it!"

"But this is somebody who doesn't know whether to kill themselves," I say.

"Just drink it," he says, exasperated. "Three or four swallows and you're going to go to sleep. Permanently. In ten minutes you'll be off this planet. Yes, I was probably pressing her to some extent. But I was pressing her to make up her mind one way or another because I can't go flying across the country week after week and have nothing come of it. I want her to either go on and live her life, or check out. But it's her choice. It's not mine."

We go for lunch. Cassandra has told me that her multiple chemical sensitivities (triggered by the 1993 spider bite) were so severe, there is only one local restaurant she can eat in where the atmosphere does not set off her symptoms. But we eat in another restaurant—an all-you-can-eat buffet—and she is fine. She eats all she can. I begin to see Cassandra as living proof that George really shouldn't help people like Cassandra kill themselves.

After lunch I tell him some people think he's on a slippery slope.

"What slippery slope?" he asks sharply.

"Not being able to stop helping people because you see it as your calling and you like to be there at the moment of death because you get something out of it. And you may consequently be encouraging them toward suicide."

"Bullshit," he says. "It just hasn't happened. Otherwise these people wouldn't be hanging on for years and years and years."

And that part seems to be true: He's always said he has clients who have been vacillating for years.

George drives off to do some real estate business and I'm left alone with Cassandra. We sit on her porch. "I see this as a business," she says. "George sees it as a calling. There's a big difference there. For me it's 'No cash, no help.'"

"What's your price?" I ask.

"Seven thousand dollars," she says.

"You're bound to get it wrong, aren't you?" I say. "And help someone who shouldn't be helped?"

Cassandra shrugs. "Probably, at some point, yes," she says.

She says George's worst crime is his financial imprudence: that he'll help people who can't afford to pay.

"George will get to a point where he'll run out of money," she says. "He won't scale down the expensive cuts of meats. He would rather kill himself than economize."

"He seems quite keen on killing himself," I say.

"I think he'll do it soon," says Cassandra. "And that's why I've been pressing him to give me a list of his current clients."

A few weeks pass. Then I get an early-morning call from Cassandra. She says the FBI has just arrested George. His partner, Thomas, woke up to find George and two men standing there. They said, 'We're putting George in prison until we can take him to Ireland.'" George didn't have the opportunity to run into the kitchen and drink his poison.

A few weeks after that (I later learn) Cassandra flew to New Zealand to help a depressed, nonterminally ill woman she had met on the Internet commit suicide. The woman had previously asked a mainstream right-to-die group called Dignity NZ to help her, but they refused. "I was of the impression that she needed assistance in living rather than advice on how to end her life," Dignity NZ's founder, Lesley Martin, later e-mails me. "I imagine you are developing a good understanding of what an absolute mess the euthanasia underground is. Unfortunately, there are 'gung-ho' individuals involved who, in my opinion, treat the matter of assisting someone to die as an exciting relief from the boredom of their own lives and do so completely ill-equipped and dismissive of the responsibility we have of ensuring that people who need mental-health assistance receive it, while still working toward humane legislation that addresses the real issues."

I visit Cassandra and ask her what was wrong with the New Zealand woman. "She had some sort of breathing disorder," she says, "and the doctors there wouldn't give her the medication that she needed. I happened to take the same medication. I gave her a little bit of mine and she was fine."

"But you helped her commit suicide, even though you helped her breathe better?" I say.

"Yeah," says Cassandra. "Isn't that ironic?"

"You shouldn't do it," I say.

"Somebody's got to pay the bills so you can have some water in that glass you're drinking," she says.

On October 25, 2007, a federal judge in Charleston, West Virginia, decrees that because assisted suicide is not a crime in twenty-five of the fifty states, he can't allow the Irish prosecutor to try George in Dublin. The extradition has failed. George is free.

I visit George one last time. I thought there wouldn't be any more twists and turns in this story. But there's a final one. "You know I provided you with a tape?" he says. He means the Shirley/Arizona telephone tape. "That was not a real deathing. I was talking to a dial tone."

"You're a very good actor," I say.

"I wanted to give you an example of how I would work with somebody," he says, shrugging. "And she was the only possibility."

He explains that Shirley was a real person, and he really had visited her on many occasions, and that she really had vacillated. All that was true.

"And guess what?" he adds. "She's killed herself now. While I was in jail." He pauses and says, sounding quite triumphant: "She really is dead now."

Is She for Real?

DAY 1: AT SEA

It is Tuesday evening and I am on a luxury Mediterranean cruise ship called the *Westerdam*. I'm in the audience in the Vista lounge. A grouchy woman is sitting on a beige and golden throne on the stage. She's complaining about builders and dispensing dietary advice. Her name is Sylvia Browne and for years I've wanted to interview her. She's America's most divisive psychic. She's become famous for telling the parents of missing children what happened to their kids. Distraught parents go to her during her weekly appearance on *The Montel Williams Show* on CBS television. Montel is like Oprah. Sylvia tells them, "Your child is dead," or "Your child was sold into slavery in Japan."

She really did once say that, in 1999. A six-year-old, Opal Jo Jennings, had a month earlier been snatched from her grandparents' front yard in Texas while playing with her cousin. A man pulled up, grabbed her, threw her into his truck, hit her when she screamed, and drove off. Her grandmother went on Montel's show and said, "This is too much for my family and me to handle. We want her back. I need to know where Opal is. I can't stand this. . . . I need your help, Sylvia. Where is Opal? Where is she?"

Sylvia said, "She's not dead. But what bothers me—now I've never heard of this before—but for some reason she was taken and put into some kind of a slavery thing and taken into Japan. The place is Kukouro."

"Kukouro?" Montel Williams asked, after a moment's stunned silence.

"So she was taken and put on some kind of a boat or a plane and taken into white slavery," Sylvia said.

Opal's grandmother looked drained and confused. Opal's body was eventually found buried in Fort Worth, Texas. She had, the pathologist concluded, been murdered the night she went missing. A local man, Richard Lee Franks, was convicted.

Montel Williams was once asked in a radio interview why he has Sylvia Browne on his show. He said, "She's great! She's a funny character! She's hysterical!" Thanks to Montel her books, such as *Adventures of a Psychic*, are frequently on the best-seller lists. She is the queen of psychics, but there are many others working in her field. "It happens every time a child goes missing," Marc Klaas told me in a telephone conversation shortly before the cruise began. "I call them the second wave of predators. First you lose your child and then these people descend. Every time." It happened to Marc. In October 1993 his twelve-year-old daughter, Polly, had two friends round for a sleepover at their California home. At 10:30 p.m. she opened her bedroom door to find a man standing there with a knife. He tied up the girls, told them to count to a thousand, and took Polly away. For the next two months, before Polly's body was eventually found (she'd been raped and strangled), Marc was inundated with offers from psychics. "I was insulated from most of them by family and police," he said, "but there had to be at least a dozen I personally dealt with. They hope you'll pay them and they hope they'll get really, really lucky and make a guess so close to the truth, they can say they solved it."

Marc did consult a psychic. He says she got it wrong but nonetheless later took credit (on a tabloid TV show) for psychically locating Polly's body. "You become increasingly desperate and afraid," he said. "Every day the police don't find your child, you think they're not doing their job. So you go elsewhere, and psychics put themselves out there as a very viable solution."

This is why, Marc said, he's not surprised by reports that Madeleine McCann's parents are considering consulting a psychic called Gordon Smith. Friends of the family have already contacted Smith, a host on Living TV's *Most Haunted*. According to a *Daily Mail* article on October 2, the McCanns have received a thousand psychic tip-offs since May.

Sylvia Browne doesn't solicit. Such is her fame, distraught parents go to her. Most famously, Shawn Hornbeck's parents went to her. On October 6, 2002, eleven-year-old Shawn disappeared while riding his bike to a friend's house in Missouri. Four months of frantic searching later, his parents went on *Montel*.

"Is he still with us?" asked Pam, Shawn's mother.

"No," said Sylvia.

Pam broke down. Sylvia said Shawn was buried beneath two jagged boulders.

Four years later, in January of this year, Shawn was found alive and well and living with his alleged abductor, Michael Devlin, in Kirkwood, Missouri. This miraculous happy ending became headline news across the U.S. Shawn's parents told journalists that one of their lowest points was when Sylvia Browne told them their boy was dead. "Hearing that," his father, Craig Akers, told CNN, "was one of the hardest things we ever had to hear."

Sylvia Browne doesn't give interviews, especially not since the Shawn Hornbeck incident. She's turned down CNN's Anderson Cooper, Larry King, ABC, and so on. A few months ago I logged on to her website and watched some of her videos. She looks and sounds like a worldly dame you'd meet in a bar in a Dashiell Hammett novel. Then I noticed an announcement on her news page: Sylvia was to be a guest lecturer on a cruise around the Mediterranean in late September. Fans could sign up for four lectures and a cocktail party.

"She can't avoid talking to me if we're trapped on a ship together," I thought. And so, impulsively, I booked myself on to the cruise.

IT'S OUR FIRST EVENING aboard and there she is. She's sitting on the throne on the stage, unexpectedly giving a rambling, grumpy lecture. "I don't like tofu," she growls. "I'd sooner eat a sponge." And: "Try to get a workman! I've always wanted to put a little solarium on the back of my house. You know. Glass. They put it on backward. People don't care anymore."

The audience listens politely. For all the times Sylvia gets things psychically wrong (which she does a lot: I sometimes think if she tells you your kid is dead, you should probably presume the child's alive, and vice versa), she still has an enormous following. Hundreds of people have paid thousands of dollars each to be cruising with her this week. This is in part because if you want to pay $750 to have a thirty-minute telephone reading with her, there's a waiting list of four years. Her critics believe her career can't possibly survive the Shawn Hornbeck debacle, but there's no sign of it diminishing on this cruise.

I don't know anything about my fellow travelers. They mainly look like retired Americans. But then Sylvia draws names out of a hat. If we hear our name called, we are allowed to ask her a single question. Only one.

"Julie Harrison . . . Joan Smith . . . Pamela Smith . . ." says Sylvia. And, one by one, they walk to the microphone in front of the stage.

"Why did my husband decide to take his own life?" asks the first woman.

"What?" Sylvia says. The woman is crying so hard, Sylvia can't understand her.

"Why did my husband decide to take his own life?" the woman repeats.

"He was bipolar," Sylvia says.

The next woman walks to the microphone.

"I have a strained relationship with my daughter," she begins. "And I want to know—"

"Your daughter is strange," interrupts Sylvia.

Sylvia doesn't pause. Other psychics will often reach around for some inner voice, but Sylvia answers each question instantly, in a low, smoky growl, sometimes before the person has even finished asking it.

"Your daughter is stubborn," she says. "She's selfish, narcissistic. Leave her alone." The woman reluctantly nods. Tears roll down her cheeks.

"Don't get too involved with her," Sylvia says. "She'll hurt you. Leave her alone. I don't like her."

"Thank you, Sylvia," the woman says.

"Am I ever going to have a better relationship with my father?" another woman asks.

"No," Sylvia replies. "He's narcissistic. He has sociopathic tendencies. Forget it. There's a darkness there."

"Thank you, Sylvia," she says.

Sylvia seems to be psychically diagnosing a lot of people with narcissism today.

"Will you tell me exactly the time and place my father died?" the next woman asks.

"Ten years ago in Iowa," Sylvia says.

"Iowa?" says the woman, surprised.

"I'm the psychic," Sylvia snaps. "I'm telling you. Iowa."

"Thank you, Sylvia," the woman says, cowed.

The next woman asks, "What happened to my dog? Is she still alive?"

"No, honey," Sylvia says.

The woman bursts into tears. There are no parents of missing children on this cruise, but every other human tragedy is well represented.

"My son . . ." the next woman says. She stops, choking on her words. "My son met a violent death," she says.

"I'm sorry, honey," Sylvia says.

"Is he around me?" she asks.

"Yes, he does come around you," Sylvia says. "In fact, he rings the phone. He also drops coins around you. When the phone rings and no one's there, that's him. People have said to me, 'That's telemarketers.' Have you ever heard of a telemarketer that didn't talk? No." (Actually, telemarketing companies use an auto-dialing machine called the Amcat. When your phone rings and there's nobody there, it's because the Amcat has inadvertently dialed your number on behalf of a cold caller who is still pitching to someone else. I feel bad mentioning it here, but it's the truth.)

"He's around you," Sylvia says. "He has beautiful eyes, an oval face. Why is he holding his head?"

"He was shot in the head," the woman says.

"That's why he's holding his head," Sylvia says.

Sylvia says this to the mother but also to us, as if to say, "See, everyone! That's my psychic gift!" It is an impressive moment.

It's dinnertime in the Vista restaurant. I sit with others from the group. Sylvia is nowhere to be seen.

"Those stories were really sad," I say.

"That's nothing," says a woman in her seventies whom I'll call Evelyn. "Three years ago I saw Sylvia give a talk in Tampa. A girl in her thirties stood up, really young. She said, 'I haven't been feeling well. What do you think is wrong with me?' And Sylvia replied, 'Do you want the truth, honey? You'll be dead in two years.'"

Everyone around the table gasps.

"The girl had to be helped from the room in tears," Evelyn says.

"I wonder if I should try to track the girl down," I think out loud.

Evelyn looks at me as if I'm an idiot. "She'll probably be dead," she says.

DAY 2: DUBROVNIK

Sylvia is having the day off and so her co-psychic, Colette Baron-Reid, entertains us in the Vista lounge. She's not grouchy and monosyllabic like Sylvia. She's bouncy and eager to please. She makes us do a "get to know the group" exercise. We have to turn to our neighbor and tell them a lie about ourselves. My neighbor is Evelyn. I really like her: She's a funny and kind old lady from New York who does amateur dramatics. She's looking forward to directing a big musical next year.

I say, "My lie is that I don't have any children."

Evelyn replies, "My lie is that I don't have really bad stomach cramps and I'm not scheduled for a colonoscopy when I get home from this cruise." Evelyn looks scared. "If Sylvia calls my name out tomorrow," she says, "I'm going to ask her about the stomach cramps. They're really bad. They shouldn't be this painful."

Later, in the Jacuzzi near the dolphin sculpture on the lido deck, I bump into the woman whose husband committed suicide.

"Did Sylvia help you last night?" I ask.

She smiles sadly and shakes her head. "No," she says. "He wasn't bipolar. He had excruciating physical pain in his legs." She falls silent. "Sylvia didn't help," she says.

She'd been too polite to say anything at the time. I think Sylvia survives in part because her audiences are often too polite to say anything.

I feel the need to escape the group. I sneak off to the ship's casino and pump money into a slot machine. From the corner of my eye I see a flash of red and gold approach in a wheelchair. It is Sylvia. Her golden hair cascades down her red dress. She starts pushing money into the machine next to me. I momentarily overhear her conversation.

"Do you think they liked it?" she asks one of the four large and quite frightening-looking men who are always around her. They look like the Sopranos.

"What?" he replies.

"The thing," Sylvia says.

"You mean the lecture?" he says. He sounds surprised, as if this isn't a conversation they have very often.

"Yeah," Sylvia says. She sounds quite sweet and anxious. "Do you think they enjoyed it?"

"They loved it," he says.

"Good," Sylvia says. She catches my eye and smiles warmly. In this moment, she seems likable, though a suspicious part of me wonders whether she knew I was overhearing and said something sweet for my benefit.

There's a website called stopsylvia.com. A computer programmer called Robert Lancaster created it as a hobby. He does it because, he writes, "I found her work with missing children to be incredibly offensive." The site assiduously details many of the notable occasions she's got it wrong. In the FAQ section, Lancaster asks:

Q: Do you think Sylvia believes she is psychic?

A: No, I do not.

Famous skeptics such as James Randi say Sylvia is not a silly, deluded person who believes herself to be psychic. They say she's a callous fraud. She's just a good cold reader.

Cold reading is the stage art of convincing a stranger you know more about them than you actually do. Good cold readers are brilliant observers. They make high-probability guesses about their subject based on their clothes, race, age, etc. They quickly pick up on signals as to whether or not their guesses are in the right direction, and alter their spiel accordingly. Of course, cold reading is easiest to spot when the psychic does it badly. This morning, Colette, Sylvia's co-psychic, seemed to be cold reading badly. She said to a man in the audience, "Why do I see a hospital around you?"

"I'm a doctor," he replied.

"That's why I see a hospital!" Colette exclaimed to the crowd.

"I'm a chiropractor," he added. "I work out of an office. I stay away from hospitals."

"I meant medical . . . uh . . . lab," Colette said. "You know the expression, to 'lab' something? To research something? That's what I meant. Are you researching anything at the moment?"

"Yes," he said.

And so on. My guess is that Colette genuinely believes herself to be psychic and doesn't realize she's actually dabbling in the dodgy art of cold reading. I think she thinks she's tapping into her psychic impulses when she picks up on her audience's inadvertent clues.

But then, perplexingly, Colette had a moment of seeming psychic brilliance. Apropos of nothing, she told a woman called Jean that her recently deceased husband loved to ride around on his all-terrain bike and enjoyed eating tuna sandwiches. Jean practically shrieked that the bike and tuna were indeed her dead husband's two very favorite things. Colette looked thrilled and you should have seen the smile on Jean's face. It lifted everyone's spirits.

Now I watch Sylvia playing the slots. She is a truly enigmatic person. She was born in Kansas City, Missouri, in 1936, to a salesman father, and has been a professional psychic for fifty-three years. In 1959, when she was twenty-two, she married a man named Gary Dufresne. They divorced in 1972. A few months ago he gave an interview to Robert Lancaster of stopsylvia.com. He said he couldn't remain silent any more after hearing about the

Shawn Hornbeck incident: "I try to get her out of my mind as much as possible, but the damage she does to unsuspecting people in crisis situations is just atrocious."

He said that one evening back in the early seventies, Sylvia held a tarot party at their home in San Francisco: "I said to her as we were washing dishes and she was wiping, I said, 'Sylvia, how can you tell people this kind of stuff? You know it's not true, and some of these people actually are probably going to believe it.' And she said, 'Screw 'em. Anybody who believes this stuff oughtta be taken.'"

In return, Sylvia has called her former husband "a liar and dark soul entity, but at least the asshole gave me children."

In 1992, she was indicted on several charges of investment fraud and grand theft. She pleaded no contest to "sale of security without permit"—a felony—and was given two hundred hours of community service.

Famous anti-psychics, such as Richard Dawkins, are often criticized for using a sledgehammer to crack a nut. Dawkins's last television documentary, *The Enemies of Reason*, was roundly condemned for making silly, harmless psychics seem too villainous. But Sylvia isn't harmless. In 2002, for instance, the parents of missing Holly Krewson turned their lives upside down in response to one of Sylvia's visions. Holly vanished in April 1995. Seven years later her mother, Gwen, went on *Montel*, where Sylvia told her Holly was alive and well and working as a stripper in a lap-dancing club on Hollywood and Vine. Gwen immediately flew to Los Angeles and frantically scoured the strip clubs, interviewing dancers and club owners and customers, and handing out flyers, and all the while Holly was lying dead and unidentified in San Diego.

DAY 3: CORFU

I'm sitting next to Evelyn, the woman with the stomach cramps. "My heart's racing to see if she calls out my name," she whispers. Evelyn has come onto this cruise specifically to ask Sylvia about her stomach pain.

"Evelyn," Sylvia calls.

She walks to the microphone.

"Uh," she stammers.

"Speak up, honey," Sylvia says.

"Um," Evelyn says.

Sylvia looks impatient.

"I—uh—think I've got a poltergeist in my house because things keep moving in my dishwasher," Evelyn says quickly. "Can you tell me the poltergeist's name?"

"The poltergeist is an older relative called Doug," Sylvia says.

"Thank you, Sylvia," Evelyn says.

She sits back down. I look at her. She shrugs.

IT'S THE EVENING of the cocktail party. We all put on formal wear and bustle around the Queen's lounge, excited about our opportunity to mingle with Sylvia. But she doesn't show up. We wait for an hour, then disperse, confused and disappointed. I bump into Evelyn on the way out. She's looking maudlin.

"What's wrong?" I ask.

"This whole Doug business has really knocked me for a loop," she replies. "Who's Doug? I don't have any older relative called Doug. I don't know anyone remotely like that." She pauses. "I used to idolize Sylvia but now I'm kind of off her. And those one- and two-word answers she gives . . ." Evelyn screws up her face. "She's so cold. And why didn't she turn up at the cocktail party?"

I spot Nancy, Sylvia's nice-looking assistant. I decide to tell her I'm a journalist and I'm on this cruise because I want to interview Sylvia.

"Sylvia doesn't like to give interviews," Nancy replies. "She says, 'Journalists can go to hell. I'm famous enough. All they do is turn on me.'" Still, Nancy says, she'll give it a go.

In the Explorations coffee bar I find Cassie (not her real name), a very likable young German woman and a huge Sylvia fan. I sat next to her on the transfer bus from the Rome airport.

"The most bizarre thing just happened," she says.

She says she and two others from the group were just in the shopping arcade when they spotted Sylvia.

"Look! There's Sylvia!" Cassie said.

"When I said it, Sylvia looked up with a start," Cassie says. "Her face immediately contorted into a kind of horrified grimace that she'd been spotted by some fans. Honestly! She looked like a vampire looks when a shaft of light hits them. She hissed 'Go!' to the man pushing her wheelchair. And—whoosh—she was gone. He spun her around and pushed her away really fast. It was nasty. Something is not sitting right with me anymore. She's not a friendly person. Did she think I was going to jump on her?"

Cassie's story resigns me to the obvious: There isn't a chance in hell Sylvia will grant me an interview.

DAY 4: SOME OTHER GREEK ISLAND

Sylvia's assistant, Nancy, rushes up to me in the lido restaurant. Sylvia has agreed to an interview. Five p.m., the Neptune lounge.

It's time for our next two-hour lecture with Sylvia. She seems in a far better mood today.

"I want to know if my son will come back safely," one woman asks.

"Yes, honey," Sylvia replies.

"I'm having cardiology work done soon," asks the next person. "Am I going to get better?"

"Yes, you are." Sylvia smiles.

"Will my daughter live past twenty-five?" asks the third.

"At least into her fifties," Sylvia says.

And so on. All this is in stark contrast to the other grouchy evening when it seemed that nobody's sick relative was going to make it past 2009. I can't help wondering whether, if Shawn Hornbeck's parents had gone to Sylvia today, she would have told them that their son was alive and well.

At 5:00 p.m., I knock on the door of the Neptune lounge. It is swanky and invitation-only—reserved for guests staying on the rarefied seventh floor. Sylvia is there to greet me, along with one of the four men who seem always to surround her. I tell her what Cassie said about her being rude in the shopping arcade. It's a relatively trivial allegation, but I'm curious to see how she'll respond.

She denies it. "You can approach me anywhere, anytime," she says. "I've never, ever been rude to anyone, anywhere. No one could ever accuse me—when I'm eating dinner and they come to me, or if I'm in the casino—I have never, ever been hateful. Never! That's one thing I've been so much against. These people put you there! To be rude to them is just terrible."

The thing is, just before the interview, I bumped into Cassie's two companions from the shopping arcade. They both told me Sylvia had been startlingly rude to them and now they're really off her.

I've wanted to interview Sylvia for years, but I suddenly wonder if it is pointless. I think she's a consummate pro who will just say anything.

"There are times," I say, "when you've got it wrong in a very bad way with missing—"

"The kid," interrupts Sylvia. She means Shawn Hornbeck. "Yeah, I believed the kid was dead." She shrugs. "What I found out later—Larry King wanted me to come on and explain but I said I'm not going to explain anything—is there were three children missing. I think what I did was I got my wires crossed. There was a blond and two boys who are dead. I think I picked up the wrong kid."

"Shawn Hornbeck," I say. "Were the other kids missing from the same area?"

"Absolutely," Sylvia says.

"At the same time?" I ask.

"Yes," Sylvia says. "I have a tiny newspaper cutting about them back in my office."

(I later realize that, of course, "three children missing" in the "same area" is annoyingly too vague to be checkable.)

"Then there was Opal Jo Jennings," I say.

Sylvia looks blankly at me.

"Back in 1999," I say.

Sylvia still looks blank.

"You said she was sold into white slavery in Japan but actually she was dead," I prompt.

"I don't remember that case at all," Sylvia says.

"Little girl," I say. "She'd been killed but you said she'd been sold into white slavery in Japan."

"No," Sylvia says. She shakes her head. "Don't remember that. Not at all. All I remember was that kid Van."

"Shawn," I say.

"Van Hornwell?" Sylvia says.

"Shawn Hornbeck," I say.

"Yeah. Hornbeck," Sylvia says. "I don't remember the Japanese girl at all." She pauses. "Look," she says, "no psychic—and this is what they don't understand—can ever be one hundred percent. That's God."

By "they" she's referring to her two biggest critics, James Randi and Robert Lancaster. She says she doesn't care what they say about her: "The whole thing about my job"—she pauses and corrects herself—"God-given career, is if you're right, you're right. If you're wrong, you're wrong. And the people that are gonna love you will love you and the people that won't, won't."

Then, just as I think how self-assured she must be not to let their attacks eat her up, she says, "I've had a private investigator on Randi and Lancaster, and I have enough on them to hang 'em." She reels off a few defamatory allegations, then adds, "But I'm not going to play that game. That's vengeance, see? Who cares? Randi is an evil little man. When I told him he was going to have a heart attack, and then he did—ha!—he wouldn't give me any kudos."

In the end it is a short interview, just half an hour. What was I thinking? That she would admit to being a fraud? I will give her this, though: I believe that she is genuinely passionate and knowledgeable about spiritual things. The only times during the interview when she becomes really animated are when she talks about Mother Goddess this and that. So I don't believe that part is fake. But there is no doubt that she makes a fortune saying very serious, cruel, showstopping things to people in distress, especially, it seems, when she's in a grumpy mood.

"I don't think people should go to a psychic to hear a fairy story," she says. "It might be nice for a time, but what about the validity in the future?"

"But when you're dealing with missing kids and you're wrong," I say, "it's very, very bad."

"Right." She shrugs.

"What do you say to people who say you're a fraud?" I ask.

"My years," she replies. "My years of validation save me." She pauses. "If after fifty-three years I was a fraud, don't you think they would have found out?"

DAY 5: DISEMBARKATION

I jump ship in Athens, two days early. I miss Sylvia's final lecture. The next day I receive an e-mail from Cassie, the German fan who went off her after she was rude in the shopping arcade. "Please call me!" she writes. "Sylvia talked so harsh about you! I wrote everything down she said!"

I phone her.

"You have no idea what that woman said about you yesterday!" Cassie says. "She got up onstage and said to the audience, 'Are you guys enjoying the trip?' And everyone yelled, 'Yeah! Whooh!' And then she said, 'Because I heard that some of you aren't enjoying the trip.' And she launched into this huge attack on you! She said, 'I had an interview with this pale little man and he said I was rude to some of you in the shopping arcade. You must have seen him around. He's a creepy little worm. . . .' She said you were a worm and a creep and a dark soul entity. She just went on and on about you. It lasted for about twenty minutes!"

"How did the audience respond?" I ask.

"People didn't know where the hell this was coming from," Cassie says. "A few of them said to me afterward, 'I didn't pay four thousand euros to listen to someone go on like that.'"

All this proves one thing to me. Now I know for sure that Sylvia isn't psychic, because I don't have a dark soul at all. I have a very light soul.

The Fall of a Pop Impresario

September 10, 2001. The Old Bailey trial of the pop mogul and former pop star Jonathan King, in which he is accused of a series of child-sex offenses dating back to the sixties, seventies, and eighties, begins this morning. Back in July, Judge Paget decided, for the purposes of case management, to have three trials instead of one. So the jury will hear only the charges that relate to the years between 1982 and 1987. There are six within this time frame—one buggery, one attempted buggery, and four indecent assaults on boys aged fourteen and fifteen.

I have been having an e-mail correspondence with Jonathan King for the past nine months, and last night he e-mailed me to say, "I think you know, young Ronson, that whichever way it goes for me you could have an award-winning story here, if you're brave. You can change the face of Great Britain if you do it well. Good luck! JK."

I have just returned from New York, and in the canteen on the third floor of the Old Bailey—in the minutes before the trial is due to begin—Jonathan King comes over to make small talk about my trip.

"Did you bring me any presents back?" he asks. "Any small boys? Just kidding! Don't you think it is amazing that I have retained my sense of humor?"

He smiles across the canteen at his arresting officers. They smile faintly back. Jonathan has always told me about his good relationship with the police, how kind they were to him during his arrest, and he looks a little crestfallen at their evident withdrawal of affection.

"The police are far less friendly than they were," he says. "Quite boot-faced, in fact. And there doesn't even seem to be a senior officer around. I'm getting quite insulted that I'm so unimportant that only constables are allowed anywhere near the case."

He looks at me for a response. What should I say? Yes, his crimes are so significant and he is so famous that it would seem appropriate for a more senior officer to be in attendance? In the end, I just shrug.

There are half a dozen journalists here today covering the case. In the lobby outside the court, Jonathan approaches some to shake their hands. "Who's the gorgeous blonde with a TV cameraman?" he whispers to me. "Sorry if this ruins my image."

"I felt terrible about shaking his hand," one reporter says a little later. "I felt disgusting. I was standing there thinking, 'What's he done with that hand?' I should have refused to shake it."

"I just asked my solicitor if it's unusual for the accused to make a point of shaking the hands of the press and the prosecution barrister," Jonathan says as we walk into court. "He said it was absolutely unheard-of!" Jonathan laughs, and adds, "You know, I fully intend to change the legal system just like I changed the pop industry."

And at that, we take our seats. The jury is selected, and the trial begins.

ON NOVEMBER 24, 2000, Jonathan King was charged with three child-sex offenses dating back thirty-two years. In the light of the publicity surrounding his arrest, a dozen other boys (now men) came forward to tell police that King had abused them, too, during the seventies and eighties. Some said he picked them up at the Walton Hop, a disco in Walton-on-Thames run by his friend Deniz Corday. Others said he cruised them in his Rolls-Royce in London. He'd pull over and ask why they were out so late and did they know who he was. He was Jonathan King! Did they want a lift?

He told the boys he was conducting market research into the tastes of young people. Did they like his music? His TV shows? Were they fans of *Entertainment USA*, his BBC2 series? He asked them to complete a questionnaire—written by him—to list their hobbies in order of preference. Cars? Music? Family and friends? Sex? "Oh, really?" Jonathan would say to them. "You've only put sex at number two?"

And so they would get talking about sex. He sometimes took them to his Bayswater mews house, with its mirrored toilet and casually scattered photos of naked women on the coffee table. Sometimes he took them to car parks, or to the forests near the Walton Hop. He showed them photographs of naked Colombian air hostesses and Samantha Fox. He could, he said, arrange for them to have sex with the women in the photos.

Sometimes, within the bundle of photographs of naked

women he would hand the boys, there would be a picture of himself naked. "Oh!" he'd say, blushing a little. "Sorry. You weren't supposed to see that one of me!" (When the police raided King's house, they say they found ten overnight bags, each stuffed with his seduction kit—his questionnaires and photos of Sam Fox and photos of himself naked—all packed and ready for when the urge took him to get into his Rolls-Royce and start driving around.)

He told the boys that it was fine if they wanted to masturbate. And then things would progress from there. Some of the boys reported that his whole body would start to shake as he sat next to them in the Rolls-Royce.

And then he "went for it," in the words of one victim. None of the boys say he forced himself onto them. They all say they just sat there, awed by his celebrity. The boys all say that Jonathan King has emotionally scarred them for life, although almost all of them returned, on many occasions, and became the victims of more assaults.

Later, Jonathan King will spend his last weekend of freedom— the weekend before the guilty verdicts—recording for me a video diary of his feelings about the charges. At one point, midway through this twenty-minute tape, he hollers into the camera about this perplexing aspect of the case. "They kept coming back to me again and again and again, although this vile behavior was supposed to be taking place!" He laughs as if he's delivering a funny monologue on some TV entertainment show. "Why on earth would anybody do that? I'd be out of that house as fast as I possibly could! I'd make damned sure I was never alone with that person again. Mad!"

When the police asked Jonathan why all these boys—who

have never met or even spoken to each other—had almost identical stories to tell, he replied that he didn't know. I am determined to ask at least one victim why he continually went back for more.

The defense argues that the police actively encouraged claims of emotional scarring when they interviewed the victims, because, without it, what else was there? Just some sex, long ago. The danger, says the defense team, is that if Jonathan is found guilty, the judge will sentence him not only for the acts themselves but also for the quantity of emotional scarring the victims claim to have. And how can that be quantified, especially in this age of the self, when the whole world seems to be forever looking to their childhoods for clues as to why they turned out so badly?

"Jonathan King," says David Jeremy, the prosecution barrister, in his opening remarks to the jury, "was exploiting the young by his celebrity."

When I first heard about King's arrest, I looked back at his press interviews for clues, and found a quote he gave *Music Week* magazine in 1997: "I am a 15-year-old trapped inside a 52-year-old body."

I talked to some of his friends from the pop industry, and one of them said, "Poor Jonathan. We were all doing that sort of thing back then."

I attended an early hearing at Staines magistrates' court. Jonathan King arrived in a chauffeured car. The windows were blacked out. Two builders watched him from a distance. As he walked past them and into the court, one of them yelled, "Fucking nonce!"

He kept walking. Inside, he noticed me on the press benches. We had appeared together on Talk Radio a few years ago and he recognized me. On his way out, he gave me a lavish bow, as if I had just witnessed a theatrical event, starring him. Outside, the builders were still there. They shouted, "Fucking nonce!" again.

My e-mail correspondence with Jonathan began soon after this hearing. In one e-mail, he asked me if I would consider it fair if, say, Mick Jagger was arrested today for having sex with a fifteen-year-old girl in 1970. I agreed that it wouldn't be. He told me that he was being charged with the same crime that destroyed Oscar Wilde—the buggering of teenage boys—and we perceive Wilde to have been unjustly treated by a puritanical society from long ago. I wonder if the reason why we look less kindly upon Jonathan King is because he sang "Leap Up and Down (Wave Your Knickers in the Air)," while Oscar Wilde wrote De Profundis.

In another e-mail, he wrote about Neil and Christine Hamilton, falsely accused of rape while being filmed by Louis Theroux, whom Jonathan sees as my great competitor in the humorous journalism market. He wrote, "Louis EVERYWHERE . . . but who on earth would want to cover the Hamiltons, famous for doing NOTHING. Still, I do hope The Real Jon Ronson will have the balls, courage and integrity to take up the crusade (whatever the outcome) that it is GROSSLY unfair for the accused person/people to be smeared all over the media. Over to you, Ronson (we don't just want a Theroux treatment, do we?)."

Later, in court, some of the victims say that Jonathan had a trick of making them feel special, as if they could do anything, as if they could make it big in show business, just so long as they stuck with him (and didn't tell anyone what had happened). Has King got legitimate grievances against the legal system, or is he simply trying to seduce me in the same way he seduced the boys?

His Jagger analogy was alluding to some covert homophobia at the heart of the case. But perhaps the real contrast lies somewhere else. Mick Jagger (or, indeed, Bill Wyman) wouldn't have needed to pretend he was conducting market research into the tastes of young people. He wouldn't have needed to have promised them sex with Colombian air hostesses. But Jonathan did not, intrinsically, have much pulling power, so he did need those extra little touches. Perhaps the real contrast, then, is one of aesthetics.

The Walton Hop closed down in 1990. There were complaints of noise from the neighbors. But the Hop's home, the Playhouse, still stands. Jimmy Pursey, the lead singer of Sham 69, was one of the Hop's most regular teenage attendees. He went dancing there every Tuesday, Friday, and Saturday night throughout the seventies. One day, shortly before the trial began, Jimmy gave me a guided tour of the Playhouse.

"It's so hard to explain to people who see in black-and-white the color that existed in this club," he said. "The Playhouse was a theater for fringe plays and amateur dramatics. But on Tuesdays, Fridays, and Saturdays it would become paradise."

Jimmy took me through the hall and toward the stage.

"It was inspirational," said Jimmy. "This wasn't table tennis. This was dancing. This was testing out your own sexuality. Normal people would become very unnormal. It was 'Welcome to the Pleasuredome.' It was everything."

He leaped up onto the stage and took me to the wings, stage right. We stood behind the curtains.

"This is where the inner sanctum was," said Jimmy. "From here, Deniz Corday would have the best view of the teenagers who were a little bit bolder, a little bit more interesting."

"Bolder and interesting in what way?" I asked.

"People like me," said Jimmy. "If Deniz liked you, you'd be invited backstage and get a little bit of whisky added to your Coca-Cola. Backstage, you see. And you'd go, 'Oh, I'm in with the big crowd now.' That's all there was to it with Deniz."

"And Jonathan?" I asked.

"He'd drive into the Hop car park, and come backstage from the side," he said. "And we'd all be going, 'God! There's a Rolls-Royce outside with a TV aerial coming from it! Ooh, it's got a TV in the back and it's a white Rolls-Royce!' Because you'd never know if it was the Beatles."

"But it wasn't the Beatles," I said.

"No," said Jimmy. "It was Jonathan King." He laughed. "A very big difference there!"

The Beatles lived on St. George's Hill, in nearby Weybridge, and were often seen driving around Walton in their Rolls-Royces.

A DISPROPORTIONATE NUMBER of celebrities who are now convicted pedophiles hung around backstage at the Walton Hop during the seventies and eighties. There was Jonathan King's friend Tam Paton, the manager of the Bay City Rollers, who was convicted of child-sex offenses in the early eighties. (It was Paton who first introduced Jonathan King to the Hop—they met when Jonathan was invited to produce the Rollers' debut single, "Keep On Dancing.")

Chris Denning, the former Radio 1 DJ, was another Hop regular. He has a string of child-sex convictions, is currently in jail in Prague, and was friendly with King and Paton.

For Jimmy Pursey, the trick was to pick up the girls who were drawn to the Hop to see the Bay City Rollers while avoiding the attentions of the impresarios who orchestrated the night.

"It was fun with Deniz Corday," said Jimmy. "Deniz would say, 'Oh, Jimmy! Come here! I'd love to suck your fucking cock!' Deniz was a silly, fluffy man. Then there was Tam Paton. I remember being back here having one of my whisky and Coca-Colas one night, and Tam turned to me and he said, 'I like fucking lorry drivers.' Chris Denning was more reckless. One time he placed his penis within the pages of a gay centerfold and showed it to my ex–bass player, who proceeded to kick the magazine, and Denning's dick, and yell, 'Come on, Jimmy, we're fucking out of here!' But Jonathan King was more like a Victorian doctor. It wasn't an eerie vibe . . . but Jonathan had this highbrow, Cambridge, sophisticated thing about him. The Jekyll and Hyde thing. There wasn't much conversation with Jonathan. And with Jonathan, you'd always had these rumors. 'Oh, he got so and so into the white Rolls-Royce.' And they'd always be the David Cassidy look-alike competition winners. Very beautiful."

"Would he make a grand entrance?" I asked.

"Oh no," said Jimmy. "It was never, 'Look at me!' He never went out onto the dance floor at all. He was much happier hiding backstage up here, behind the curtains, in the inner sanctum." Jimmy paused. "The same way he hid behind all those pseudonyms, see? He's always hiding. I think that's the whole thing of his life. He always says, 'That was me behind Genesis! That was me behind 10cc! That was me behind all those pseudonyms.' But what do you do then, Jonathan? Who are you then, Jonathan?"

Jimmy was referring to the countless pseudonymous novelty hits Jonathan had in the late sixties and seventies—the Piglets' "Johnny Reggae," for instance, and Shag's "Loop Di Love." These came after his hugely successful 1965 debut, "Everyone's Gone to the Moon," which was recorded while he was still a student at Cambridge. (Before that, he was a pupil at Charter-house.) It was a remarkable career path: a lovely, plaintive debut, followed by a string of silly, deliberately irritating hits.

One of King's friends later suggests to me that it was his look—the big nose, the glasses, the weird, lopsided grin—that determined this career path, as if he somehow came to realize that it was his aesthetic destiny. He's sold forty million records. He's had a hand in almost every musical movement since the mid-sixties—psychedelic, novelty bubblegum pop, alternative pop, Eurovision, the Bay City Rollers, 10cc, *The Rocky Horror Picture Show*, Genesis, Carter the Unstoppable Sex Machine, the Brit Awards, and so on.

Within two years of leaving Cambridge, he was running Decca Records for Sir Edward Lewis, with his own West End offices and a Rolls-Royce parked outside.

"Genesis," he once said, "would have become accountants and lawyers if I hadn't heard their concealed and budding musical talent when they were fifteen years old."

He is at once seen to be the quintessential Broadway Danny Rose—the buffoonish loser who was forever nearly making it—and also a powerful multimillionaire whose influence is as incalculable as it is overlooked. He's hosted radio shows in New York and London, presented the successful and long-running *Entertainment USA* TV series for the BBC, written two novels, created a political party—the Royalists—and published *The Tip Sheet*, an influential online industry magazine that, he claims, is responsible for bringing the Spice Girls, Oasis, Blur, The Prodigy, R. Kelly, and others "exploding on to musical success. We find and help break new stars around the world."

In 1997, he was honored with a lifetime achievement award by the Music Industry Trust. In a letter read out at the ceremony, Tony Blair acknowledged King's "important contribution to one of this country's great success stories."

A galaxy of stars—Peter Gabriel, Ozzy Osbourne, Simon Bates—came out to praise him, although no galaxy of stars is willing to do the same now that he's been accused of pedophilia.

Nonetheless, he seems to delight in being the man we love to hate (theatrically speaking; he is mortified when he thinks his arresting officers really do hate him).

"I love to infuriate," Jonathan told me over coffee in his office, shortly before the trial began. "I deliberately set out to irritate."

"Of course," I said, "should you be convicted, people will hate you in a very different way. This is not a good climate in which to be accused of pedophilia."

"Well," he said with a shrug, "it's not as though I'm sitting here thinking, 'Oh, I'm such a nice person. Will everybody please be nice to me.' I know I tend to provoke extreme reactions, so I'm not at all surprised when they arrive."

"So you see what's happening now as a *continuation* of your public image?" I asked him.

"Absolutely," said Jonathan. "And it is so. And it would be absurd not to regard it as so."

"But there's a difference between bringing out a novelty record that nobody likes and being accused of buggering an underage boy," I said.

There was silence. "Let's not discuss it further," he said.

September 11, 2001, day two of the trial, and things are already looking hopeless for him. The first victim—now a painter and decorator from the suburbs of North London—takes the stand. I'll call him David. Jonathan approached David in Leicester

Square when David was fourteen or fifteen. Although David had no idea who Jonathan was, Jonathan quickly told him he was famous.

"It was exciting," says David.

Jonathan gave David the questionnaire, the one that ranked boys' hobbies in order of preference. He filled it out. Jonathan invited him back to his house and asked him if he and his friends masturbated together. Jonathan showed him pornographic movies on a cine projector.

"We were talking about masturbation," says David. "He told me to relax. He undid my trousers. He tried to masturbate me, which didn't arouse me at all. He told me to do it myself, which I proceeded to do. I felt very awkward."

David returned to King's house on three occasions. Similar indecent assaults occurred each time. Later, Jonathan wrote David a series of letters.

"He made it sound like I would be famous," says David.

The prosecuting barrister asks David to read one of these letters to the jury.

"'Maybe you will go on to be a megastar. Now I am in New York. I will call you when I next hit town. In the meantime, keep tuning in on Wednesday at 9pm for *Entertainment USA*, the greatest TV show in the world.'"

David says that Jonathan King has emotionally scarred him for life. He says he cannot hold children. He says it makes him scared and uncomfortable to hold and play with his girlfriend's little boy.

After lunch, Ron Thwaites, Jonathan's defense barrister, begins his cross-examination of David. His tone is breathtakingly abrasive.

"We are going back sixteen years because you decided not to make the complaint until nine months ago," he says. "You're not asking for sympathy for that, are you?"

"I was the one that was assaulted," David replies, shakily.

"Do you think it's easy for a man to be accused of a crime after twenty years," says Thwaites. And then: "Are you interested in money?"

"I am nervous up here," says David. "You are putting me under pressure. I was sexually assaulted by that man over there."

"You must have been fairly grown up to go to London on your own," says Ron Thwaites. "You can't have been a boy in short trousers, mewling for your mother."

And so on. We are unaware that, during this cross-examination, New York and Washington, D.C., are under attack.

That night, I receive an e-mail from Jonathan: "Makes whether or not I put my hand on a teenager's knee 15 years ago seem rather trivial, doesn't it? Are you dropping KING for the World Trade Center? Boo hoo! What do you think of the jury? A lot of ethnic variation which, I think, is probably a good thing. Not Ron's best day, but not terminal! See you tomorrow. Love JK."

A week later, Jonathan posts a message on his website, kingofhits.com: "Well, it's been a fascinating couple of weeks. Not many people are fortunate to discover first hand exactly what Oscar Wilde went through! This week is the crucial one for me—keep praying. And just one oblique thought . . . when you look at the teenagers from 15 years ago who grew up to be terrorists who killed thousands in America, wonder what changed them into mass murderers. Then wonder what turns other decent teenagers into mass liars."

King's demeanor remains cheerful throughout our time to-gether. "I am living in clouds and happy flowers and love and beauty," he tells me one day. "And if I go to prison, I shall enjoy myself."

Even on the one occasion that Jonathan all but confesses to me—"I'm sure you've got skeletons in your own closet, Jon. 'Honest, guv! I thought she was sixteen!'"—he says it with a spir-ited laugh.

When the *Guardian*'s photographer takes Jonathan's portrait early one morning before a day in court, he is frustrated to re-port that during almost every shot Jonathan stuck his thumbs up—as if he was doing a Radio 1 publicity session—or grinned his famous, funny, lopsided grin into the camera. This was not the image anyone wanted. We were hoping for something more revealing, sadder, perhaps, or even something that said "child sex," or "guilty." But Jonathan wouldn't oblige.

One day during the trial, I hear a story about Larry Parnes, Britain's first pop mogul. He discovered Tommy Steele and Marty Wilde. Like many of the great British impresarios back then, he based his business judgments on his sexual tastes.

"If I am attracted to Tommy Steele," he would tell his associ-ates, "teenage girls will be too."

Parnes's West End flat was often full of teenage boys hoping to be chosen as his next stars. If he liked the look of them, he'd give them a clean white T-shirt. Once he'd had sex with them, he'd make them take off the white T-shirt and put on a black one.

Wham!'s manager Simon Napier-Bell—who was once invited by Parnes to put on a white T-shirt—has said that the great dif-ference between the British and American pop industries is this: The American impresarios are traditionally driven by money, while their British counterparts were historically driven by gay sex, usually with younger boys—and that British pop was conceived as a canvas upon which older gay Svengalis could paint their sexual fantasies, knowing their tastes would be shared by the teenage girls who bought the records.

Deniz Corday is desperately worried that the Walton Hop, his life's work, is about to become famous for something terrible.

"Jonathan didn't want me to talk to you," he says, "but I must defend the Hop with all my life."

Deniz is immensely proud of the Hop. There is Hop memorabilia all over his flat, including a poster from a Brooklands Museum exhibition, "The Happy Hop Years 1958–1990. An Exhibition About Britain's First Disco: The Walton Hop."

"Every day, someone comes up to me in the supermarket," says Deniz, "and says, 'Thank you, Deniz, for making my childhood special.' Some say the Hop was the first disco in Great Britain. It was terribly influential. Oh dear . . ." Deniz sighs. "This kind of thing can happen in any disco. The manager can't control everything."

Deniz says he knows it looks bad. Yes, an unusually large number of convicted celebrity pedophiles used to hang around backstage at the Walton Hop. But, he says, they weren't there to pick up boys. They were there to conduct market research.

"Tam Paton would play all the latest Roller acetates and say, 'Clap for the one you like the best.' Same as Jonathan and Chris Denning. It helped them in their work."

Deniz turns out the lights and gets out the Super 8 films he shot over the years at his club. Here's the Hop in 1958. Billy Fury played there. The teenagers are all in suits, dancing the hokey pokey.

"Suits!" laughs Deniz, sadly. The years tumble by on the Super 8 films. Now it's the mid-seventies. Here's Jonathan at the turntables. He's playing disco records, announcing the raffle winners, and grinning his lopsided grin into Deniz's Super 8 camera. He's wearing his famous multicolored Afro wig. Now, on the Super 8, two young girls are on stage at the Hop, miming to King's song "Johnny Reggae." "These were the days before karaoke," explains Deniz.

For a while, we watch the girls on the stage mime to "Johnny Reggae." It turns out that Jonathan wrote it about a boy called John he met at the Walton Hop who was locally famous for his reggae obsession. David Jeremy, the prosecutor at the Old Bailey, says that Jonathan's "market research" was simply a ploy, his real motive being to engage the boys in conversations about sex. But I imagine that the two endeavors were, in Jonathan's mind, indistinguishable. I picture Jonathan in the shadows, backstage at the Hop, taking all he could from the teenagers he scrutinized—consuming their ideas, their energy, their tastes, and then everything else.

The Super 8s continue in Deniz's living room. Here's Jonathan again, in 1983, backstage at the Hop. He's put on weight. He doesn't know the camera is on him. He's holding court to a group of young boys and girls on a sofa. You can just make out little snippets of conversation over the noise of the disco. He chews on a toothpick, looks down at a piece of paper, turns to a boy and says, "Whose phone number is this?"

He spots the camera. "It's Deniz Corday!" he yells. "Look who it is! Deniz Corday! Smile at the camera!" He lifts up his T-shirt and Deniz zooms in on his chest.

"In thirty-two years," says Deniz, "we never had one complaint about Jonathan and young boys, and suddenly, after thirty-two years, all these old men—grandfathers, some of them—come forward and say they've been sexually abused and it's been bothering them all their lives. I think there's something deeply suspicious about it. Jonathan's a really nice guy and definitely not a pedophile. Anyway, I think it should be reworded. I think a pedophile should be someone who goes with someone under thirteen."

The clothes and hairstyles change as the decades roll past on the Super 8s, but the faces of the thirteen- to eighteen-year-olds remain the same. They are young and happy. Deniz says that, nowadays, we have an absurdly halcyon image of childhood. He says that the youngsters at the Walton Hop were not fragile little flowers. They were big and tough and they could look after themselves. He rifles through his drawer and produces some of the police evidence statements. He reads me some excerpts.

"'There was a crate of Coca-Cola kept backstage, and it was people like Jonathan King and Corday who hung around there. If you were invited back there you would get a free Coke with a shot of whisky.'"

Deniz pauses. "Now, how ridiculous can you get? I'm going to give the kids of the Hop a shot of whisky with a Coke?"

There is a silence.

"Well," he says quietly. "If I gave them a little bit of whisky once in a while, they're not going to put me in jail for it. I used to call it 'Coke with a kick.' Anyway, we're not talking about me. We're talking about Jonathan. Have you heard of any charges against me?"

"No," I say.

"Exactly," says Deniz. "This is about Jonathan. Not about me."

Deniz continues to read. The victim making the statement describes life at the Walton Hop and how Jonathan once went out of his way to talk to him.

"'I was obviously excited to be talking to Jonathan King. He offered to give me a lift home, which I accepted. This was the first of many lifts King gave me, and I recall that he always drove me home in a white convertible Rolls-Royce. It was an automatic car and the number plate was JK9000. We talked about music, and he often told me that he needed a young person's point of view. King drove me home on a couple of occasions before he eventually assaulted me. The first assault occurred at a car park, which was situated on the left-hand side of the Old Woking Road. Next to the car park was a field and a wooded area. King seemed familiar with the location. I believe he had been there before. I was sat in the front passenger seat and King was in the driver seat. I noticed that King had started shaking, and I presumed that he needed the toilet.'"

Deniz laughs.

"Well, you can laugh occasionally," he says.

He continues to read. "'He then leaned over to where I was sat. To my horror he started pulling at my trousers. He wrenched my trousers open and he just went for it.'"

Deniz reads the statement with mock, burlesque horror.

"'He had his face in my lap and he was performing oral sex on me by putting his mouth around my penis. I was so shocked.'"

Deniz looks up. "He doesn't say if he had an erection!" he laughs.

"'After a while he stopped performing oral sex on me, and although my penis was erect I did not ejaculate. I then noticed that King had his trousers undone with his penis exposed and he started masturbating himself. I remember looking out of the window and contemplating walking home. I did not because I just hoped that once he was done he would drop me home. King eventually came and he then drove me home. I didn't want Jonathan to tell Deniz what had happened, because I thought he'd want to do the same thing.'"

"No thanks, mate," says Deniz, before carrying on with the statement.

"'I felt sick and ashamed about what he had done to me, and I remember looking in the mirror the next day and wondering if you could see what had happened in my face. The second assault on me by King took place near the car park which had been previously described. This time he buggered me. . . . Once at the location, we got out of the car and he then led me about fifteen yards to a dip in a wooded area. King led me by placing one hand on the back of my neck and the other on my arm. King was shaking. King then took my trousers and underwear down. He then forced his penis inside my anus and penetrated me. I would describe King as frantic at the time. He was totally uncaring. I honestly believe if I had said no, he would have forced me. King had his underwear and trousers down by his ankles and he used no lubrication. I can also say that he did not have a huge penis.'"

Deniz laughs. "I'm glad to hear that, mate!" he says.

"'Although he was rough, it was not painful. I was in a state of shock. King eventually came inside of me and it was all very quick. Not only did I wash that night, but I constantly washed myself that week. I hated what he had done to me and I felt dirty. It may be that King grabbed some of my hair, because for about a week I washed my hair every day, which was most unlike me. I even remember my dad making some comment about me using so much shampoo. The third time King assaulted me was . . .'"

Deniz looks up angrily. "How many times do you have to go back before you decide that you don't like being fucked? Does it take three sexual experiences for you to realize it was bothering you? 'The third time King assaulted me was, again, following a lift home from the Hop. This time it did hurt and I told him that, but he did not stop. I even asked him if he used Vaseline, and he replied, "Oh no, you'll do with spit." It all happened very fast, and he was very surgical and physical. I would also like to add that King never kissed me or showed me any affection. Many years later I attended the Brit Awards, and while I was there I saw Jonathan King. On seeing me, he gave me a long stare and then walked away. I believe he is dangerous and I want to stop it happening to other children.'"

Deniz looks up, in fury, from the evidence statement.

"He wasn't a child!" he says.

"How old was he?" I say.

"Fifteen," says Deniz.

In the end, Jonathan is acquitted of this particular charge. The victim admits on the witness stand that he was probably sixteen when he knew Jonathan, and the prosecution can't prove that the sex was nonconsensual. While there is no statute of limitations for underage sex—or for sexual assaults—a sixteen-year-old who has had consensual sex with an adult must, by law, complain within a year of the offense for the adult to be tried. This boy waited twenty-three years, which is why his case is abandoned.

The day after I see Deniz, I receive an e-mail: "Hope you'll remember Deniz is not quite as worldly wise as others—don't hurt him. JK."

I always find it hard to look Jonathan in the eye after hearing some detailed recital of his sexual behavior. But I wonder whether any act of sex, when described with such precision, would sound equally unpleasant. The evidence Deniz read me constitutes probably the most serious charge of all sixteen complaints, and even it is not as black-and-white as one might like. Why, for instance, did the victim return on two occasions?

I would like to ask Jonathan his views on the intricacies of these sexual power plays, but he professes his innocence so adamantly that he won't be drawn on the subject. I do, however, get to ask another of his victims, Nick McMeier, these questions. One morning in November, I sit in Nick's flat in Kingston, Surrey, and he shows me some of the presents Jonathan bought him during their time together.

"Whenever I visited, I'd end up with two or three records," says Nick. "So I guess you can calculate how many times I visited him on that basis."

I look at the pile of records. "There must be thirty or forty records here," I say. "Or more."

"And he gave me a copy of his book *Bible Two*," says Nick. "And a guitar. And a biography of Edie Sedgwick."

Jonathan also took Nick on trips—to the Walton Hop, for instance, and to Deniz's house, although nothing happened there. He gave him driving lessons in his TR7 in the car park of Chessington World of Adventures. "He enjoyed being assertive. He was never particularly shy about name-dropping or describing just how famous he was." Nick laughs. "There was one occasion where we were in his Rolls-Royce in London and he pulled out in front of somebody and they beeped him and he turned round and said, 'Do you mind? There's a famous person here!' And we carried on driving. It made me laugh at the time because it was true. He was a famous person."

"Do you think that if you'd stopped being starstruck, he would have lost interest in you?" I ask.

"Yes," says Nick.

Nick is thirty-four, and very good-looking. He tells me how they first met. He was between fourteen and sixteen—he can't exactly remember—and he was cycling home from Richmond Park when Jonathan King pulled over in his Rolls-Royce and asked him directions to the Kingston bypass.

"I gave him the directions and then he said, 'Do you know who I am?' 'Actually, no.' He said, 'You do realize who I am?' And I said, 'Yeah. I do.' I tried to act as un-starstruck as I possibly could."

As they stood there on the road, Jonathan asked Nick to phone the BBC and tell them just how much he enjoyed his TV shows and could they please commission more from him. Nick agreed, although he never did phone.

They swapped phone numbers and Jonathan called several weeks later and invited him to his flat.

"We listened to some records, had a bit of a chat. He showed off his mirrored toilet. He said, 'Take a look in there, it's pretty impressive.' So I went in there and was duly impressed. And that was pretty much it."

This was the only time that no sex took place. On every other occasion, Jonathan buggered Nick. "Why did you keep going back?" I ask.

"I don't really know. Well, I was getting records every time.

But I was also enjoying the sexual gratification. I wasn't racked with guilt. At that age, you've got the hormones raging around inside you. And I felt taken care of. I knew that wasn't how grown-ups normally took care of children, but he had a kind of invincibility about him. A self-assurance."

Nick's relationship with Jonathan King lasted eighteen months. In the intervening years, he has come to identify the extent of the emotional scarring those months caused him. He has just completed six weeks of therapy, which, he says, has barely scratched the surface.

"It caused a division between my emotional side and myself," he says. "It was like I put my emotions in a room and shut the door. It's not even something I was aware of happening until I spoke to the police and they came to interview me. And two days later this incredible dark cloud came over me, like a black dog. It also bothers me quite a lot that I was lying to my parents. He even came round one Christmas and met the whole family. We got together a Christmas stocking for him with a pound coin in the bottom of it and a satsuma."

Nick says that he has seen the message Jonathan posted on his website, comparing his victims to the terrorists who attacked the World Trade Center.

"I think he's rather a sad, impotent man," says Nick, "whose chickens have come home to roost." He laughs. "But that's probably a coping mechanism for myself to disenfranchise him of any power."

On day five of the trial, one of the victims says in court that Jonathan had a blue door, when in fact his door was white. This presumably trivial inaccuracy gives rise to the following e-mail from Jonathan: "The accusers have provenly lied on oath—blue front door etc. Will the CPS prosecute them for perjury? Rather doubt it. If the verdicts are guilty, they collect their cash from the Compensation Board. . . . Is this right or fair? A topic you may feel inclined to raise in your wonderful story. See you later. JK."

Most of the conversations that occur in the Old Bailey canteen among the journalists center not on Jonathan King but on Ron Thwaites, his extraordinary, shocking, charismatic defense barrister.

"Ron could get the Devil off," one veteran Old Bailey tabloid reporter tells me.

Before the trial even started, during the preparatory hearings in July, Thwaites had great success reducing the charges against his client. "Lots of people," he said to Judge Paget, "don't enjoy sex."

Lots of people don't enjoy sex—but this doesn't mean that assaults have been committed against them. Where's the guilty mind if the boys appeared to acquiesce? An assailant, he argued, must know he's committing an assault for a crime to have occurred. But there were no protestations. Nowhere in the evidence did a boy admit to saying "No!" or "Stop!" And if they really hated it—if it scarred them—why wait twenty years to come forward! Thirty years!

David Jeremy, the prosecution barrister, argued that the look on their faces would have suggested protestation.

Thwaites contended that if King was having anal sex with them, he wouldn't have seen the look on their faces. Yes, said Thwaites, King approached boys. He approached thousands of boys.

"These encounters," he said, "are the tip of the iceberg."

But he did not approach them for sex. He approached them

for market research. "My client interacts with his public," he said, "on a grand scale." I looked over at the arresting officers. They chuckled wryly at the words "tip of the iceberg."

Then Thwaites attacked the police, accusing them of under-handed tactics. If a complainant said he was between fourteen and sixteen when the assault allegedly occurred, the police wrote that he was fourteen. He asked for six of the complainants to be struck off the charge sheet, and the judge agreed to four of them. Thwaites also asked for three trials instead of one, for the purposes of "case management."

The prosecution, startled by this suggestion, argued that this would harm their best evidence—the pattern of King's seduction. But Judge Paget agreed to split the trials.

"Oh, fuck," whispered an arresting officer, putting his head in his hands, when the judge announced his decision.

The unspoken assumption, shared by all parties, was that there would never be three trials. The prosecution was likely to throw in the towel after trials one or two, whatever the outcome. So the preparatory hearing turned out to be a great victory for King and Thwaites.

Every day in the Old Bailey, Ron Thwaites launches another merciless attack on anybody he can think of who is not his client. The victims are "cranks" who "came out of the woodwork" seeking "compensation." This includes one who cried in the witness box. "Crocodile tears!" he snarls. Others are "drug addicts and fantasists and liars." One is "completely mad."

Admittedly, Thwaites does have something of a point here. One of the victims, Chris Sealey, admits within five minutes of cross-examination that he sees black cats that nobody else can see and thinks that Gypsies are going to come to his house to rip out his throat. Chris also admits that he came forward solely for the money. He hopes to sell his story to a newspaper. (He does: to the *Sunday People*, embellishing his testimony with extraordinary relish.)

Chris's argument is "So what?" Jonathan King got something out of him, so why shouldn't he get something out of Jonathan King?

Thwaites even brings me into the mix at one point. During his summing-up he points in my direction and says to the jury, "I cannot prove that there is a contract in which [the complainants] have agreed to appear on TV or in the newspapers. . . ."

His implication seems to be that the Ronson-Victim financial pact is so cunning that the poor, justice-seeking defense team cannot break through its steely ramparts. The real reason why Thwaites cannot prove this contract exists is, of course, because it doesn't (Nick does not want to be paid for our interview), but I cannot let the jury know this. I just have to sit there. From a distance, the game-playing between prosecution and defense in an Old Bailey trial might seem impressively ingenious, but close up I sometimes find it quite horrible.

But Thwaites does highlight some of the unfortunate aspects of the case. There is no material evidence. No DNA. How can King defend himself against crimes that occurred so long ago?

"Justice delayed," says Thwaites, "is justice denied."

Nonetheless, for all of Thwaites's mini-victories, Jonathan tells me he has already packed his bags, all ready for a guilty verdict. He says he has bought every book on the Booker Prize short list in preparation for life in jail.

It takes the jury three days to reach a verdict. The night before they do, Jonathan sends me an e-mail that reads: "Pray for me."

I don't e-mail him back. I have grown to like Jonathan King, but he is guilty. As likable as he is, he did it. Perhaps there is some homophobia in this case. Bill Wyman, after all, got away with having sex with a younger girl. Is it unfair, as Jonathan claims, that his initial high-profile arrest was simply a way for the police to advertise for more victims to come forward? Most observers agree that the prosecution would never have secured a conviction with the initial complainants' allegations, and that the police were hoping for more reliable witnesses to come forward. Is it unfair, or clever police work?

I don't see Jonathan in the canteen or the lobby on the day of the verdict, but I do see him in the dock as the jury files in. He smiles at me. Every male juror makes a point of looking at Jonathan as they take their seats. The women all look away. The clerk of the court asks the foreman for the verdict on the first count, and he says, "Guilty."

Jonathan nods.

Then it is time for count two—the most serious charge. Buggery. This is the charge that relates to Chris Sealey. The foreman says, "Guilty."

Jonathan nods.

There are six guilty verdicts in total. A clean sweep. Judge Paget says that, under these circumstances, bail must be revoked. Within seconds, Jonathan is led downstairs from the dock and straight to Belmarsh prison.

LITTLE KELLERSTAIN, Tam Paton's large, outlandish, rural bungalow near Edinburgh Airport, his home for twenty-seven years, give or take his twelve months in jail for child-sex offenses and the years traveling the world in Learjets and limousines with his young charges, the Bay City Rollers, is noisy today. You imagine it to have always been a noisy place. Indeed, the old neighbors, the now-dead rich couple who lived next door at the grand Kellerstain House, used to complain bitterly about their eccentric legendary pop-impresario neighbor, the packs of screaming Roller fans forever camped outside his electric gates, the parties, the teams of police officers searching his house for clues of pedophile activity, and then more screaming—the screams of the headlines: "Sordid Secrets of Twisted Tam," "Tam's Night in the Sauna with the Boys."

Today, the place is noisy with dogs and boys. The dogs are Rottweilers. There are four of them, and they seem to hate one another. There are about half a dozen boys living with Tam. They live in spare rooms and in trailers in the garden. They are all around eighteen years old. Tam is sixty-three now. He is polite to a fault, almost humble. It is as if the years of being considered a pedophile have reduced him to a position of constant subservience around strangers. The Tam Paton of today is nothing like the fearsome Svengali you would see on television during the Roller years.

I have come to see Paton because of the similarities in his and Jonathan King's crimes. They were friends and colleagues, and would visit the Hop together. The boys Paton "indecently assaulted" were not that young like Jonathan. The youngest was fifteen. I know it will take Jonathan years to settle into his new role in life as a convicted celebrity pedophile. Paton has had twenty years to do this. So I imagine that meeting him will be like meeting Jonathan in the future.

"I was jailed for six years for underage sex," says Tam. "Underage sex. Under the age of twenty-one. This was 1981. I served a year. My victims were . . . one was fifteen. I never even touched him. There was nothing physical in that particular charge. The chap was deaf and he had a speech impediment. He came to my house and he saw a pornographic movie, a heterosexual porno-graphic movie."

"What was it called?" I ask.

"Tina with the Big Tits," says Tam. "This happened right here in this very room. It was all to do with women's boobs. Big boobs. All sizes of boobs. And he'd had two lagers. The charges that were raised against me was that I'd subjected a fifteen-year-old handicapped boy to pornographic movies and supplied him with stupefying alcohol with intent to pervert and corrupt. I got six months right there for that."

Tam takes me to the scene of more of his crimes—his sauna room. It was built in the seventies, in what used to be his util-ity room. He turns on the Jacuzzi. It bubbles into life. "I got six months for putting my hand on a guy's leg in the sauna," says Tam. "And then I got another two years for a chap who willingly came up here. He was sixteen, educated, a nice guy. He came up in a taxi. I gave him a bottle of Lambrusco."

Of course, the stigma of being imprisoned for underage-sex crimes remains with Tam. Just last week, one of his friends—who has a three-month-old baby—was visited by social services and warned that the baby should be kept away from Tam.

"A tiny little baby!" says Tam. "People look at me like I'm an animal. People who don't know me judge me. I always remember going up to visit someone in prison, and this woman was sitting there. She was looking at me, growling a bit, and I could imagine what she was thinking: 'There's a pedophile!' Anyway, I later discovered about her character. And I'll tell you, it outweighed anything I'd ever done."

"What had she done?" I ask.

"Shoplifting," says Tam.

There is a silence.

"People have their own little guilt trips," says Tam. "They look around. 'Who's a beast? Who's a pedo?' Now it's on my record for the rest of my life. If I want to go into business, I have to state that I was done for lewd and libidinous. Gross indecency. People think, 'Oh my God! He must have been crawling about in a nursery.'"

"Can I ask about the boys who live here?" I say. "What do they do?"

"They clean up," he replies, a little sharply. "They feed the dogs. They take them for walks. They help me with my property business. They are eighteen years of age, and I don't have a relationship with them. You can interview them until the cows come home. Maybe I just like nice people floating about. We don't have orgies. There's no swinging from the chandeliers. Even if there was," he adds, "it would be legal."

Tam believes he was targeted because of his fame, because he was a celebrity Svengali. He blames his arrest, then, on the pop business. And now he is out of it. He has become a property millionaire, with forty flats in Edinburgh's West End.

"I do get myself upset," he says. "I've given away all the Roller albums to charity. I want to forget it all. I've had two heart attacks. And now the same thing is happening with Jonathan. A foxhunt. Everyone wants to see the death of the fox. They would never have gone after us if we were heterosexual. But if you're a poof, my God."

I change the subject.

"Do you think you have emotionally scarred any of the boys for life?" I ask.

"Oh my God," he says. "I hope not."

IN MID-OCTOBER 2001, I have coffee with Jonathan King's brothers Andy. He's just visited Jonathan in Belmarsh for the first time.

"How is Jonathan doing?" I ask.

"Great," says Andy. "He seems really cheerful. Talking ten to a dozen."

"Really?" I ask.

"He's wearing pink pajamas as a silent protest," Andy tells me. "He says it's aesthetically reminiscent of the way gays were treated under the Nazis."

On November 20, things take a turn for the better for Jonathan. He is acquitted of buggery and indecent assault in the second trial—the witness admits on the stand that he was sixteen and not fifteen. The Crown Prosecution Service announces that same day that it won't proceed with any more trials—this includes the allegations from boys who said Jonathan King had picked them up at the Walton Hop.

The next morning, Jonathan is sentenced to seven years. Judge Paget says that the case is a tragedy. This otherwise honorable man, he says, this successful celebrity, used and abused his fame and success to attract impressionable teenagers. But there was no violence, no threats used.

Jonathan smiles and nods as he is sentenced. One journalist says that he looks smug; another says that he looks pale and beaten. His name is placed indefinitely on the sex offenders' list. The police say he may have abused hundreds of boys over the past thirty years.

POSTSCRIPT

Jonathan King wrote to me throughout his prison sentence, and sent me Christmas cards, etc. I wasn't the only one. The *Observer*'s Lynn Barber published a brilliant article about their pen-pal friendship. Her husband, David Cardiff (who was my teacher at college), was dying, and Jonathan had proved to be a "wonderful confidant," she wrote. She visited him at Maidstone prison and reported that he was walking around wearing a T-shirt that read "I'm a celebrity—get me out of here!"

"The very qualities—the relentless cheeriness, bumptiousness and optimism—which made him seem quite irritating on the outside seem absolutely heroic in prison," she wrote.

Just before Christmas 2001, a few weeks after the *Guardian* published my story about the case, I received a telephone call from the former Radio 1 DJ Chris Denning. Back in the seventies, Denning and Jonathan were best friends and business partners. Denning had, days earlier, been released from a three-year jail sentence in Prague for child-sex offenses. The night before his deportation from the Czech Republic, I met him at a down-at-the-heels hotel off Wenceslas Square. He wouldn't say which country he was going to. (It turned out to be Austria.) He faced a number of similar offenses in Britain, and he told me he'd be arrested if he ever returned here.

He turned up with a boy. He introduced him as one of the boys he'd just been in prison for, and he said he brought him along to prove they were still friends. The boy had the flu, and throughout the interview he sat on the bed, sniffing, and looking bored and ill.

I asked Chris Denning if Jonathan King had learned how to pick up boys from him.

"That's possible," he said. "He did steal some of the things I did."

"Like what?" I asked.

"I would make funny remarks," he said. "I'd be walking down the street with a couple of my younger friends and I'd say something absolutely absurd to a passerby. I remember one joke I had. I'd say to a passerby, 'Excuse me, do you know where so-and-so street is?' And they'd say, 'No. I'm sorry, I don't.' And I'd say, 'Oh, I can help you! It's just down there on the left . . . !' And for young people—for somebody like me to make a joke like that—it was hilarious."

Chris Denning—despite his various jail sentences and the fact that he'd been sleeping rough in a Prague cemetery for the past week, on and off—still had the looks and voice and demeanor of an old-style Radio 1 DJ.

"But Jonathan's humor always had a streak of cruelty," Denning added, "and I've always tried not to do that. I hate that kind of thing. Once, I was going along in his car to Brighton. He'd invited a couple of young people I knew. He'd said, 'Why don't you bring them along for the trip?' He had a chauffeur. He said, 'James! To Brighton!' I was sitting in the Rolls-Royce with my shoes half off and he grabbed them and chucked them out of the window. I said to the chauffeur, 'James. Can you please stop? I want to get my shoes.' Jonathan said to him, 'If you stop, you're fired. Drive on.'"

"What did the boys in the car think of it?" I asked.

"I don't think they liked it," he said. "It was funny, you see, but it was cruel."

Chris Denning asked me if I wanted to know the worst thing about being attracted to underage boys.

"Sadly," he said, "they grow up. They disappear. The person you were attracted to has gone. He doesn't exist anymore. You can never have a lasting relationship with them. It's very sad."

In August 2005, Chris Denning returned to London from Austria. He was arrested at Heathrow Airport and in February 2006 was convicted of child-sex offenses dating back to the seventies and eighties. He was sentenced to four years in prison. That same week, I received the following e-mail:

Dear Jon,

I was abused by King's mate Chris Denning who, as you know, has just been banged up. I recently sent this e-mail to King. You may find it amusing.

Dear Jonathan, I see your old mate Chris Denning has been given another serve of porridge. Hardly seems fair that he only got four years and you got seven, but then again you are an extremely repulsive and smarmy cunt and one can't really blame the judge for wanting to shaft you.
    You are no doubt aware that your ex employer the Sun has published a piece linking you to Denning as members of a "paedophile ring." May I make a suggestion Jonathan,

this could be a blessing in disguise, an opportunity to restore your tattered reputation. Why don't you sue the Sun Jonathan? How dare they link you to that vile pervert Denning! After all you are a wronged man, a "victim" of your own celebrity. A modern day Oscar Wilde. And after all it's not your fault that twelve year old boys are so damn sexy, and of course they all wanted it, why wouldn't an adolescent boy want to be pawed and fucked up the arse by a slavering, fat, ugly pig like your good self. I expect they were beating down your door Jonathan, how unfair that you should be persecuted for providing these boys with a "service." Such a cruel world.

My dear sweet Jonathan I am not sure what lies beyond the great divide, I try to live a good life and I hope to die with honor. I am however sure of one thing. That is this. When you die you will be met by them and welcomed, the suicides, and the ones who chose to die slowly by bottle and by needle. And they shall take you in their arms dear Jonathan, and embrace you for all eternity.

Your friend,

Simon

PART FIVE

JUSTICE

"Look at your face. You look like a slave."

—*From "Amber Waves of Green"*

Amber Waves of Green

As I drive along the Pacific Coast Highway into Malibu, I catch glimpses of cliff-top mansions discreetly obscured from the road, which is littered with abandoned gas stations and run-down mini-marts. The office building I pull into is quite drab and utilitarian. There are no ornaments on the conference-room shelves—just a bottle of hand sanitizer. An elderly, broad-shouldered man greets me. He's wearing jogging pants. They don't look expensive. His name is B. Wayne Hughes.

You almost definitely won't have heard of him. He never gives interviews. He only agreed to this one because—as his people explained to me—income disparity is a hugely important topic for him. They didn't explain how it was important, so I assumed he thought it was bad.

I approached Wayne, as he's known, for wholly mathematical reasons. The same goes for everyone I meet for this story. I've worked out that there are six degrees of economic separation between a dishwasher making less than $8 an hour and a *Forbes* billionaire, if you multiply each person's income by five. So I decided to journey across America to meet one of each multiple, to try to understand their financial lives and the vast chasms that separate them. Everyone in this story, then, makes roughly five times more than the last person makes. There's a minimum-wage guy in Miami with an unbelievably stressful life, some nice middle-class Iowans with quite terrible lives, me with a perfectly fine if frequently anxiety-inducing life, a millionaire with an annoyingly happy life, a multimillionaire with a stunningly amazing life, and then, finally, at the summit, this great American eagle, Wayne, who tells me he's "pissed off" right now.

"I live my life paying my taxes and taking care of my responsibilities and I'm a little surprised to find out that I'm an enemy of the state at this time in my life," he says. He has a big, booming voice like an old-school billionaire, not one of those nerdy new billionaires.

"Has anyone said that to your face?" I ask him.

"Nobody has to say it," says Wayne. "Just watch what they're doing."

"You mean the Occupy Wall Street crowd?"

"Those guys are a bunch of jerks," Wayne mutters, giving a dismissive wave that says, "They're just a sideshow." "Politically I'm on the enemy list. And I'm not so naive not to recognize it. I've lived my whole life doing what I thought was right and now I'm an enemy of the state."

Is he, though? It's true that income inequality is a big campaign issue. Obama in a recent speech: "What drags down our entire economy is when there's an ultra-wide chasm between the ultra-wealthy and everyone else." Whereas Romney called Obama's attacks on the super-rich, "the bitter politics of envy. I believe in a merit nation, an opportunity nation where people by virtue of their education, their hard work and risk taking and their dreams—maybe a little luck—could achieve great things."

The reality, though, is rarely are enemies of the state treated so incredibly well. Their tax rate is at a seventy-year low. In the 1950s and 1960s, the top tax bracket paid more than 80 percent. It was 70 percent when Reagan took office, 39 percent under Clinton, and now, under Obama, it's 35 percent. But the very, very rich don't pay even that. By utilizing a variety of loopholes, like awarding themselves dividends instead of income, the four hundred richest Americans pay, on average, 18 percent tax.

Wayne won't reveal exactly what he pays now that he's at the top, but he's happy to tell me he began at the bottom. "Have you read *The Grapes of Wrath*?" he says. "That was my family. My dad was a sharecropper in western Oklahoma. When the dust storms came and everything got wiped out, they came to California. The guys with the mattresses on the top of their cars in the movie? That was the way it was."

They had nothing. His father got a job winding coils that went into refrigeration units. Wayne grew up in East Los Angeles, went to college, joined the navy, drifted around. For a while he worked for unglamorous-sounding businesses with names like the Frieden Corporation, but nothing stuck. He got married, had two children, and wasn't thriving. He had to do something.

And then he had an idea.

Maybe "idea" is the wrong word. He had a realization about a very no-frills aspect of American life: "You could rent a storage unit out for more than you could rent an apartment out, and with none of the overheads."

"How come?" I ask.

"Supply and demand," he replies, shrugging. "People needed them and were willing to pay for them."

This was 1972. He put a down payment on a building in San Diego and divided it into two hundred units. "After that, it was just building the units up, one at a time. For years and years. That's all. You don't get money unless you have a lot of talent, which I don't have, or you work hard, which is what I do. We don't have any golden touch here."

"How many buildings have you got now?" I ask.

"Maybe twenty-three hundred," he says. "With five or six hundred units inside each."

Wayne says he never once stopped to contemplate the amount of money he was making. "I was just looking at getting the best locations I could and getting the buildings opened and getting the tenants and getting the cash flow and on and on," he says.

"You never once thought, 'This money is cascading in. I am worth FOUR BILLION DOLLARS?'" I ask.

He shakes his head. "I don't spend any time at all thinking about my personal wealth. I suppose if I had nothing I might think, 'I have nothing.' But when we decided to go public and I saw how much money there was, I was very surprised."

In 2006, Wayne was America's 61st richest man, according to *Forbes*, with $4.1 billion. Then the recession hit and now he's now the 242nd richest (and the 683rd richest in the world), with $1.9 billon. He's among the least-famous people on the *Forbes* list. In fact, he once called the magazine and asked them to remove his name. "I said, 'It's an imposition. *Forbes* should not be doing that. It's the wrong thing to do. It puts my children and my grandchildren at risk.'"

"And what did they say?" I ask.

"They said when Trump called up, he said the number next to his name was too small."

When Wayne is in Malibu, he stays in his daughter's spare room. His home is a three-bedroom farmhouse on a working stud farm in Lexington, Kentucky. "I have no fancy living at all," he says. "Well. I have a house in Sun Valley. Five acres in the woods. I guess that's fancy."

I like Wayne very much. He's avuncular and salt of the earth. I admire how far he has risen from the *Grapes of Wrath* circumstances into which he was born; he's the very embodiment of the American Dream. I'll return to Wayne—and the curious way he views the world—a bit later.

But first let's plummet all the way down to the very, very bottom, as if we're falling down a well, to a concrete slab of a house on a hot, dusty, potholed street in a downtrodden Miami neighborhood called Little Haiti.

THE AIR IS SO DRY it hurts your teeth, unlike Wayne's Malibu air, which is enlivening. As it happens, the view down the street includes not only used-car lots but also storage facilities—the idea that made Wayne his billions.

A young man peers into a crack of sunlight that emerges from behind one of the sheets that block out all his windows. His name is Maurose Frantz, but he goes by Frantz. He can't afford air-conditioning, hence the sheets, so it's very dark and stuffy in here with old air. Six people live here—Frantz and his parents, grandparents, and little brother—and it's the size of my living room.

"Outside is dangerous," Frantz says. "One time someone

pulled up and said to me, 'Do you need a gun?' He showed me a *gun*! I said, 'I can't hear you, man.' Another time my grandpa—they jumped him. They took his wallet. They slotted him. He cried, he cried, he cried."

Frantz is Haitian. His accent is very strong. Throughout our time together, I'm constantly asking him to repeat what he said.

"They did what to your grandpa?" I say. "They slotted him? Slattered him? Sorry?"

"*Slapped* him," Frantz replies. "*Slapped.*"

Frantz washes dishes at Miami's Capital Grille restaurant, a posh steakhouse right on the harbor in Miami's financial district. He makes $180 to $200 for a twenty-seven-hour week. That means he makes in an hour what I make in 2.4 minutes, and what Wayne makes pretty much every time he breathes in and out.

At the end of the week, Frantz gets an ATM card with his pay already loaded onto it. He receives no health benefits or sick leave or anything like that. Sometimes when he clocks out at the end of the night, he finds he's already been mysteriously clocked out by someone else. The Restaurant Opportunities Centers United (ROC), a restaurant workers' advocacy group, say this practice has been reported in Capital Grilles across the country, so they've launched a class-action suit against Darden—the restaurant chain that owns Capital Grille—for such "wage improprieties." Frantz says he's repeatedly requested some kind of paper breakdown of how many hours he's been paid for and how much tax has come off, but they never give it to him, so he's stopped asking. He's also stopped asking for a promotion to busboy. He says they told him they'd let him know, but they never did. According to ROC, the Capital Grille is notorious for denying promotions to dark-skinned people. It's possible for a black worker to become a busboy, Frantz says, but he's never seen a black server.

Last night, one of Frantz's coworkers threw away his shoes.

"I checked everywhere," he says. "I checked in the garbage but I couldn't find them. I called the sous-chef and I told him, 'I put down my shoes. Somebody threw them away.' He said, 'Frantz, you know me. I'm cool with you. I treat you like a man. I give you all the respect you need. I talk to you about your life.' I said, 'I know, Chef.' He respects me, the sous-chef. He said, 'I don't know what happened to your shoes. I can't tell you nothing.'"

Frantz talks a lot about respect and the opposite of respect—humiliation. Like the other day, he says, he was working so hard the busboy told him, "Look at your face. You look like a slave." He says that insult really stung. It's as if he's lowered his ambitions to the level that he can take all sorts of awfulness as long as people talk to him with a little respect. It occurs to me that his life would be better if he spent less time worrying about feeling disrespected and more time actively working to improve his conditions, but then I realize he is doing all he can. Putting his head above the parapet to talk to me is a brave step. (ROC asked for volunteers on my behalf and he was the one to agree.) But I can't see how his life will improve anytime soon. According to ROC, he receives no food stamps or government assistance of any kind. He's so far down America's financial ecosystem, he barely registers on it.

I ask Frantz to show me his neighborhood. He says there's nothing really to see. He rarely goes out—only to work and church and to play soccer. Everywhere else is too dangerous. When we head outside, I scurry from his front door to the car. A smashed-up police cruiser lies abandoned on the corner. We take a drive past one place on earth he has some fun: the soccer field in the public park. Six miles later, we reach the Capital Grille. Usually he catches the bus, which takes an hour. When he works late and misses the 1:00 a.m. bus home, he has to stand there until the next one comes at 4:00 a.m.

"Do you ever wonder what the customers' lives are like?" I ask.

"I don't know nothing about the customers," says Frantz. "I've never seen them."

I look at him. "You've never seen a customer?" I ask.

"Never," he says.

"Do you know how much the steaks cost?" I ask.

"I never saw a menu," he says. "They're in the restaurant, not the kitchen."

His last words to me, before I leave to go and visit someone who makes five times what he does, are "If I get money, I'm going to leave."

FIFTEEN HUNDRED MILES away from Frantz's neighborhood is a lovely, leafy, middle-class Des Moines suburb called Urbandale. There's mist and dew and the lawns are so green they look painted. Any slapping that occurs in this neighborhood will be child-on-child slapping, quickly dealt with by the parents. It's 7:00 a.m. and deserted and unseasonably cold—a tornado will pass through in a few hours—but I'm sure in warmer circumstances I'd see children running around, in and out of one another's homes, and riding their bikes to school. Sometimes I dream of raising my family in a place like this. In poorer—and richer—neighborhoods, people isolate themselves. The $900-a-week family that lives here—Dennis and Rebecca Pallwitz and their two babies—has a ground-floor apartment on a nice block with a communal pool. Most of the properties here are detached family homes—theirs is an exception. I sit in their kitchen and tell them about Frantz.

"Oh," gasps Rebecca sympathetically.

"I know," I say. "Imagine living in Miami and earning a fifth of what you earn. The stress must be unbelievable."

"It's another world," says Rebecca.

The Pallwitzes' fifth anniversary is approaching. "We'd like to go to the east of the state where we had our honeymoon," Dennis says. "But"—he glances at Rebecca—"that would cost gas and food and a bed-and-breakfast stay, so maybe we'll stick around here, save the gas money, and get a hotel room for a couple of days."

"You can't afford to drive across the state?" I say in a startled screech. I sound like the Dowager Countess from *Downton Abbey*. In fact, last night in New York City, I got to see something Frantz has never seen: the inside of a Capital Grille restaurant. (I'm guessing Dennis and Rebecca have never been to one, either.) It was delicious and I didn't even think about what it cost. There were stag heads and sculptures of horses and fine oil paintings of generic earls and lords and foxhunts. The milieu was very English country gentleman, although an English country gentleman would never put an "e" at the end of the word "grill." Almost every waiter was light-skinned, but I did see one dark-skinned black man serving. So that was nice.

"But there's lots of stuff to do here in the Des Moines area that we still haven't done," Dennis says, brightening. "So . . ."

"I know what I want to do," says Rebecca.

"What's that?" says Dennis.

"The drive-in movie theater and then the Incredible Pizza," she says. "The Incredible Pizza's got games and a buffet. You can pay thirty dollars, eat as much as you want, then play games until the money runs out. They have this tunnel thing going on. That doesn't cost anything. Our son can take his shoes off and run in there for a while. . . ."

Dennis smiles, but I can tell he thinks Rebecca has evoked a crappy way to spend a fifth anniversary.

Dennis installs, maintains, and repairs "a wide variety of home medical equipment, oxygen equipment, wheelchairs, a smattering of everything." Rebecca stays home with the children. She says their problems are twofold: taxes and health insurance.

"He gets paid every two weeks," says Rebecca. "For state and federal taxes they take about a hundred eighty dollars. Then for health insurance they take about three hundred seventy-five."

"The health costs go up every year," says Dennis. "And not just the regular four percent for inflation. It could be ten percent, seventeen percent . . ."

I ask them if they feel worse off than they did a few years ago. Rebecca says, "Yes, a little. The cost of everything, like health insurance, gas, and groceries, has been going up by leaps and bounds. Some things have even seemed to double. Versus our income not changing that much."

I tell them about the health system in my native UK—free health care for everyone. I say I remember Glenn Beck trying to scare America by saying that if Obamacare went through, things would end up like Britain, with a savage, failing, socialist health-care system.

"But it's not failing," I say. "It's great. And nobody has to pay anything." (Actually, it's funded by national taxation, and some parts of it work more efficiently than others, but you'd be hard-pressed to find a Brit who doesn't feel essentially proud and defensive of the system.)

Dennis and Rebecca look at me warily, as if I might be pretending for some nefarious European socialist reason that the UK National Health Service is a functional thing. But it really is.

So they're going nowhere for their anniversary. Instead they've started seeking help at the local Food Pantry, a charity offering food to the needy. Rebecca says she was amazed that somewhere like Urbandale even needed a Food Pantry. But it does. And when she queues up, she doesn't see only derelicts. She sees middle-class families just like them.

Dennis says he wishes they were better off, but there are positives about being poor. It makes people community-spirited, he says. Plus, money can turn a man wayward. Dennis runs a church support group for sex and drug and alcohol addicts. Why did some of those men fall into a hedonistic abyss? "Because they could afford to," he says.

This is a little heartbreaking to hear. It reminds me of Frantz. He rationalizes his place in the ecosystem by saying it's manageable as long as people talk to him respectfully. Dennis rationalizes his position by saying that, if he had more, who knows what pleasure-seeking scrapes he might succumb to?

And there's something else Dennis and Rebecca have in common with Frantz. They, too, say they leave the house only for work and church and to go to the park. They haven't been to the movies in a year.

"I hope you're not offended," I say, "but your lives seem unexpectedly similar to Frantz's."

"I don't find it surprising that we have the same struggles," says Rebecca.

"How do you feel when you hear stories of the super-rich getting away with paying hardly any tax?" I ask them.

There's a short silence.

"I'd probably do it, too, if I could," Dennis shrugs. "But I can't." He pauses and shrugs again. "So."

FIVE TIMES Dennis and Rebecca, there is me. I make $250,000, double that in a good year—if, say, George Clooney is turning one of my books into a movie. Which doesn't happen often. Just the once, in fact. Being a panicker, I live my life convinced poverty and disaster lie just around the corner unless I constantly and frantically work. Which I do.

But I have none of Dennis and Rebecca's struggles. I can vacation anywhere. I haven't noticed rising gas and grocery prices other than hearing myself murmur a vague "Oh. That seems a bit more" and then forgetting about it. I have never felt so rich and so fortunate as I do as I drive away from Urbandale that morning.

THE WOMAN who makes roughly five times more than me— $1.25 million in a bad year, up to $3 million in a great one— wants to remain anonymous. I'll call her Ellen. She's a New York producer: movies, TV, Broadway. I meet her in London. She's over on business. She's brassy and loud and restless and alarmingly energetic and tough-looking and she talks incredibly fast. She says it would be "too weird and stressful" to reveal her name to the world in the context of what she makes. If you're super-rich or super-poor, everyone can see that. But in the top-middle, one stays covert. Plus she doesn't want letters begging for money. She once had one from her father, who is a "pathetic gambler."

"How does it feel to make what you make?" I ask her.

I notice a strange tone in my voice. The usual chirpy sense of inquiry isn't there. Instead I sound weirdly tense, as if the true reason for our meeting is for me to discover what I'm missing out on.

"Good," she says, nodding. "Happiness is having twenty percent more than what you need. The trick is not to be too rich."

"Why not?" I ask her.

"People want to go on your private plane," she says. "You fall asleep in the middle of conference calls. There's a certain discombobulation when you have too much."

Maybe Ellen's right. Maybe it would be bad to have your own plane. But for a second Dennis flashes into my mind, with his own imagined perils of having more money. I remember that Karl Marx line about religion being the opium of the people—his idea that the elites keep the masses subdued with illusory happiness. But Dennis and Ellen have both suggested to me, surely fallaciously, that greater fortune might lead to unexpected sadness. So we're actually very good at inventing our own opium.

Personally, I wish I was better at opiating myself. Instead I'm sort of glaring at Ellen in a hostile manner, wondering how I might scramble up to her level.

"So what can and what can't you do in terms of luxury living?" I ask her.

"If you're really rich, you can buy your doctors," she says. "Mike Ovitz famously bought a couple of cardiac surgeons."

"You don't have anything like that, do you?" I say.

"No, of course not," says Ellen.

"Thank God," I think. Becoming aware of what's just out of your reach can pull the rug from under your feet. It's comforting to know that having my own doctors would be massively out of my reach.

"But I know a guy who knows a guy," says Ellen. "I'm at a level where I don't have to suffer. I've been sick. I had cancer. If you have money, you call the guy who knows the guy who's the head of the department. The truth is, rich people with cancer versus everyone else with cancer? Longer life! And I didn't think about bills at all! I have a bill? I throw it in the box. And that box goes to my business manager. This is a key item if you have money. You don't look at the bills. When I got money I vowed, 'Never again will I suffer the small stuff.' To me, paying a bill is the small stuff. 'I don't care how the fuck it happens, someone pay that fucking thing!' It's a good feeling."

I listen and nod and think, "I very much need a business manager." "How much do you pay your business manager?" I ask.

"A very small amount of money," Ellen says. "A hundred thousand dollars a year."

There's a silence. "That's a lot," I say.

Ellen looks at me surprised. "No, it's not," she says.

She explains that her business manager performs many tasks for her: He runs her office, does her bookkeeping, oversees her investments, files her taxes. And even though she pays him what can amount to 10 percent of her income, she has some money in the bank, so she can afford him.

Rarely has an interview awakened in me so many dormant desires. Before meeting Ellen I had no idea I needed a business manager and a friend who knows top surgeons personally. I was a lot happier before this interview began.

"I still worry about bills," I say, sadly. "And I get knots in my stomach when the tax is due. Really big knots. Have you worked out how to pay less tax like really rich people do?"

"No," Ellen replies. "I pay forty-two percent."

"Good," I say.

FIVE TIMES Ellen is a man named Nick Hanauer. His taxable income is, he tells me, "tens of millions. In a bad year it can be ten million." We speak via Skype. I'm in London. He's at his home in Seattle. What little I can see of it looks lovely. He's in some kind of an office/den with an electric guitar in the corner. His parents made good money from the pillow trade. After college he set up a few OK businesses, but then one day he met a girl who was dating a guy. She said, "You two are going to be friends."

The guy had a business idea. Nick loved the sound of it. He invested all the money he had in it—$45,000 cash. The guy was Jeff Bezos and the business was Amazon.com.

Nick asks me about the woman beneath him on my income list. "Is Ellen a highly paid salary person?" he wonders.

"Yes," I say.

"She has to go to work every day?"

"Right."

"If she stops going to work, she's out of business?"

"She has a bit of money saved, but basically yes," I say.

Nick smiles. "While we sit here, during this charming conversation, I will make twenty-five thousand dollars," he says.

I look at Nick. "That's terrible," I say.

Nick roars with laughter. "That's the difference between me and her! Hahahaha!"

Nick has just been holidaying in Cabo. His life is ceaselessly luxurious, and always will be, because of one insanely clever realization—that Jeff Bezos was onto something—and the smart, subsequent ways he invested his Amazon profits.

"Ellen says she doesn't want to be any richer because you've got problems," I say. "People want to go on your plane. You fall asleep during conference calls."

"Hahahaha!" Nick literally slaps his thigh. "People do want to come on my plane, and my wife and I make every effort to bring everyone we can."

"How much tax did you pay last year?" I ask.

"Eleven percent," says Nick.

"Do you feel awful about that?" I ask.

"Yes," says Nick.

There's something unusual about Nick, in that he's come to believe that the system he benefits so richly from is built on nonsense—specifically the idea that "the markets are perfectly efficient, and allocate benefits and burdens perfectly efficiently, based on talent and merit. So by that definition the rich deserve to be rich and the poor deserve to be poor. We believe this because we have an almost insanely powerful need to self-justify."

And the biggest nonsense of all, he says, "is the idea that because the rich are the smartest, and because we're the job creators, the richer we get, the better it is for everyone. So taxes on the rich should be very, very low because we're essentially the center of the economic universe, the font of productivity." Nick pauses. "If there was a shred of truth to the claim that the rich are our nation's job creators, then given how rich the rich have gotten, America should be drowning in jobs!"

"So if the rich don't create the jobs," I ask, "who does?"

"The middle classes!" Nick roars. "A huge middle class will produce an unbelievable opportunity for capitalists."

I tell Nick about Rebecca and Dennis in Iowa, about how their health-insurance costs are preventing them from driving across the state to celebrate their anniversary, thus denying themselves happiness and small businesses across Iowa their money.

"I fly around in a twenty-five-million-dollar Falcon 2000," he replies. "And they can't afford to drive across the state to celebrate their anniversary? It's not fair, and it's terrible for business. The best ideas in the world aren't worth jack shit unless you have someone to sell to.

"I don't even know how much my health-care costs are," he continues. "It doesn't matter! For them it's the difference between celebrating an anniversary and not celebrating an anniversary."

The solution, Nick says, is to raise taxes for the rich. He says a 50 percent rate for people like him seems about right. It would pay for the likes of Dennis and Rebecca's health care and enable them to drive across Iowa, creating jobs at whichever bed-and-breakfasts and gas stations and tourist attractions they happen to stop off at.

"If you're so concerned about it, why don't you write a check?" I ask.

"You can't build a society around the effort of a few do-gooders," he replies. "History shows that most people would not do it voluntarily. People have to be required to participate."

So instead, he says, he's dedicated his life to something more meaningful. He's trying to persuade everyone he can—business journalists, etc.—that the system needs a radical change. He's published a book about it: *The Gardens of Democracy*.

"The view that regulation is bad for business is almost universally held," he says. "But in every country where you find prosperity you find massive amounts of regulation. Show me a libertarian paradise where nobody pays any taxes and nobody follows rules and everybody lives like a king! Show me one!"

AND SO I JOURNEY to a place where that libertarian ideal is imagined in a soft, warm glow: B. Wayne Hughes's unassuming Malibu office. As it happens, Wayne is a substantial donor to Republican causes. For example, he has given $3.25 million to American Crossroads, a super PAC started by Karl Rove and Ed Gillespie that pays for GOP campaign ads. You'll see a lot of "Paid for by American Crossroads" tags on your TV in the coming months. But I didn't know his politics when I approached him. My first inkling that his libertarian philosophy is practically spiritualist in its passion comes when he happens to mention some old novel from 1939 he likes.

"Read *Doctor Hudson's Secret Journal*," he says. "It'll tell you how to make your life a very satisfying thing. But it doesn't have a damn thing to do with money."

"Oh, OK, thanks, I will," I reply politely. Then I instantly forget about it. The recommendation of a silly-sounding novel doesn't seem at all relevant to my story. But later, just as I'm about to wind down the interview, a weird thing happens. It's when I ask him if he has any advice for wannabe billionaires.

"I don't know anything worth knowing," he says. Then he pauses. A mischievous look crosses his face. "I gave you a secret in this interview already on how to make your life way better and you went right by it."

I look at him, befuddled.

"Hahahahaha!" he says.

"Was it that thing you said about *Mr. Hudson and the . . .* ?" I say.

"Exactly right!" he roars. "*Doctor Hudson's Secret Journal.* Read it! You'll see!"

And so I order it from some secondhand-book place. It's out of print. It arrives, ancient and battered. It's kind of pulpy, the story of a Dr. Hudson who encounters a mysterious gravestone engraver named Randolph.

"I now have everything I want and can do anything I wish!" Randolph tells the doctor. "So can you! So can anybody! All you have to do is follow the rules!" Randolph hands Dr. Hudson a "magic page" upon which is written the secret, the rules for "generating that mysterious power I told you about . . ."

You can imagine how excited I am when I get to this part of the novel. But the secret turns out to be underwhelming. It is this: If you perform anonymous good deeds, greatness will visit you. But the philanthropy must be carried out with "absolute secrecy." That's the key.

When I read my B. Wayne Hughes transcript, I see that it's peppered with covert references to *Doctor Hudson's Secret Journal.* When I asked him which charities he donates to, he said, "I have over the years supported charities." Then he fell mysteriously silent. Then he said, "If you talk about things you've done that you think are worthwhile, you subtract from yourself. And so therefore I will only say my principal charity is children's cancer and I've been doing it for twenty-two years."

"You don't want to say how much you've given away?" I asked.

"I don't want to subtract from my pleasure," he said. "I especially don't want it written up. It would be a disaster for me. It would hurt me."

"Why?" I asked.

"It would subtract from me," he said.

Then, later, he said, with an anguished look, "Don't you think I have an urge to say, 'I did this and I did that and I got studies going in twenty hospitals . . .' I have an urge to say that but I'm sitting on it. Why? Because once I say it, I've lost it! It's gone. Forever. The whale doesn't get harpooned until it rises to the surface to blow. If you do a good deed, a deed you're proud of, and you don't tell anybody, it will be the most difficult thing you've ever accomplished, but with the highest payoff. You feel good about yourself. It gives you happiness and satisfaction. It makes you different from other people in ways people don't realize. If you follow the rule, I promise you it is a life-changing event."

It was a lovely, engaging, strange philosophy. But there's another side to it. Dr. Hudson chooses whom to bestow his graciousness onto. It's entirely his choice. Taxation takes that decision out of his hands and gives it to the state. It screws up the formula completely.

Wayne's avuncular manner deserted him when he talked about what to do about the have-nots. "I remember an advertisement with an Indian in a canoe in a harbor," he said, "and tears are running down his face because he sees all the trash in the water and he sees what's happening. That's how I feel about America. It's an emotional thing for me." He paused, and that's when he said, "I'm a little surprised to find out that I'm an enemy of the state at this time in my life. They talk about your 'fair share.' 'Are you paying your fair share?' Fair is in the eyes of the beholder." He paused. "I hope I don't come off like some big person . . . so conservative . . . I believe in spreading it around, but I believe in doing it myself. . . ."

"So the trash in the river is higher taxes?" I asked.

"It's the idea of entitlement," he snapped. "That idea wasn't there in the history of this country. I remember passing a building and my father saying to me, 'That's the poorhouse. You don't ever want—'"

And then we were interrupted by his daughter, a woman in her forties. She came into the room, kissed him, and asked him if he was going to walk along the beach later. He said he was. She kissed him again and left and he didn't return to the "poorhouse" anecdote. Instead he said, "When the politicians said, 'Everybody is entitled to a house,' you saw what happened. And now you have 'Everybody is entitled to go to college.' Which is stupid! When I went to college I had to drive a truck to pay. I had a partial scholarship, but I took care of myself."

"So you're saying everybody is entitled to college, but they should have to pay their own way?" I asked.

"Some people don't belong in college!" he said. "That should occur to you."

I understand why Wayne's great love in life is his stud farm. There's something very Thoroughbred-horses about his view of the world. Perhaps the different ways Nick and Wayne made their money may explain their politics. Nick sees an economy of luck. He got lucky, and he understands that fragility for what it is. Wayne sees an economy of earning where those with exceptional talent or exceptional grit rise, as they should, to the top.

For Wayne's philosophy to work, though, he needs to see those who don't make it as kind of deserving of their ill fortune. He talked to me about "derelicts on welfare" in Los Angeles who check themselves into the hospital because they're "bored" and "want feeding" and "we're paying for all that kind of activity." He said too much tax money is spent on "guys going to chiropractors, guys getting massages all over the country! On us! Give me a break. Guys getting Viagra!" He talked about "Los Angeles bus drivers who are on permanent stress leave because someone spat on them when they got on the bus and now they're emotionally upside down. More than half the bus drivers are out on stress leave! Systems like that cannot work!"

Later, I hunt for published data that back up Wayne's feckless-bus-driver nightmare scenario. I can't find any. I do find something else, though—plenty of statistics showing that a guy with Wayne's level of wealth has never had it so good in America. And yet, of all the people I interview, Wayne is the only one who seems angry about the politics of his situation. Frantz, Dennis, Rebecca—those at the bottom looking up—showed no animosity at all.

The government used to tell people like Wayne exactly what to do with huge chunks of their income: Hand it over and we'll decide how to use it. Today, America's richest citizens have won the right to control these decisions themselves, and that's a big reason why income inequality is so dire. For every secret philanthropist like Wayne, there are many who give little or nothing back. Meanwhile, Dennis and Rebecca continue to tread water, and might even drown.

Wayne's heart is in the right place. He's not parsimonious. He started from nothing and he wants to give back, but he wants to choose how. He genuinely believes that higher taxes ruin society. But I can't help thinking that when he talks about bored derelicts and emotionally weak bus drivers, he's really—even if he doesn't know it—talking about Frantz.

The Man Who Tried to Split
the Atom in His Kitchen

Angelholm is a pretty southern Swedish town, famed for its clay-cuckoo manufacturing, a clay cuckoo being a kind of ocarina, which is a kind of flute. The crime rate here is practically zero. Except one of its residents was last year arrested for trying to split the atom in his kitchen. His name is Richard Handl and he buzzes me into his first-floor flat.

I wanted to meet Richard because I keep seeing reports of home-science experimenters clashing with the authorities. There's been a spate of them this past year or two.

I glance into Richard's kitchen and recognize his cooker from the news. It was horrendously, alarmingly blackened then, but it's clean now.

"So, you aren't currently doing any experiments?" I ask him.

"I'm banned," he says.

"By whom?" I ask.

"My landlord," he says. "And the Swedish Radiation Safety Authority."

When Richard was a teenager, everything, he says, was fine. "I had friends. We'd go partying. I have Asperger's, so I was a bit of a nerd, a geek. My interests were chemical experiments. I'd make solutions that changed color. When I was thirteen, I made some explosives in the garden, using gunpowder, stuff I got from a paint store and from my father's pharmacy. He had sulfuric acid, nitric acid. Visiting my father in his pharmacy was very exciting."

His father assumed Richard would grow up to be a pharmacist too. He was, Richard says, happy and proud of his son, as it was his dream to raise a boy to follow in his footsteps. But something unexpected happened to Richard fourteen years ago, when he was seventeen: "I became very aggressive to people," he says.

"In what way?" I ask.

"It was toward my father," Richard says. "Sometimes I hit him."

"In response to what?"

"Very small things. Like if he was late and didn't call."

"Was he worried about you?"

"Yes, he was quite worried about me. He took me to the hospital, so I could talk to psychiatrists. They said I was depressed. And I had some paranoid disorder."

"And all this just came from nowhere?"

"It just happened," he says, shrugging.

Richard worked in a factory for four years, but his disorder meant he spent most of his time in his flat. His love of chemistry continued undimmed, but the possibility of him becoming a pharmacist had practically gone. So, instead, he decided one day to start a collection: He would scour the Internet and buy an ampoule of every chemical element. He quickly realized he had to downgrade his ambition. "There are some very unstable radioactive elements, like polonium and francium, that last just a couple of minutes and then decay. They're impossible to get."

But he persevered with the others.

"Do you have any of them still here?" I ask.

"Sure," he says. "Would you like to see them?"

He disappears into his bedroom and returns holding a basket filled with ampoules of gold and silver and platinum and thallium and beryllium. Some are solid blocks, some glittering shards, others shining slivers. The basket looks like a treasure chest.

"This is the most amazing one," Richard says, picking up an ampoule marked "Cesium." It looks like solid gold. "Watch," he says. "If you warm it up . . ."

He closes his fist around it for thirty seconds. Then he shows it to me again. It has melted. We both look at it, amazed, as if we've just witnessed a magic trick.

"And then," Richard says, "I began to collect radioactive elements like radium and uranium and americium."

Richard was Googling "americium" one day when he found a story, in *Harper's* magazine, about a Michigan boy named David Hahn who grew up in the 1990s. Both boys spent their childhoods blowing things up in the garden. Hahn once turned up at a Boy Scouts meeting with a bright orange face due to an accidental overdose of canthaxanthin. Hahn also got expelled from camp for dismantling a smoke detector (he was trying to extract the americium—pretty much everything you need to split the atom you can find on eBay or in smoke detectors and antique luminous-dial clocks).

Those were the days before the Internet, so getting hold of information about how to build a nuclear reactor was more complicated for Hahn than it would turn out to be for Richard. He learned how to do it by writing to the U.S. Nuclear Regulatory Commission and pretending to be a physics teacher. Did they have any pamphlets on how to split the atom?

"Nothing produces neutrons as well as beryllium, Professor Hahn," they wrote back.

And that's how David Hahn managed to turn his potting shed into a nuclear reactor.

It wasn't long before the Michigan police cottoned on, and in June 1995, eleven men in protective suits descended on the dangerously irradiated shed. He was shut down.

Sixteen years later, in Ängelholm, Richard read the Hahn story and felt inspired to try it out himself. This is how Richard went about trying to split the atom. First, he got a saucepan. Into it he put his radioactive elements—the americium and radium. He mixed them up with sulfuric acid and beryllium and turned on the stove. The mixture bubbled up crazily, splashing all over the cooker and the floor. He quickly turned off the gas and posted a picture of the carnage on his blog, with the caption "The Meltdown!"

His plan, he says, was to repeat the experiment, but this time to collect into a test tube the neutrons that were emanating from the concoction. Then he'd have fired the "neutron ray" at a chunk of uranium sealed in a glass marble.

"What does the neutron ray look like?" I ask.

"It doesn't look like anything," Richard says. "You can't see it."

"How do you know it's there?"

"You have to measure it with a Geiger counter," he says.

"So what you're saying is, you'd point the test tube filled with neutrons at the uranium marble, and that's what would split the atom?"

"Yes," Richard says.

Richard never did collect the neutrons into a test tube. After the meltdown, he decided to e-mail the Swedish Radiation Safety Authority to double-check that what he was doing was aboveboard.

"Hello!" read his e-mail of July 18, 2011. "I'm very interested in nuclear physics and radiation. I have planned a project to build a primitive nuclear reactor. Now I'm wondering if I'm violating any laws doing so?"

They e-mailed him back on August 11: "Hi. The short answer to your question is that if you build a nuclear reactor without permission, you are violating strict laws. It is a criminal offense and can lead to fines or imprisonment for up to two years."

Richard was surprised. "The amount I had was very small," he says, "so far away from the amount needed to make a dirty bomb or something like that. To get it to explode, you must have something called a critical mass, which is fifty kilograms of radium or six kilograms of plutonium. I had five grams. The worst that could have happened was I might have got radiation in me."

"And got cancer years later?" I ask.

He shrugs. "Yes."

Even though it took the radiation authority three weeks to respond to Richard's e-mail, everything moved very quickly after that. Within days, they'd turned up at his flat with the police.

"They told me to get out with my hands up. They scanned me with Geiger counters. There was nothing. They measured the whole apartment. They said I was arrested for a crime against the radiation-safety law."

And that's it, so far. Sixteen weeks have passed and nothing has happened to him, besides making headlines all over the world.

"I don't regret it," he says, "because it was exciting. I'm sad I can't do it anymore."

We glance at his basket of elements. "There are no other experiments you could do with these?" I ask.

"I can," he says, "but I don't want to."

"What could you do?" I ask.

"I could . . ." Richard pauses. "This thallium is very, very poisonous. If you break the ampoule, it would start to react with the air and oxidize. Thallium oxide. Very poisonous. If you get it on your fingers, you can die."

"But you would never consider . . ."

"No, no," Richard says. He pauses. "Actually, I'm thinking of trying again to become a pharmacist. I'm going to read up on some courses from the high school and begin to study in the university."

I RECEIVE a slightly alarmed e-mail from Jason Bobe, who runs DIYbio.org, an online community for home-science experimenters. I'd e-mailed him as part of my research. He says he's worried my story may discourage home science. Maybe, he suggests, I should talk to Victor Deeb, whose experiments in his basement went disastrously wrong in a very different way and whose story might offer a counterbalance.

Deeb lives in a small Massachusetts town called Marlborough. He's retired, in his mid-seventies, and although he's lived in the U.S. almost all his life, he still has a strong Syrian accent, which gets stronger as he becomes more incensed over the phone.

Three years ago, on August 5, 2008, a policeman happened to be driving past Deeb's house. "He saw smoke billowing from the air conditioner in an upstairs room, so he called the fire department." Deeb speaks in short, exact phrases, as if he considers our conversation to be like a chemical experiment, requiring complete precision.

A plug had shorted in the bedroom. The fire department put out the fire, glanced into the basement, and immediately called for emergency reinforcements.

"The whole fire department came," Victor says. "The FBI. Even the CIA was here. It couldn't have been any more crazy. They went into the sewer system to see if I was dumping anything down the toilet."

What they had found in the basement was a hundred bottles of chemicals. None was hazardous. There was nothing poisonous. "I was working on a coating for the inside of beverage cans containing no bisphenol A," Deeb says.

BPA, he explains, is standard in beverage-can coatings. The problem is that it can seep into the drink and play havoc with our hormones, causing men to grow breasts and girls as young as seven to have periods. Back in 2008, he says, "there were few references in the media to the negative effects of BPA. Currently, there is a deluge of articles. So my desire to eliminate BPA was ahead of its time." He pauses. "I spent an enormous amount of time with the authorities, trying to explain what I was working on, but they had no perception. No concept."

And so he watched as they hauled away all the chemicals and test tubes in a truck. "I had a box full of files and notes and comments," he says. "Twenty years' work. They hired two Ph.D. chemists to go through the box, looking for confirmation that there were hazardous materials in the basement. When they couldn't find anything, they left the box out in the rain. It destroyed all my notes. Twenty years of my life and work and efforts to help others down the drain."

"When they realized their mistake, I presume they apologized and paid you a settlement," I say.

"The opposite!" he says. "They're suing me for the cost of emptying my basement."

For America's online community of home-science experimenters, the most outrageous moment of all came when the enforcement officer, Pamela Wilderman, explained her decision-making process to the local paper: "I think Mr. Deeb has crossed a line somewhere," she said. "This is not what we would consider to be a customary home occupation."

"Allow me to translate Ms. Wilderman's words into plain English," wrote Robert Bruce Thompson, the author of *Illustrated Guide to Home Chemistry Experiments.* "'Mr. Deeb hasn't actually violated any law or regulation that I can find, but I don't like what he's doing because I'm ignorant and irrationally afraid of chemicals, so I'll abuse my power to steal his property and shut him down.' . . . There's a word for what just happened in Massachusetts. Tyranny."

Before I hang up, Victor Deeb says he wants to remind me of something. He says that for every David Hahn and Richard Handl, there's a Steve Jobs and a Charles Goodyear. "They started at home. Goodyear developed the vulcanization process by mixing sulfur with virgin rubber on his wife's stove in their kitchen."

And then he is gone, to do—he says—what he spends every day doing. He's going to try to remember what he'd written on the pages in the box that was left out in the rain.

Lost at Sea

The Port of Los Angeles, October 23, 2011. At the Goofy Pool on deck 9 of the *Disney Wonder*, the Adventures Away celebration party has begun. "Good-bye, stress!" the cruise director shouts. "Hello, vacation!" The ship's horn sounds out "When You Wish Upon a Star" to indicate that we're about to set sail, to Mexico.

I'm standing on deck 10, looking down at the dancing crowds of guests and crew. There are 2,455 passengers this week, and 1,000 employees. You can spot the Youth Activities team in their yellow tops and blue trousers. They look after the children in the Oceaneer Club on deck 5.

There's no talk of it, but many people on board know something terrible occurred on this route—to Puerto Vallarta and Cabo San Lucas—earlier this year. At 5:45 a.m. on Tuesday, March 22, a CCTV camera captured a young woman on the phone in the crew quarters. Her name was Rebecca Coriam. She was twenty-four, from Chester, and had recently graduated with a sports science degree from Exeter University. She'd been working in Youth Activities on board for nine months, and apparently loved it. But on the phone she was looking upset.

"You see this young boy walk up to her to ask her if she's all right," her father, Mike, told me a few weeks ago, sitting in the family's back garden in Chester. "She said, 'Yeah, fine.' Then she put the phone down. She turned around. She had her hands in her back pockets, which she always did. Then she put her hands to her head like this, pushing her hair back. . . ." Mike did the movement. It looked normal. "And then she walked off."

And that's the last anyone has seen of her. She just vanished.

When she didn't report for work at 9:00 a.m., the crew Tannoyed her. They searched the ship and called the Mexican coast guard, who searched the waters, all to no avail. That was seven months ago.

"Now, whenever we call anyone, all they say is 'The investigation is ongoing,'" Mike said. "We've tried e-mailing, telling them how we feel, how it's getting harder . . ." He pauses. "But nothing. Just 'It's ongoing.'"

Mike and his wife, Ann, have created a website, Help Us To Find Rebecca (rebecca-coriam.com), and have organized fundraising events. The day I visited, the house was filled with raffle prizes, chocolates, board games, and soft toys, donated by wellwishers. Mike said on some days they were just functioning, but on others they didn't know if they were coming or going.

They said only one police officer has ever been assigned to investigate Rebecca's disappearance. He flew in from Nassau in the Bahamas, fifteen hundred miles from the ship—just one man charged with conducting a forensic investigation and interviewing three thousand passengers and crew. He took charge because the ship is registered in the Bahamas, for tax reasons. It wasn't deemed relevant that it's based in Los Angeles, the company's head office is in the UK, Rebecca was British, and she went missing in international waters between the U.S. and Mexico. (For European passengers, this holds true for all cruise liners, but a law passed last year means if a U.S. citizen disappears on a cruise ship, the FBI now has jurisdiction.)

Mike and Ann have met the Bahamas officer only once. They flew to Los Angeles on March 25 to meet the ship as it arrived back. The Disney people showed them the CCTV footage and introduced them to the policeman.

"I asked him, 'Are you going back on the ship now?'" Mike said. "He said, 'No, I'm going back to the Bahamas.' I thought, 'Hang on, you only got to the ship on Friday.' He had just Saturday there and that was it. The passengers weren't questioned."

"Not at all?" I asked.

"No. Not many of the crew, either," Ann said.

I told Mike and Ann that I would book myself onto the cruise, ask a few questions, just see what I could find out. They said they'd be pleased for whatever help they could get.

In the atrium on deck 3, passengers queue for Mickey Mouse's autograph. I overhear an adult passenger ask a crew member, "Exactly how many Mickey Mouse symbols are there on board?" He looks taken aback. There are about twenty within our immediate vicinity—art deco mouse ears on the frosted-glass doorways, swirly mouse ears on the carpet. "I don't know," he replies. The passenger looks annoyed that his question can't be answered. "I can point out some hidden Mickeys," the crew member adds. It's a Disney tradition to embed tiny mouse symbols into the architecture. Fans love to spot them.

I wander into one of the bars and get talking to a waiter. "What's it like working here?" I ask.

"It's all about the show," he replies. "When you're out among the guests, you're always on show. Even if you're a waiter, or a cleaner, or a deckhand."

"How long have you been on board?" I ask.

"Seven months. I'll be going home in forty days—forty-four, to be exact." He laughs. "Seven months is long enough. Being away from your family is hard."

"Were you on board when Rebecca Coriam vanished?" I ask.

"I don't know anything about it," he says. There's a long silence. "It didn't happen," he says. He looks at me. "You know that's the answer I have to give."

It's a beautiful, clear night outside on deck 4. Ahead of us are the lights of another cruise ship. A few days later—when we reach Puerto Vallarta—I spot it again. It's called the *Carnival Spirit*. Forty-three people have vanished from Carnival cruises since 2000. Theirs is the worst record of all cruise companies. There have been 171 disappearances in total, across all cruise lines, since 2000. Rebecca is Disney's first. A few days ago, Rebecca's father e-mailed me: "Would like to inform you the number of people missing this year has just gone up to 17. A guy has gone missing in the Gulf of Mexico. The Carnival Conquest." By the time I get off this ship, the figure will have gone up to 19.

When someone vanishes from a cruise ship, one of the first things that happens to their family members is they receive a call from an Arizona man named Kendall Carver. "When you become a victim, you think you're the only person in the world," Carver told me on the phone. "Well, the Coriams found out they aren't alone. Almost every two weeks someone goes overboard."

Carver says the numbers have reached epidemic proportions and nobody realizes it because it's in the industry's power to hush it up. He lost his own daughter, Merrian, back in August 2004, from the *Celebrity Mercury*. Even though the cabin steward reported her missing on day two, Carver said, no alarm was ever raised. "He reported her missing daily and they told him to forget it."

So the chocolates piled up on her pillow. When the *Mercury* docked in Vancouver—as Carver later testified at a U.S. Senate subcommittee hearing—nobody from the ship said anything: not to the police, the FBI, nobody. They just quietly placed Merrian's belongings in storage, then gave them to charity. "If we hadn't eventually traced her to that ship, she would have vanished," he said.

At the time, Celebrity Cruises issued a statement saying, "Regrettably, there is very little a cruise line, a resort or a hotel can do to prevent someone from committing suicide." But as Carver points out, the case is still open. Later the company added, "There is probably nothing we or any company could do that would make the parents feel the company had acted sensitively enough."

Now Carver leads a lobby group called International Cruise Victims. Over the phone, he told me theories of murder, negligence, and cover-ups. Sometimes he sounded angry and xenophobic; at other times he was compelling.

"Think of where those cruise workers are from," he said. "They're low-paid, from Third World countries, on those ships for nine months at a time. The sexual crime rate is fifty percent higher than in the average American city."

It's true that passengers on just one ship—the *Carnival Valor*—

reported nine sexual assaults to the FBI in less than one year. "You're on a ship," Carver said. "There's no police. Once you leave the port, you're in international waters. Who do you think is attracted to working on those ships?"

"Do you think your daughter was murdered?"

"The answer's yes," he said. "That's the story among the crew." He paused. "Put murder to one side. Just think about the drinking. Royal Caribbean has just started a policy of unlimited drinks for one price. Celebrity is doing it."

I don't think drunkenness is an issue on the *Disney Wonder*. You'd have to drink a frozen piña colada the size of a glacier to get drunk, such are the measly measures they serve here.

"There's a man in Ireland had a fifteen-year-old daughter," Carver said. "One cruise served her eight drinks in an hour. She went to the balcony and threw up and went overboard. She was gone."

He's talking about Lynsey O'Brien, who went missing on January 5, 2006, while on a cruise with her family off the Mexican coast. The cruise liner, *Costa Magica*, conducted its own investigation into her disappearance and decided there was "no evidence of an accidental fall," that Lynsey had shown the bartender ID stating that she was twenty-three years old, and that her death was caused by "underage drinking." While they "continued to extend their deepest sympathy" to the family, they claimed their report cleared them of any wrongdoing.

"In other corporations, police get involved," Carver said. "On cruise ships they have, quote, security officers, but they work for the cruise lines. They aren't going to do anything when the lines get sued. We came to the conclusion cover-up is the standard operating procedure." He paused. "And the Coriam girl. Where is the CCTV footage?"

According to articles published at the time of Rebecca's disappearance, in the *Los Angeles Times* and *Cruise Law News*, Disney claims to have no footage of Rebecca going overboard. They refuse to "disclose the number of CCTV cameras or their locations for security reasons."

"If there's a video that shows your daughter going overboard," Carver said, "that's the end of the story. There's no way someone can go off a ship and it not be recorded."

At 7:00 a.m. on Tuesday morning, I stand on deck 4 as we pass the stretch of ocean where Rebecca went missing. A school of dolphins leap into the air, doing backflips. Passengers around me gasp. A young crew member from Ireland passes and I ask her about life in the crew cabins. "It's like being inside Harry Potter's closet," she replies.

She means it's magical, but tiny and dark. Their cabins are windowless, below sea level, like steel boxes. Crew members are contracted to work seven days a week for four-, six-, or eight-month stretches (according to how high up the ladder they are) before being allowed a few months off. At 10:00 p.m. one night, I see some women from Rebecca's department, Youth Activities, playing with kids on the stairs. It seems they're on duty as long as there are kids who need entertaining. A former member of staff, Kim Button, has written a blog about life on the *Wonder*: "I don't think it's possible to imagine how tiny a crew room is without actually seeing it! Seriously, your mind can't even fathom such things. We had staff meetings at 2am, the only time when one of us wasn't working, so even if your work day ended at

10pm, you couldn't get much sleep because you had to be in a meeting at 2am. . . . The crew pool is literally one of the few places where crew members can just hang out and be themselves, without fear of acting improperly in front of guests."

Even though life on board is, for a guest, assiduously magical, with constant Broadway-style high-budget shows, bingo, origami and acupuncture classes, films under the stars, and shore excursions to snorkel with tropical fish and ride horses through Mexican rain forests, from time to time I detect tiny flashes of cabin fever. I watch a children's entertainer try out a move in which he throws a stuffed pelican to his assistant. It accidentally hits her in the face. "You're supposed to catch the pelican!" he snaps.

"My boss," she mutters, looking embarrassed.

On a shore excursion, a Mexican crew member asks some passengers to stand in a straight line, two by two, while we wait for the bus. Every passenger feels the need to say something facetiously passive-aggressive in response.

"Oh, a straight line!" one says.

"Can it not be a little crooked?" says another.

And so on, practically all the way down the line. The crew member looks upset and embarrassed.

I've decided the only place Rebecca could have fallen from is the deck 4 jogging track. The railings everywhere else are just too high. She was a keep-fit fanatic. My theory is that after the 5:45 a.m. phone call, she went for a jog and slipped. So I'm surprised to spot four CCTV cameras on deck 4—two on the port side, two on the starboard—evidently capturing every inch of the deck. They're hard to see at first, as they're shaped like long tubes and look like some kind of nautical equipment.

A man in yellow overalls is varnishing a railing. I glance inside the atrium. There's a big Cinderella party going on. Someone is singing a song about how we have to have "faith, trust, and pixie dust." There's a crew party going on somewhere too—I hear screeching and laughter from behind a steel door. It sounds very different from the guest parties, like a pressure cooker letting off steam.

I sidle up to the man doing the varnishing. "That girl who went missing back in March," I say. "She must have fallen from this deck?"

He looks surprised: "No, she went from deck 5."

"But there's no outside space on deck 5," I say.

"Go to deck 10, walk to the front of the ship, and look down," he says. "You'll see the crew swimming pool. That's where she went from. The starboard side."

"How do you know this?" I ask him.

"I was on the ship that day. Everyone knows."

"How?" I ask.

"They found her slipper," he says.

I walk up to deck 10 and look down. And I see it. The crew swimming pool looks nice—bigger than some of the guest pools. But it's the swimming-pool equivalent of an inside cabin. There is no view of the ocean because behind the railings is a high steel wall. It reaches well above head height. There is no way someone could accidentally fall from there. You would have to make the effort to climb up. It would be difficult. It would take time.

Back on deck 4, the man is still varnishing.

"I saw it," I say.

"God bless her," he says.

"It must be a very intense life, working on the *Disney Wonder*,"

I say. "You've got those tiny, claustrophobic cabins. The passengers are very demanding. You work every day for six months. You have to be a Disney-type person the whole time, even when you're varnishing railings. . . ."

He looks at me as if I'm nuts. "We don't spend any time in our cabins," he says. "We just sleep and shower there. We spend our free time in the mess hall or by the crew pool."

A group of his fellow deck workers joins us. "Disney aren't slave masters," one says. "We get to go onshore. We get breaks. Everything you've got up here, we've got down there." He points to the bowels of the ship. "We've got a library, a gym, a games room, a swimming pool. I don't have a flat-screen TV or a gym at home. I have them here. The only thing I miss is my family."

"But all that having to be on show for the guests all the time . . ." I say.

"All the big smiles and happiness," someone replies, "it's all real. You couldn't act that."

"Disney wouldn't hire you if you weren't that sort of person," someone else says.

"But what about Rebecca Coriam?" I say. "Did you know her?"

A few of them nod. "She was a lovely girl," one says. "Not emotional. Just like everyone here. Nice and friendly and happy."

"Then why . . . ?" I say.

"I don't know," he shrugs. "But there's nothing dark or sinister going on. This is Disney."

Over the next few days I ask more people, and every time I get the exact same response: She jumped from the front of deck 5, at the crew pool.

"Disney knows exactly what happened," one crew member

tells me. "That phone call she had? It was taped. Everything here is taped. There's CCTV everywhere. Disney have the tape."

"What's in the tape?" I ask her.

"I don't know, but I know someone who knew her well. Would you like me to introduce you?"

And so, after everyone has gone to bed, I have a brief conversation with one of Rebecca's closer friends from the ship.

"Do you know what was in the tape?" I ask him.

He shakes his head. "Not exactly. I know she was having a fight with her partner." He pauses. "What's it ever about? It's about love, relationships. There's no mystery. She was just a lovely girl with underlying sadness."

The next morning, as we sail back into the Port of Los Angeles, a crew member beckons me over. He says he's heard I've been asking questions about Rebecca Coriam and he wants me to know that suicide is not the only possibility. Maybe, he says, after the phone call she took a walk to clear her head and the wind lifted her away.

"But the steel wall is so high down there," I say.

"I was on the ship that day," he says. "It was a rocky day. One time a friend of mine was called early in the morning. The deck by the crew pool was really windy and slippery, and someone was walking there, and my friend was called to get them inside. Disney took it really seriously. The guy got sent home."

"So she could have fallen?" I ask.

"She could have fallen," he says.

We pull into the port. This is where Mike and Ann came on March 25 after receiving a call from Disney executive Jim Orie to say Rebecca was missing. They were here in time to see the passengers disembark.

"We were hoping we could have spoken to some of them, but we never got the opportunity," Mike told me back in Chester. Ann added: "They kept us in a car with the windows all blacked out."

"Did you get the feeling they were deliberately keeping you away from the passengers?"

Mike: "Well . . ."

Ann: "Probably."

"But Disney were being polite and helpful and sympathetic?" I asked.

"Oh yeah," said Mike.

After the passengers had disembarked, Mike and Ann were taken on board. They were put in a room that quickly filled with Disney executives and the girl Rebecca had spoken to on the phone at 5:45 a.m.

"Did you ask her what they'd talked about?" I asked. "Why Rebecca had been upset?"

They shook their heads. "We would have liked to have asked more, but by the time we'd flown over we were jet-lagged," Ann said. "We hadn't slept since the Tuesday. We flew out on the Friday. We hadn't eaten. . . ."

"With hindsight, it might have been better if we'd gone out a little later," Mike said.

"When you were more able to ask questions?"

He nodded. "But your daughter's missing, so you don't think like that, do you? Also, we wanted to be quick to meet some of the passengers."

Mike remembered thinking, as he sat in that room on the ship, that their uselessness at getting information wouldn't be a problem because there would be plenty of other opportunities to ask questions. They had no idea they would never have another chance.

The next day, November 1, Rebecca is discussed in the House of Commons. Her MP, Stephen Mosley, says Disney was "more interested in getting the ship back to sea than in the case of a missing crew member" and "it's appalling" that only one policeman from the Bahamas—"an authority internationally recognized as almost toothless"—was called to investigate. He said "flag of convenience" countries such as the Bahamas, as they're called in the shipping world, shouldn't be left to conduct these kinds of investigations.

I call Disney. Their spokesperson tells me, "If you talked to crew members, you'll know Rebecca's disappearance has been difficult and heartbreaking for everyone." And beyond that, they can say nothing much else except "The police in the Bahamas are also telling us the investigation is still ongoing. They have not shared a timeline with us, either."

"Is it true the telephone call Rebecca made shortly before vanishing was taped?" I ask.

"That pertains to specific details about the investigation and so it's not appropriate for us to share that kind of information," she replies.

"Is there anything you can tell me?" I ask.

"I can tell you we wish we knew what happened as much as anyone," she says.

The officer in the Bahamas, Paul Rolle, doesn't return my calls.

I call Mike and Ann. I tell them about my week on the ship. When I get to the part about the waiter saying, "It didn't happen," Mike sighs and says, "Oh. Yeah."

I tell them about all the CCTV cameras and Mike says, "They could have had them fitted since." (It's a measure of him that he'll not descend to conspiracy theories about Disney.) I tell them about the high steel wall on deck 5, about how that sadly points to suicide, although not definitely. I ask if I'm telling them things they didn't know.

"No, we've been through all this," Mike says.

"Was there any underlying sadness?" I ask.

"No, no, no," Mike says. "There isn't."

"A crew member told me Disney have a tape of the telephone conversation," I say.

There's a silence. "Did they say . . ." Mike pauses. "Was there any idea . . . ?"

"No," I say. "No idea."

I say I regret never talking to one of her really good friends on board. And then, later that night, a woman telephones. I'll call her Melissa. She says she'd never have talked to me had Mike and Ann not asked her to.

"When did you last see Rebecca?" I ask her.

"It was at eleven p.m. the night before she went missing. We'd both just finished work, and she was trying to pull my false eyelashes off." She laughs. "She had her head on my knee and we were chatting and messing about."

"Where was this?" I ask.

"In the secret corridor," she says. "There's a whole different world underneath the ship deck. We have parties down there, private showings of films. It's absolutely brilliant. Bex said, 'Are you going to the bar?' I said, 'Yeah,' but I didn't for some reason. And that was the last time I saw her." She pauses. "She was the most amazing little burst of energy. You were completely drawn to her. She loved life. Bouncing around all the time. She was one of my best friends, but it could get a bit much." She laughs again. "You come in from a heavy night and she'd be zapping around everywhere. Playing tricks on you. She's very mischievous."

"Someone told me she'd had a fight with her partner," I say.

"That ship absolutely seethes with rumors," Melissa says. "Yes. She was in a relationship, and there were problems, and it was upsetting her. It was a very, very intense relationship. It was great and then it was awful. They were both fiery, passionate personalities."

"Do you think that's what the call was about?"

"I can't think of any other reason why she'd have been upset and wandering around by herself at six a.m.," Melissa says. "From what I've heard, she was on the phone to a mutual friend. Not the girl she'd been having the relationship with."

And then Melissa starts telling me some odd little things. She says after Rebecca went missing, Disney had a little ceremony. They put flowers at the wall next to the crew pool, "where they think she might have jumped from. But they didn't say. They put these flowers down but refused to answer any questions as to why. It was left unsaid. It really stirred things up. Why are they putting them there? Nothing was clear."

"I thought they knew she went from there because they found her slipper," I say.

"Those weren't her flip-flops," says Melissa. "Mike and Ann showed them to me. They were too big. They weren't her style. They were pink and flowery and Hawaiian. I'd never seen her wear them. Why didn't Disney come to me or her girlfriend and say, 'Can you identify these as Bex's?' Instead they put them in her room for when her parents got on board. Who does that?"

She pauses. "Disney swear they've told us everything they know, which is that they don't know anything, but most of us think, 'Bullshit. Someone must know something. Someone's covering something up.'"

Melissa has her own theory. "Bex was a bit of a risk taker. She was always pouring soap over people. Classic Bex. I was welcoming a family on board one time and she came over and rugby-tackled me to the ground!"

Melissa thinks Rebecca went to the crew pool at 6:00 a.m. to be alone, with no intention of harming herself. "She loved deck 5. It's where we always used to go. I bet she climbed onto the wall and sat on the ledge in a 'I need to feel like I'm off the ship for a second' way. She wouldn't have thought, 'It's very high. I might fall.' She'd have just sat on it and thought, 'Oh crap. What have I done?' And fell." She pauses. "Security on that ship is ultra-tight. You can't get on or off without your ID card. Down by the crew pool there's HR offices, the crew gym, the crew office that deals with passports, money, documentation. And they're saying there's no CCTV cameras?"

"But why would they suppress that?" I ask.

"To try to protect the brand. If it was six a.m. and they were doing their job and watching the front, someone must have seen her go over. Or if they didn't, they're covering up why they didn't." She falls silent. Then she says, "Bex made hundreds of people happy. The passengers loved her. They all loved her. You'd think Disney would give something back. They owe it to her to find out what happened."

ABOUT THE AUTHOR

Jon Ronson's books include the *New York Times* best seller *The Psychopath Test*, as well as *Them: Adventures with Extremists* and *The Men Who Stare at Goats*—both international best sellers. *The Men Who Stare at Goats* was adapted as a major motion picture, released in 2009 and starring George Clooney. Ronson lives in London.